TALES OF MY TIME

Tales of My Time

RAYMOND BAXTER

In collaboration with Tony Dron

GRUB STREET · LONDON

Published by
Grub Street
4 Rainham Close
London
SW11 6SS

First published in hardback in 2005
This edition first published 2007

British Library Cataloguing in Publication Data
Baxter, Raymond
   Tales of my time
   1. Baxter, Raymond 2. Television personalities –
   Great Britain – Biography 3. Television journalists
   – Great Britain – Biography
   I. Title II. Tony Dron
   791.4'3'092

ISBN-13 978 1904943 70 9

Typeset by Pearl Graphics, Hemel Hempstead

Printed and bound by MPG Ltd, Bodmin, Cornwall

Grub Street Publishing only uses
FSC (Forest Stewardship Council) paper for its books.

NB: All photographs in the book are from the author's collection.
With thanks to the BBC, British Aerospace, Imperial War Museum,
Royal Air Force and various friends.

Contents

Foreword

More than 20 years ago my wife urged me to write this book, "for the sake of the family". It grieves me deeply that she is not with me now, as I accede to her request. She died of cancer on 2nd September 1996. We had been married for 51 remarkable years – remarkable not least for the fact that she tolerated me for so long, and at what personal sacrifice. She was an intrinsic part of my adult life and is in the background of my mind constantly as I reminisce in these *Tales of My Time*.

And so this book is truly dedicated to her memory and to our family.

But the words would not have got to paper without the incalculable assistance and co-operation of my friend, Tony Dron – brilliant motoring editor and journalist, and fearsome racing driver. Eleven years ago he wrote four consecutive and very flattering articles about me in *Classic Cars* magazine. Thereafter I described him as my Honorary PRO, but I had no idea that he would accept with declared pleasure my plea for his assistance in what – when I came face to face with it – appeared a task beyond my current capability.

So now, for what it is worth, 'tis done – at the rate of 4,000 words per week in writing time, not to mention my living time – and I am deeply grateful to the Almighty, as well as expert medical opinion, for the fact that I am still alive and able to tell my *Tales*.

Raymond Baxter,
Henley-on-Thames

Introduction

It was the voice, the voice that defined an era for so many British people. Raymond Baxter remains a hero, especially to those of us born shortly after the Second World War and much of his life reads like an adventure story. An operational Spitfire pilot throughout much of the war, he went on to become the voice of motor racing on radio and television and, as such, was the live commentator at countless events which have become legendary in the history of motor sport, including the Le Mans disaster of 1955 and Fangio's extraordinary winning performance in the 1957 German Grand Prix.

As a competitor, he had hair-raising escapades on major international rallies and, as the voice of Farnborough Air Displays on the BBC for 30 consecutive years, he astonished us time and time again, not only with his clear descriptions of the latest military aircraft but also with his ability actually to fly some of them himself as he spoke to us.

His commentaries on great state occasions, including the Coronation and Sir Winston Churchill's funeral, managed to convey all the relevant facts in a delivery that was not merely interesting but also a perfectly balanced mix of dignity and a reflection of the emotional feelings of the British people.

Above all, I suspect, he is remembered best today as the long-serving presenter of the science programme which rapidly became a big hit with British viewers, *Tomorrow's World*.

It is now less than two years since Raymond's *Tales* were committed to print; and it's a mere five months since he passed away, on 15th September 2006. It still seems somehow significant that he left us on Battle of Britain Day. Raymond worked hard and played hard to the end. As soon as the manuscript for *Tales* was completed to his satisfaction, he set off for Dunkirk in his Little Ship, *L'Orage*, for the 2005 Return of the flotilla, remembering and honouring those desperate days of May 1940. As ever, his journey to France began on the River Thames, from the bottom of his garden near Henley, where *L'Orage* was moored.

On his return, Raymond continued to enjoy a busy schedule of public engagements and, indeed, he was still working mere days before the end of his life. He spoke over the public address system at the Goodwood Revival on Saturday, September 2nd, commentating on the World War Two aircraft there. That wonderfully appropriate setting proved to be his final public appearance.

One of the Spitfire pilots at Goodwood, John Romain, volunteered to perform a flypast at Raymond's funeral at Ewelme on September 29th. This idea was welcomed immediately by Raymond's son, Graham, and the whole of the Baxter family. On the day, the sight and sound of a Spitfire flashing over the church at the end of the service was a very moving moment indeed.

It was a huge privilege to have been invited by Raymond Baxter to help in recording his life story and I recall his delight on learning that it would go into this second edition. I hope you enjoy reading Raymond's *Tales* as much I enjoyed working with him.

Tony Dron
Cambridge
February, 2007

Chapter 1

Opening Sequence

One evening in early March 1945 Squadron Leader Max Sutherland DFC, CO 602 (City of Glasgow) Squadron, gathered his four senior pilots to the bar at RAF Ludham. After the first round of drinks, his brown eyes blazing with challenge, he said, "Listen chaps, I've got an idea." Our minds became concentrated; we knew Max to be unpredictable, to say the least.

At that time we were flying our socks off in Operation Big Ben – the anti-V2 campaign. On several occasions during those ops we saw the white trail of V2 rockets arcing up at incredible speed and height towards their indiscriminate targets. It made us the more determined to strike back as hard as we could. Equipped with Spit 16s we were dive-bombing every reported or suspected launch site, and dive-bombing, skip-bombing and strafing interdiction targets throughout occupied Holland. In addition we were committed to normal fighter duties, readiness, bomber escort (US & RAF), air-sea rescue, and shipping and reconnaissance patrols. Four sorties per pilot per day were not uncommon.

"Just outside The Hague," said Max, "is the former HQ of

Shell-Mex. It is now the HQ of VI and V2 operations. I have worked out that the width of the building equals the total wing-span of five Spitfires in close formation." He paused to let it sink in. "I reckon we could take it out."

Then he said, looking me straight in the eye, "What do you reckon, Bax?" I took a long slow draught from my Guinness and said, "Might be a bit dodgy, Boss."

The concentration of heavy and light *flak* from Den Helder to the Scheldt was our daily experience, and later we learned that no less than 200 batteries of well-manned guns would lie in our path.

"Yeah, I know," said Max. "But we'll get 453 to lay on a diversion and we'll go in flat and low."

453 were the Australian squadron in our Wing, led by Squadron Leader Ernie Esau, another major character. They were our neighbours on the airfield, with whom we had developed a close bond both in the air and at the pub.

So it was agreed and, somewhat surprisingly, approved by Group. After a disappointing abort, because cloud obscured the target on 18th March 1945, the attack was delivered precisely according to plan. We peeled off from 453 at about 8,000 feet, crossing the Dutch coast, and Maxy transmitted the seldom-used codeword, "Buster" (full throttle), and "Close Up".

He then led us in a perfectly judged diving arc, in which the controls became increasingly heavy and, therefore, more demanding for close formation. We flattened out at about 100 feet with the target dead ahead and square in our gyro-sights – range about 300 yards. We let go with our 2 x 20mm cannon and 0.5in machine guns and released our 1 x 500lb and 2 x 250lb, eleven-second delay bombs "in our own time".

Then, as I cleared the roof of the building, I looked ahead. And approaching me at eye-level, and near enough 400mph, was this black cockerel atop the weather vane on the church spire across the road! I can see it to this day.

The PRU (Photographic Reconnaissance Unit) photograph, which we had studied, showed the church (which we were determined not to hit), but not the height of its spire. With no space to turn, I could only tweak the stick and say, in my head, perhaps two seconds later, "Thank you, God."

Then the Boss damn' near got his tail shot off. Our pre-attack briefing had been that the moment we cleared the target we should fan out, continuing at rooftop height. So five Spitfires swept at extremely low level across the centre of the Dutch capital. This, as was hoped, presented the anti-aircraft gunners with such a variety of fast-moving targets that the amount of *flak* we encountered was comparatively light. Unfortunately, however, Max Sutherland – as he had done on many occasions previously – decided to pull up to have a look back and assess the extent of the damage which we had inflicted with our 11-second delay bombs. This, of course, attracted the concentration of anti-aircraft fire onto him. Nevertheless, he had the satisfaction of observing that the whole of the Shell-Mex building was occluded by a cloud of smoke, flame and dust.

But, almost immediately, Max called us again, saying: "Tarbrush [I think that was the call-sign], proceed as planned to re-arm and re-fuel. I have been hit. Bax, please come and have a look at the damage."

So, clear of the built-up area where the *flak* was, Max pulled up to about 3,000ft and, as the rest of the formation sped towards their refuelling point, I closed to him and had a careful look at his tail.

"Boss," I said, "you've got a big hit on your starboard elevator."

"Is it still flyable, do you think, Bax?" he said.

"Up to you, Boss," I said, "but I'll keep a careful eye."

"I will continue at bale-out height," he replied. "Please stay close." So I did that, at about 3,000ft and on his starboard side, slightly behind and below, keeping a very careful eye on that severely damaged tail. We made it to the circuit – at Ursahl, our planned refuelling point near Ghent in Belgium – and as Max had his airspeed indicator and flaps working I remained close and watched him make a perfect landing. Then I followed him in and we had time to take a look at what we had achieved by comparing notes with our mates, who were all safely down and undamaged.

Max got a Bar to his DFC for that, and the rest of us got a Collective Mention. The BBC Nine o'clock News that night reported, "During the day, RAF fighter bombers continued their attacks on selected ground targets in occupied Holland." Just so!

Years later my friend Michael Turner, the distinguished aviation artist, read about my cockerel and said he'd like to paint a picture of it. Rummaging about in my box of goodies in which I keep my logbook, imagine his delight when I found the original PRU photograph on which our attack had been based. The resultant painting was shown in the Guild of Aviation Artists' Exhibition a few years ago and is reproduced in this book.

A few months after that Michael received a letter from a total stranger in Holland requesting my address. It transpires that, totally by chance, Aad Devisser had visited an exhibition of WWII aviation art, seen Michael's painting and realised that he too was there on 18th March 1945.

As a 16-year-old, he was doing his best to avoid deportation to a labour camp. With his parents he lived in caretaker quarters in the Shell-Mex building. As he described it, "I heard you coming... and looked into your eyes."

Mercifully, although we destroyed their home, he and his family survived, including the dog. Aad became my friend and before his death wrote to me of "the admiration and gratitude he and his fellow Dutch men and women felt for the RAF pilots who were risking their lives for us."

Chapter 2

This is Your Life

At 11am on 14th February 1998, I was in the recording booth of a film/TV production company in Soho where I had worked many times before. But as I approached the completion of my task I became aware that something curious was going on. Recording 'post-production commentary', often written by myself, had been part of my job for many years, both for the BBC and elsewhere.

The arrangement is simple. The commentator sits in a soundproof booth, separate from the production team. The film, or tape, cut and edited, is projected so that both the production team and the commentator view the images separately but simultaneously. That may sound complicated but in reality it is not. Given high standards of professionalism on both sides, the commentary 'to picture' can and should be a routine procedure. Imagine therefore my puzzlement on this day when I began to perceive that odd things were happening on the other side of the screen.

First the producer apologised for a break because the sound-recordist had to go for a pee. This took quite a while. Then I was asked to re-record a sequence of several minutes because "it was not quite right". By this time I could feel my back-hair rising.

Throughout my career in broadcasting I have taken great pride getting it right first time. I can indeed claim that, in my day, amongst BBC film crews I was known as 'One-take Baxter'. So when, after a further pause, I was asked to re-record a few paragraphs for no apparent reason, I was on the edge of hitting the roof. Still, checking my impatience, I got on with the job.

As it approached completion and my eyes were on my monitor screen, a voice in my headphones said:

"You're approaching the finishing line, Raymond, but there's a big red one coming up behind you." Instantly, I recognised the voice of my old friend, Stirling Moss, but how on earth did he manage to do that? I wondered. Nice one! I was considerably puzzled but then the producer, on the far side of the screen, said:

"Look over your left shoulder, Raymond."

There, squeezed into the tiny recording booth behind me, sure enough, was Stirling, together with Michael Aspel, a friend and colleague of many years, and a film cameraman who had crept in without me noticing because I was so engrossed in what I was doing and, anyway, with the headphones on I was deaf to any small noises behind me.

Thus were uttered the celebrated words, "Raymond Baxter, This is Your Life."

Never have I been so surprised. Immediately it was clear that the reason for my having been messed about was that the *This is Your Life* team had laid their well-proven plot to catch their subject unawares, in this case timed to a zero hour of noon. They most certainly succeeded, despite the fact that I had completed my job more than 15 minutes quicker than they had calculated.

Therefore, while I was totally concentrated on my work, in the street outside Michael had arrived at the wheel of a Jaguar XK120 to be met, literally on the doorstep, by Stirling. After a brief exchange of greetings, all covered on film, they entered the building together as planned. Then they had crept, undetected, into that small recording booth behind me and the trap was sprung. There was applause, I remember, from the production team who had clearly enjoyed every minute of their role in the conspiracy.

For my part, events thereafter assumed a dreamlike quality. I was absolutely delighted by the realisation that this was all happening, and to find my friend Stirling at the centre of the plot increased my enjoyment. But after the initial shock my mind turned to practicalities.

"Excuse me," I said to a charming girl who was clearly in charge. "When is this going out?"

"Tonight," she said.

"Tonight? Oh my God, but what about my clothes?" I was casually dressed for 'out-of-picture' work.

"All taken care of," she said. "Your daughter has given us the suit from your wardrobe she thinks right for the occasion, together with shirt, a choice of ties and shoes."

"Has she, indeed?" I said, and the penny dropped in a major way.

The fact that I appeared on *This is Your Life*, I owe entirely to my daughter, now Jennifer Douglas and a successful professional fencing coach. She and her husband, Paul, and two daughters had moved into the large house which my wife and I bought in Henley in 1985. A primary motivation for our choice was that the house included the potential for a downstairs flat. This, we hoped, might be acceptable for Jenny, then unmarried.

In fact, what happened was that when a film crew came to my house to shoot a contribution to the *This is Your Life* programme of Murray Walker, of all people, unknown to me Jenny had said to the producer: "Why don't you do my father?"

"We had the impression that he wouldn't play," she replied.

"That was a long time ago," said Jenny. "The programme was different then and I knew that my mother would not have liked that at all. But I think it would be all right now."

That was the start of a quite extraordinary sub-plot. Several months later, when the programme makers approved the project, their first task was to inform Jenny without my knowledge – not at all easy when you remember that we all lived in the same house. Thereafter the speed of the operation was quite breathtaking. Only ten days elapsed between the second approach to Jenny and the programme's appearance live on screen. There was no particular necessity for Jenny to let my son Graham know what was afoot and she gave the production team a contact list of those she thought were potential contributors.

Then, all unwittingly, my sister presented a major problem. I had arranged to go down and stay with her at Frome for a few days, returning two days before I was booked to record the commentary in that Soho film studio. Jenny dared not tell my sister under those circumstances. On the day I was to leave Frome there was widespread fog. I rang Jenny and told her I had decided to stay in Frome for an extra day. Her voice in no way disclosed what must have been her total consternation at this late torpedoing of her meticulous planning.

The film company had agreed to send a car to Henley for me on the morning of their recording so getting me, in all innocence, to the right place and the right time appeared to be a gift. But the manner and speed with which the *This is Your Life* team got it all together despite all setbacks amazes me to this day.

However, there I was in an environment with which I was totally at ease – a film recording studio in Soho – until this explosive intrusion by Michael and Stirling Moss. From there I was whisked away to an excellent lunch in a quiet restaurant off Kew Green. Clearly the staff were familiar with the circumstances; they'd done it all before. Thereafter to the Teddington studios of Independent Television, and I sensed at the time that I was being smuggled in. The security guards knew precisely the routine, which they had no doubt executed time and time again. Shown to my dressing room for the first time in private for four or more hectic hours, I put my feet up and began to think about what lay ahead.

I began by speculating on who might be in the programme –

17

my family obviously – and I hoped the grandchildren; someone from *Tomorrow's World* – could it be James Burke? Sadly the choice would be limited in that context. Could they get someone from my family in America? Someone from motor racing was already involved. In any event I resolved to make the most of it! Play it as far as possible my way and milk it for laughs. A male dresser came into the dressing room as promised – and boosted my morale no end by admiring my suit.

"You can tell bespoke tailoring at a glance," he said, and indeed from the earlier days of *Tomorrow's World,* on the advice of Mike Latham – the second editor of the series – I had bought my suits made-to-measure from Messrs James & James of Albany Street – not quite Savile Row, but close enough – and indeed over the years the brothers became personal friends of mine. Next I was taken to the studio, shown the set and told that Jenny would be sitting on my right as I entered and that I was to take the vacant seat on her right. That was the sum total of my briefing before I was smuggled back to my dressing room and told that the make-up girl would be with me in about 45 minutes; and would I like a cup of tea? Not 'arf!

I have tapes of the programme, both the unedited version and the 'P as B' – Programme as Broadcast – as we used to say in the BBC. Again, the sheer professionalism of the production team is in my view, as a fellow pro, just outstanding. The on-stage performance overran by more than 20 minutes, due almost entirely to my own self-indulgence, yet the necessary cuts are quite unnoticeable.

On reflection, I have decided not to attempt a transcript of the show here, the printed word in this case being but a hollow shadow of the magic of the originals. I choose the word 'magic' for that it most certainly was, for me – if for no-one else. Having participated in three or four other people's *This is Your Life* programmes, I was fully aware of 'the rules of engagement'. Even so, standing alone backstage and listening to the introduction, filmed only those few hours before, I felt a mounting excitement, quite different from the rising heart rate

I have experienced in the few minutes before the start of any television or radio programme in which I have played a role.

Came the words, "Raymond Baxter – This is Your Life." Loud applause from the audience – on cue – and from the semi-darkness behind the set I stepped into the brilliantly lit arena. There, on the right with the empty place beside her, sat Jenny, looking absolutely radiant, elegantly dressed and beautifully made up. Behind her, Paul my son-in-law; my son, Graham and his wife, Bridget; my sister, Doreen and her husband – all as I had expected. But in addition on both sides a host of friends whom I could not wait to greet – so I didn't. Instead of sitting down by my daughter as instructed I set off on a little tour, shaking hands, leaning forward to give a kiss to my sister and to Bette Hill (Graham Hill's widow) and finally crossing the set to shake the hand of my old friend and colleague, Robin Richards who, I was slightly shocked to see, was in a wheelchair.

Book in hand, Michael Aspel stood aside, smiling patiently and waiting – as I was sure he would – until I settled down beside my daughter. She 'opened the batting' by saying:

"My father is incapable of growing old gracefully." Fair enough, I thought.

My sister spoke of our very happy childhood; my son spoke of his mother, describing my romance with Sylvia as "the stuff that dreams are made of." I had prepared myself for what I knew and indeed hoped was almost inevitable – a picture or pictures of Sylvia. But there, on the big screen, was the only photograph we have of our wedding. I felt myself beginning to 'choke up' but a reassuring squeeze of my hand from Jenny helped me immeasurably and thereafter I knew I could cope emotionally. So, from now on it was fun time.

And so it proved. To this day, when I watch again a particular moment, I say to myself, "Gosh, how beautiful they are." That moment came when my grandchildren made their entrance. To the left, Tom, my grandson – tall and handsome – with a sleeping little Saskia, my youngest grand-daughter, over his shoulder; Anna and Holly, Graham's other two children, strikingly attractive teenagers; and Rebecca, Jenny's first-born, who immediately 'broke rank' and scampered forward, ignoring me totally, to jump onto her mother's lap. Next day, asked by Jenny what she would like to do that morning, Rebecca said:

"I think, Mummy, I should quite like to go and make some more television."

Sir Stirling, already involved from the outset, told a nice little tale. After some complimentary observations about our time together in motor sport, he recalled a particular long distance race – he thought, the Goodwood 9Hrs – in which he realised the car he was driving had a radio. This was, of course, long before car radio transmitters became a commonplace in motor racing. Stirling said: "My pit people were telling me where I was in the race, but I wanted to find out how other people were doing. So I switched on the radio and listened to Raymond's commentary!"

James Burke, my original partner on *Tomorrow's World* – and in writing two of our *Tomorrow's World* books – recalled the first time he had to do the programme without me. I had been called away during the morning's rehearsal to rush to my father's bedside in Monmouthshire. James was, he said, terrified.

The accepted routine in *This is Your Life* is that each guest speaks his or her introductory lines out of vision backstage, makes their entrance, is interviewed by Michael Aspel, shakes hands with the host and goes to an allotted seat. I deliberately broke the rules. When each of my guests had said their piece I joined them centre stage, facing the audience, and did my best to reciprocate the compliments which I had just been paid. So, after our handshake, as I retained my hold on him, James Burke muttered:

"What are you doing, Raymond? Let me go!"

"Oh, no," I said, and told the audience that this was the first man to treat a television audience as a group of intelligent individuals rather than two or more groups of known and differing views whose reaction would be totally predictable. This he did in the series of *Burke Specials*, which he left *Tomorrow's World* to make. These were very successful and he then embarked on a series called *Connections*, based on major advances in scientific knowledge and the way in which they interconnected. Brilliant in my view, the BBC declined to renew his contract so he set about working in America in the public service channels, made an immediate impression and earned far more money than he would have done had he stayed with Auntie who, as I have written elsewhere, was – and I believe still is – a bit of a bitch.

My friend Len Holdstock, of our flying training days together on the far side of the Atlantic, told how when we were in a 'Holding Camp' in Moncton, New Brunswick, we were told that we going to Miami. Whoopee! But the Miami at which we arrived after a two-day train journey via Chicago turned out to be in the Panhandle country of the Mid-West. I told the audience that Len had enjoyed a brilliant career in civil aviation, introducing the Lockheed Tri-Star to British Airways and had been elected Master of the Guild of Air Pilots and Air Navigators, of which I am proud to be a liveryman.

My 602 Squadron days were recalled by Mike Francis who introduced himself with the words:

"Tarbrush Leader, Tarbrush Leader, this is Tarbrush Blue Two." That had Aspel puzzled, so Mike explained about R/T call-signs and code.

"Bax," he said, "was my flight commander. He was a very good flight commander, both in the air and on the ground. He taught us all the songs which our mothers had not taught us." Indeed, I had. *The Shaibah Blues*, the *Ball of Kirriemuir, There was an Old Monk...* and others which had no place in family reading. I told the audience that Michael had become a successful professional artist, having been commissioned amongst other works to paint a portrait of The Princess Royal for the University of London Air Squadron.

My dear old friend Bobby Farran spoke of the school plays which I had produced and I told the audience he was the finest jazz pianist I knew and if anyone wanted to book him, to contact me – with a backhander gesture behind my back, which got a nice laugh.

My Irish rally partner, Ernest McMillen told the tale of

when driving for the famous BMC Mini Cooper team we started the Monte from Minsk in the Soviet Union. Good businessman that he is, as well as being an excellent driver and brimming with the Irish *craic*, he decided we should buy a large tin of caviar with a view to selling it at a huge profit in Monte Carlo. In the event, though it travelled well – half-frozen in the back of our Cooper – no-one wanted to buy it for more than our purchase price. Sylvia and I and the children were eating caviar morning, noon and night for weeks.

My river neighbour on the Thames, Vince Hill, the singer (remember Edelweiss?) spoke of boating and the Association of Dunkirk Little Ships, although he does not own one. He was so anxious to get the title right that he wrote a prompt on the palm side of his thumb. He still managed to get it wrong.

A huge compliment came in the shape of a filmed greeting from The Royal National Lifeboat Institution. The spokesman was Ray Kipling, then the deputy director and former PRO. We had become very good friends during my service on the PR committee of the Institution, and later on the executive. Afloat in the Poole Lifeboat, he led the crew in a chorus, "Thank you, Raymond." Coming from a group of men whom I admire perhaps beyond all others, that too very nearly choked me up.

My longstanding friend and colleague of the British Forces Network and the BBC, Cliff Michelmore, reminded us of a somewhat historic experience we shared in Hamburg in 1948. He had done the commentary and I the inter-round summaries on a heavyweight contest between what Cliff described as two elderly gentlemen called Max Schmelling and Walter Neusel. Their world title aspirations had been interrupted by the war.

Another filmed insert had the New York skyline in the background and the distinctive features of my nephew, Carl Andre, in the foreground. Carl was, and still is, a groundbreaking sculptor of world repute. He created the Tate Gallery 'Bricks' which caused such a furore. I admire enormously his towering intellectual independence. Sylvia 'babysat' him and his two sisters when she was a teenager. Their loving relationship, in which I came to share with my son and daughter, have survived time and distance and have if

22

anything become closer during the ensuing years.

But perhaps the most magic of magic moments came with the appearance of the tall and well-built figure of the man who taught me to fly all those years ago in America. I was able to say to the audience, "To me, this man was God. One day he said to me, after we had landed, 'Gee! I can't figure you out Raymond. Sometimes you fly like an angel and sometimes you fly like a son of a bitch!'" And I knew Bob Swanson was right.

So the programme drew to its close and I was presented with the Red Book which, it transpired, is not a transcript of the words, but a beautiful collection of coloured pictures of everyone invited to attend, whether or not they spoke during the programme. It is an album of my most happy memories and I had photocopies made of all the pictures to send with my thanks to each of the participants. Some, who had sent their greeting from afar, said, "Have a great party!" Boy, did we ever.

Chapter 3

Childhood

I was into motoring at an early age, judging by the photograph taken when I was about four. My father, whom I revered, was a remarkable man and he endeared himself even more to me by building with his own two hands my first car. I was born in 1922 – so this was well before mass-produced cars for the young crowded every toyshop.

The car had a wooden frame, metal coachwork and was chain-driven to the rear wheels by rotating pedals. I couldn't pedal it backwards, so there was a freewheel drive. Turning round on the narrow paved pathway in our back garden was no problem. I merely put my feet on the ground, picked the car up and we both turned around together.

My pride in that little car was unmatched in my experience. Perhaps Malcolm Campbell might have known it in relation to one or more of his famous Bluebirds. My car, I remember, was repainted Bluebird blue in his honour. Driving it taught me much, as well as developing my skinny legs. For example, as the photograph reveals, I was some 30 years ahead of Sir Stirling Moss in the stretched-arm driving position for which he is given credit. Stylists may also note the wooden steering wheel which clearly places my father well ahead of fashion.

As to performance, certainly I was prepared to stretch it to the limit. I hurled my little car into corners at ever increasing speed to determine at what point it might turn over. We never did, thanks to my father's demonstrable skill as a designer. Perhaps more constructively, that car made me aware at a very early age of the third party hazard. Intent upon my own record round the block, that is to say the rectangular block of suburban houses where we lived – and I have no idea how I could possibly have timed my alleged record – I was thundering along, enjoying enormously the 'dumpty-dumpty-dump' of the solid tyres over the cracks between the paving stones in the pavement.

I hurtled round a familiar corner only to find myself slap between the legs of a very large and impressive gentleman. Felled by the single blow, he collapsed, sitting heavily on my car and denting my bonnet. He was by no means amused. In those days to have one's name and address taken by the police could leave no course open to any respectable family other than to flee the country or, at any rate, the county. Such was our respect for respectability. But my anger at the outrage to my car was heightened by the haunting fear of Dreadful Consequences and I pedalled away even faster than I had arrived.

Inevitably, and soon, I literally grew out of that little machine and there followed a barren period in my life in which I did not own a motor car. I drove other people's cars, not least a Morris 10 belonging to the father of one of my close friends. As 15-year-olds, we took it secretly out on the public highway, mercifully avoiding both accident and discovery. Of course that would be a terrible thing to do today but in those days there was so much less traffic and I don't think – I really don't think – that we presented a serious danger to anyone, even ourselves.

The corner on which I had that accident in the pedal car was on my route to school – Christchurch Road Elementary – a quite striking late Victorian building. The school celebrated its centenary a couple of years ago and I was invited to make a speech to the assembled children in the playground which I remembered so well.

I didn't go to school until I was seven, by which time I could read and write, and do sums. Both my parents were teachers and they taught me at home. I remember very clearly my first day at that school: I walked hand in hand with my mother and she said goodbye with a kiss at the tall iron railings and into the throng I went for the first time all on my own. But I quickly got the hang of it and thoroughly enjoyed the experience. I was very lucky, I guess, because I was happy at school. And after that initial walk hand in hand with my mother, I ran to school and back home every day. I ran almost everywhere at that time, I have to say. We were summoned to school by a bell hanging high in a tower on the roof of the school and I could start running as the bell started to ring, entering the playground before it stopped. I suppose that was, what, three minutes – not more.

In the infants' school we had mixed classes, of between 32 and 34. We sat at individual wooden desks, with a lid and a hard seat, and virtually all the teaching was done with the teacher in front of the class talking and the pupils writing in pencil. I had three remarkable lady teachers – Miss Evans, who was the redoubtable headmistress; Welsh, stern, forbidding but just so kindly. She loved her job and she loved the children. My class teacher was a Miss Crofts – medium height, running slightly towards the stout – she could not have been more different from the headmistress, and although I didn't really understand such things, I sensed the difference was politically based.

I have the impression now that Miss Evans was a strict Tory – we observed Empire Day with a special assembly – we assembled for prayers first thing every morning and her general tenor and flavour was very much of King, Country and Empire. Miss Crofts, on the other hand, I believe to have been a Liberal. She formed, in our school, a children's branch of The League of Nations. I was appointed, rather than elected, the chairman, and the secretary was a very pretty little dark-haired girl called Eileen. We were taught how to conduct a meeting – taking the chair, writing the minutes – and of course all this was way, way ahead of its time, done in the name of The League of Nations and the fact that I grew up believing firmly in the viability of, and indeed necessity for, The League of Nations is of interest in itself.

The third of my very special teachers was Miss Searle. She taught me singing and, indeed, my mother paid her to come to our house to continue my lessons. I had a good boy soprano voice, I sang in the church choir, I was Decani Primus – those who know their church terminology will know what I mean – the front boy on the right hand side facing the altar, and that position was also virtually the Head Boy, and I sang solos. But, thanks to Miss Searle, I also entered local singing competitions and quite recently when I was going through my box of forgotten treasures I found a little silver medal which I won in the Barking Musical Festival – that could be aptly named now I come to think of it – in about, I suppose, 1934.

We lived in Wellesley Road, Ilford, a street of terraced houses mostly double-fronted, that is to say with a central front door and rooms either side of the central passage. We also had a greenhouse, built onto the back of the house, which had a grapevine in it for many years, with grapes which were delicious. But it also housed the mangle for when my mother was doing the washing, and our bicycles and various other bits and pieces; so it was an extremely useful adjunct to the house.

My father was a very keen and creative gardener and, by the standards of the day, we had a big garden. It was the full width of the house and, I suppose, 35 yards long. My father arranged it in quite a formal manner and I remember when I was still quite young he dug a sunken garden with a big pear tree as its central feature and I helped, wheeling my little wheelbarrow during the excavation process, and again when building the dry brick walls which formed its circumference. We had fruit trees, and we had a shed at the bottom of the garden which again was pretty much multi-purpose but it was also my father's toolroom. We burned our rubbish in an incinerator at the bottom of the garden. There was no worry then about pollution. Our neighbours were all our friends; it was, as I say, a very respectable and self-respecting neighbourhood.

Our street and those surrounding us were virtually devoid of parked cars. There were one or two garages built on the flanks of the outer gardens but cars were few and far between. Consequently the bicycle was my typical everyday mode of transport and it was so for my father too. He was a teacher in West Ham, he taught science and cycled to and from school, departing in the morning at about eight and getting home at about five o'clock. And I remember when I was still quite little being allowed to go and meet Daddy as he came round past Ilford Station. I would wait for him on the corner by what was then the Super cinema and when he arrived I would jump onto the back of his bicycle with one foot on a tiny projection from the rear hub – it couldn't have been more than a couple of inches. My right knee rested lightly on top of the mudguard of the rear wheel and my hands grasped my father by the waist. It sounds very precarious and of course it would be instantly frowned upon today.

Anyway, away we would go and my father, I know, took particular delight in sweeping extra fast into the two or three right-angled turns which we had to make, so the bicycle was banked right over and I truly wonder if that very early experience did not increase my capability to understand co-ordinated turns when flying an aeroplane – that is to say to get the bank right according to the rate of turn, to avoid slipping and skidding: expressions not entirely inappropriate to a bicycle!

Another happy and loving recollection is of tea-time on Sundays and setting up my model railway under the dining room table. I had been encouraged to develop an interest in railways, again by my father. When we went on journeys by train he would always take me up to say thank you to the engine driver, knowing full well that the chances were that one of those kindly men would invite this little boy and his father onto the footplate, to gaze with some fear at the roaring fire and listen to the hiss of steam. And so my interest in railways stemmed from my toy train and my interest in steam stemmed from my stationary steam engine, which was another pride and joy of my youth. Fired by methylated spirit, the boiler length was about 18 inches and it was a very powerful little machine

– I still have it, although I haven't run it for years.

And from it I would drive the models which I made in Meccano, such as cranes and coal-mine pithead gears, and also a whole range of miniature machine tools: I had a lathe, I remember, a circular saw, and also a dynamo which actually lit up an electric bulb and that was a pretty exciting achievement.

When I was about ten I was given a paperback book called *Burst Tyres* and it had a pronounced influence on my life. It was about the boy hero who won everything from the Land Speed Record to the Mille Miglia and Brooklands; it captured my imagination totally. There were villains in it, who were of course Germans even then.

I had a great friend, Clifford, who lived within easy running distance and we both had Meccano sets; he built a Meccano Bluebird and I built a simpler, smaller car based roughly on an ERA. We raced them on the pavement and I won because I could run faster; we drew up the regulations, there was a speed hillclimb at Valentine's Park, the 'Measured Mile' was between two lamp posts and our Mille Miglia was all way round the block, which was really very adventurous. That was how I got interested in motor racing.

My early upbringing was very much associated with technology: I fell in love with aeroplanes at the age of about six because a favourite uncle took me to Croydon, which was then London's airport, and I can still see the big biplanes trundling in... Imperial Airways... Ensign run up over the cockpit on landing... all the crew standing to attention as those wonderful people stepped elegantly out. It really impressed me.

The looming political situation did not escape me completely. I mentioned Ilford Station and I well remember youngish and middle-aged men in black shirts selling a sort of newspaper; and my father told me that they were not nice people at all because they were fascists – Oswald Mosley's lot wore black shirts as part of their uniform when they were formed in Britain.

On one occasion, I think by accident, my father and I were in the presence of a major riot in Aldgate, when the fascists were confronted by communists. There were mounted police and my father kept me well out of danger – there were scenes of very considerable violence and I remember being horrified when I saw a man throw a bag full of marbles onto the road so that the police horses would skid on them and come to grief. That offended me beyond speech, let alone the political implications; and I also saw one protester – no, I won't use the word protester; they were rioters – and it may have been the chap who threw the marbles who was grabbed by the collar by a policeman on foot and punched very hard under the chin and, at the same time, let go so that he went backwards through a plate glass window. These were very disturbing times for a young boy but my father taught me the difference between right and wrong and about civil liberties.

I must also mention the other two members of my immediate family. My sister, who was four years older than me, went to a different school. She was sent as a fee-paying pupil to the local Ursuline Convent, a Roman Catholic school, where she received a very good education indeed and I know that she looks back with the same degree of affection to her schooldays as I do to mine. Until very recently she was in close touch with two of her particular schoolfriends, so that speaks for itself.

Like tens of thousands of our generation, my sister and I listened avidly to the daily BBC *Children's Hour* on the radio. We were the first among our neighbours to have 'a set'. Our father had rigged a single-wire aerial, running the full length of our garden, and built a recharging unit for the batteries – then called accumulators – in the cellar using a carbon filament bulb. We were duly enrolled as members of the *Radio Circle*, and had our birthdays read out by Uncle Mac, the great Derek McCulloch.

The *Toytown* serial plays were our delight, with Larry the Lamb, Denis the Dachshund, Ernest the Policeman and Mr Growser – all parts played by the uncles and aunties of the Children's Hour family. There was also a regular summary of news and international events, brilliantly presented by Commander Stephen King Hall. He always ended with the words: "Be good, but not so frightfully good that someone at

once says, 'Ah, and now what mischief have you been up to?'
– but fairly good, you know." It was the epitome of middle-
class Britain in the 1930s, and certainly influenced a considerable proportion of the generation which fought and won the
Second World War.

And my mother. If I worshipped my father I adored my mother.
She was the most loving, understanding creature in the whole
of creation as far as I was concerned. She was so soft to the
touch and so sympathetic. I really think she was a perfect
mother. Unfortunately she did not enjoy very good health and
I'm not sure that that wasn't as a result of my birth. My father
was disinclined to talk about that but I think my mother had a
very bad time. We lived, the four of us, together as a very
happy family and my father, when I was still quite little, would
tease me for being a mother's boy because after tea on Sundays
I would creep up and snuggle up onto her lap. I can remember
to this day the wonderful warmth of that all-embracing caress.
I loved her most deeply. And when she died in the 'flu epidemic
of 1933, I was desolated. My father was very nearly destroyed.
   It was my mother who taught me my love of music. She also
taught me the legends of Ancient Greece and Rome which she
read from two books, written in a rather romantic style, I
suppose, and of course she taught me from the Holy Bible. But
she did introduce me to music in so many ways: she played the
piano and on very special evenings when my Uncle Albert, my
mother's brother, was still alive, he would come to stay with us
over the weekend and we would have a musical evening. My
mother would play the piano and my father and Uncle Albert
would sing duets. My uncle was a tenor, my father had a good
baritone voice and they would sing the ballads of a slightly
earlier period, songs like *The Two Grenadiers* and *Trumpeter,
What are You Sounding Now?* These were songs of battles, and
moved me almost to tears. I would say:
   "Uncle and Daddy, don't sing that song again, it's so sad",
but they of course were enjoying themselves enormously, the
three of them. They were very good friends quite apart from
their family relationship.

31

It was also my mother who taught me my love for animals. My father wouldn't allow us to keep a dog because of the potential damage to his precious garden but he in no way inhibited my enjoyment of other people's animals. One of my earliest equine friends was the greengrocer's horse – big, black, called Bob – and I think they came once a week. I was encouraged by my mother to go out, reach up and pat Bob's nose and give him a piece of carrot or an apple. Consequently, as soon as they arrived at our house, Bob knew exactly where he was and Mr Gurr the greengrocer did not have to pull him up. In fact he would come halfway across the pavement, waiting for me.

When we went on holiday to the little village of Jevington in Sussex I got to know the local farmer very well, thereby becoming friends with his two, big, beautiful Shire workhorses, called Flower and Prince, and in the book is an absurd picture of my little legs stretched to the ultimate, sitting on the huge, broad back of Flower. It's not surprising, therefore, that as soon as I was old enough I cycled to a riding school behind the famous King's Head pub at nearby Chigwell, in Essex, and there I was taught to ride. Equally not surprising, as soon as I was able to I had horses of my own and it is for that reason that I never took up golf. I had had a crack at the sport as a young man and thought, 'I could really fall for this', but I realised that I simply did not have the time to play it, spend time with my family and have our own horses.

A major influence in the young lives of my sister and me was our Great Aunt Lena. She was Miss Lena Mohr, the sister of my maternal grandmother and, like her, she was born in Germany. And as did so many young women of her age she became a lady's maid and later the beloved companion of a wealthy lady called Miss Corry. They travelled together in Europe by rail and boat, as was the custom of the time, and my aunt excited my imagination with stories of the lovely places they had visited. After our mother died Lena came to live with us. In later life we referred to her affectionately as our Victorian Great Aunt.

Such indeed she was, and she certainly looked the part. I can see her in my mind's eye very clearly: grey hair swept back rather severely, and tied in a bun at the back. She always wore a lace front with a little velvet choker, often with a very pretty cameo brooch at her throat. She was in a way quite a severe person. I remember her saying things like: "Oh, Raymond, don't be so tedious" or, "Don't be so trying" or, "Don't be so disagreeable." She was a very beneficial influence on our lives. Effectively she took care of us two young teenagers until my sister was old enough to take over the reins as housekeeper.

Aunt Lena then went to live in a flat in a nearby road in Ilford, at which time her furniture was taken out of store and, as a result of her background, she had some most beautiful pieces including monographed silverware, a very beautiful clock and one piece of furniture which fascinated me as a small boy. A sort of reading desk, it revolved and on its shelves were bound copies of *Punch* going back to the year dot – and I could put these on a kind of sliding stand, integral with this reading desk, to browse through the pages from all those years ago. For a young boy, growing up, it was an extraordinary insight into the humour of the period.

Reverting to my schooldays, I suppose by modern standards the conditions were pretty primitive. For example, the toilets were outside and on the far side of the playground, forty yards from the main school building. So in the winter, or if it was raining, this was a considerable discouragement against an excuse to get out of lessons for a minute.

At the age of nine or ten, we divided. The girls went upstairs to the first floor whilst the boys went to the third – and this all-male environment was a considerable change. Again I was extremely fortunate with my teachers. My class master, who followed along from year to year, was called Mr Kempson. He was young and short. There was a rumour that he had been an officer in the Machine-gun Corps in the First World War but in those days anyone who was greatly admired would be so credited.

He was an excellent teacher but a very firm disciplinarian who actually gave me the cane – not a pleasant experience. The charge was that I was leading a gang in the playground. My defence was that we had a 'chasing club' – pretty ingenious as an excuse, but it was really just a game. Whenever we caught whoever we were hunting, we didn't knock him about or anything. It really was the simple joy of the hunt, I suppose.

Anyway, gangs were forbidden, I was accused of leading one and I was duly punished. I was called out in front of the class – because it was a public ritual – and told to raise my right hand to shoulder height, fully extended. I think Mr Kempson said: "Look at me"; anyway I did, I looked him squarely in the eye and there was a swish and a really sharp, sharp pain in my right hand. It was a very light cane and it was used most infrequently because it was the ultimate sanction. So I went back to my seat with tears burning in my eyes but determined not to blub under any circumstances. I told my parents when I got home and, contrary to the stories which one reads today – of children being punished and parents protesting in no uncertain manner at the school – my parents invited Mr Kempson to tea. They were fellow teachers, they understood each other and also I know my father used the cane, again very infrequently, at his school to deal with any unruly boy who needed to be put back very firmly in his place.

The way the cane was used at both my schools, I'm sure, did no one any real harm and did the whole lot of us a great deal of good. It was the ultimate lifeline of discipline. Writing 100 lines is one thing but the short sharp shock of the cane is a very different matter. And, after all, what I was accused of – I realise as an adult – was a form of bullying which, of course, was in no way to be tolerated in those days any more nor less than it should be tolerated today.

The year in which I was eleven years old was by far the most eventful of my young life. In fact, all too eventful. The King George V hospital in Ilford was amongst the finest of its kind at that time. Built in the early 1920s, it stood well back from the South End Road, in its own grounds. Its wards were wide and lofty and well lit by daylight. And in it, I very nearly died.

I developed appendicitis, a quite common illness among children at that time, and the necessary operation was followed by a curious condition called 'ether pneumonia'. This was, as its title explains, a product of the quite primitive anaesthetic of those days, literally a cotton wool pad on a frame, pressed over one's face on which ether was sprinkled, and out you went.

The operation was successful but I developed difficulty in breathing and I had pain in my chest. I became very ill indeed. And I knew it. What made matters worse was that, while I was lying in hospital, all my friends were off on a school visit to the Hendon Air Display. My passion for flying was already strong and I had really set my heart on seeing that.

It was my father who really kept me going, as he cycled to work. Every morning after leaving home, instead of setting course for his school he did a diversion to a point on the far side of the main road from the hospital, where he knew I could see him from my bed. I simply could not wait to see him arrive on his bicycle, wave to me a couple of times and then ride away again. I waved back but of course he couldn't see me. It was such a caring gesture that I marvel at it to this day.

There was no bed available in the children's ward – I guess there was hospital overcrowding even in those days – so I was put into a men's ward. It was very long and very wide and the men who spoke to me were all extremely kind and sympathetic, telling me I was plucky and that kind of thing. And that too, I have no doubt, assisted in the recovery which I duly made.

Another event of major significance in that year was my confrontation with what later came to be called the 11-Plus but in those days was known as the Scholarship Examination.

The prize was to go to the Ilford County High School and wear a burgundy blazer with a crest on the pocket. I knew that my parents were very anxious that I should do well in this examination and I was equally keen not only to earn their good wishes and congratulations, but also because I recognised the importance of this major step in my little life.

In practical terms it was no big deal because the Ilford County High School building was literally adjoining the Christchurch Road Elementary and Junior School which I had just left. And again it was a building of the same period: tall ceilings, with light classrooms thanks to large windows. And the heart of the school in more ways than one was the Hall. There we assembled every day, there was Speech Day and the other ceremonies of school life and there too was the war memorial with the names of past pupils inscribed on a wooden field. These were victims of the First World War, and there were a lot of names.

I suppose I must have done reasonably well in the examination because I went into Form 1A. Each form or year was divided into three – A, B and C – really it was a system of streaming. Every year one was regraded and if you didn't make the grade you would drop out of the A form into the B or alternatively the boys in the B, if they did well, could come up. I think there were about three or four alterations every year, probably not more.

The headmaster was a Mr Digby and he replaced Mr Kempson in my affection and regard. Unfortunately, after two or three years, the school moved to a new building at Barkingside on the far side of the borough, almost on the edge of the countryside.

Already I had discovered the pain of long-distance running. The cross-country started and finished at the school but went down the road, round Valentine's Park and back to school. I had established myself more or less as quite a competent sprinter, the 100 yards and 220 yards, as they were in those days, and also the long jump and the high jump. But no doubt owing to my pulse-rate cross-country running was always a crucifixion. So I know exactly – although at a much, much lower level – the pain barrier we hear so much about in the commentaries on contemporary marathons and other long-distance events.

The new school buildings at Barkingside were at the time the last word and, even by contemporary standards, I think very good indeed. I could ride from my home to school in less than twenty minutes. Needless to say I rode as fast as I could all the time, always. The alternative was a journey, originally by tram, along what is known as Ley Street, running from Ilford Station effectively to the Barkingside terminal which was only a few hundred yards from the school. Later it was by trolley-bus, that being the means of transport if the weather was really bad or if one was suffering from a cold.

In contrast to my attitude and affection for Mr Digby I did not like the headmaster at the new building and I have to say he did not like me. Indeed he effectively terminated my time at that school. I was very bitter about that although, no doubt, it was my fault. Suffice to say, however, that my other masters at that school all won my heartfelt admiration, loyalty and attention in class, particularly my form master, Mr Bill Barrett.

This man was without doubt a major influence in my life. He taught English, which was my favourite subject, and at which I have to say I was rather good. He also taught boxing, which I therefore took up, meeting some success because, being tall and skinny, I had a long reach for my weight. He was ahead of his time in many ways and set, I think, advanced standards. For instance, on one occasion I remember he asked a small group of us to go and take tea at his flat with his wife and this of course was a tremendous compliment. We all smartened ourselves up no end and cycled over; and, really, he was going as near as he could to the ways of a public school.

He was also the drama master and I appeared in three school plays: *Twelfth Night*, *Julius Caesar* and the *Merchant of Venice*. In *Twelfth Night* I played Viola. I still had a treble voice – and boys whose voices hadn't broken quite simply took the girls' parts – and I remember very clearly a scene in *Twelfth Night* in which Mr Barrett demonstrated to me, and the boy who was playing the prince, precisely how to execute a particularly intimate sequence.

"I can see I'll have to show you both how to do this," he said. "Now watch closely." And he took both my hands in his and held them up, clasped them to his chest and he said:

"Go on, Baxter, speak your line." So, looking into his eyes, I said, "And I my Lord, to please Your Grace, a thousand deaths would die." And to my utter astonishment he said, "Oh goodness, don't look at me again like that Baxter or we might both be in serious trouble." I had no idea what he meant until years later.

I sang in that production, *She never told her love* and I remember a sense that the audience was really captured, a magical feeling which once experienced from a stage is never forgotten, however young one may be at the time.

In *Julius Caesar* I played Caesar's wife, Portia, but my big role was Shylock in *The Merchant of Venice*, and I really revelled in that. After that production, the local newspaper, *The Ilford Recorder*, wrote: "If this boy maintains his interest in theatre, one can safely predict a great future for him."

I loved our amateur dramatics and my sister became involved with me later, when we were teenagers, in productions in an amateur dramatic society centred on our local church. We produced incredibly ambitious plays on that tiny stage: one set was in a railway carriage and the elaborate scenery had to be re-arranged in a very few minutes between acts.

I also played in the school orchestra. My grandfather had given me a violin some years previously. I had been taught in an after-school class by Mr Collier at our junior school and I was also given private lessons at home by a young woman who came to our front gate accompanied by her boyfriend, with whom she would dally for some time – to the part-annoyance, part-amusement of my parents. Anyway, she did her best with me – I just made the school orchestra, where I learnt a bit more, but I knew I wasn't very good.

We played in a concert performed by a thousand child musicians in the Crystal Palace which was a great outing and I think it's just as well there were 999 other musicians apart from me. One of my colleagues, Eric Sawyer, was already a very, very good violinist who became, in adult life, a distinguished concert soloist.

At Ilford County High School I acquired schoolboy county standard at 100 yards and 220 and in the high jump and the long jump. One summer we were visited by a party of boys from Germany. Already, my father had told me that he feared that war with Germany was inevitable and these blond, handsome boys certainly had the swagger typical of the German Hitler Youth of that day. We competed against them creditably, and were by no means a pushover, but it was a strangely challenging experience.

The bicycle was a very important element in my young life. In a street of not-yet completed houses a few hundred yards from our school at Barkingside, my friends and I played bicycle polo using walking sticks and a tennis ball – fiercely contested games after school and very good, innocent fun.

The road was totally deserted because, being unfinished, it didn't go anywhere. But there was another estate, virtually on the way to Mr Barrett's flat, where the rectangular roads to surround a block yet to be built were paved. And this provided us with a splendid circuit for every kind of bicycle race including pursuits and 'madisons' and everything we knew about bicycle sport. My father had taken me to Herne Hill, the Mecca of bicycle racing in those days, on which the great Reg Harris cut his teeth. Or rather, his tyres.

When I was about 15, one of my friends from our choirboy days had a Claude Butler bicycle which I bought from him. To us it was the equivalent of a Porsche Carrera today. It was craftsman-built and beautiful, with the lugs, the joints between the tubes, filed away into little Prince of Wales feathers to save weight. It was also equipped with a derailer – or *dérailleur* – gearchange and that French invention was still comparatively rare. Nowadays, of course, it is commonplace, and infinitely more complex. I think I had three or maybe four speeds at my disposal. But this high-performance bicycle brought me enormous pleasure and increased my experience to a much broader horizon.

I had two very close friends at school – Alec Mehrer, whose nickname was Dougan, goodness knows why, and Bobby Farran whom I have already mentioned, who became a brilliant pianist. He had a bicycle too but he wasn't nearly as keen as Dougan and me. And thanks to the introduction by one of my cousins to the mountains of North Wales, Dougan and I accepted the challenge of quite long-distance touring.

As a small boy I had learned to love the mountains, from our family holidays in Wales and later in Switzerland, and our bicycles gave us the opportunity to explore and enjoy the ranges of the Lake District and Wales to our hearts' content; not only on the mountain roads and off-road tracks which we explored extensively but also by changing our shoes and doing a bit of what we called 'scrambing' – which was a cross between fell-walking and rock-climbing. We climbed all the celebrated peaks in the Lake District: Scafell and Scafell Edge, the Langdale Pike and the other notable mountains which were well within our capability to scale.

We toured in the strict sense of the word, staying bed-and-breakfast in farmhouses for the most part. When we first started I remember bed and breakfast in a farmhouse for two young boys would cost us three and sixpence (18p) each: with immaculate bedclothes, charming motherly farmers' wives and an excellent breakfast to send us on our way.

Taking our bicycles with us in the guard's van, at no extra charge, we travelled by train to Chester, for the mountains of North Wales, or Preston for the Lake District, and enjoyed wonderful adventures.

Indeed, the day war broke out, at 11 o'clock on 3rd September 1939, Dougan and I were sailing a dinghy off Walton-on-the-Naze in Essex. Offshore, we heard an air-raid siren so we immediately hurried back on our bicycles towards Ilford. Approaching London, we looked anxiously, half expecting the sky to be black with smoke from the first air raids, which of course did not happen until later.

Back at school, my friends and I had established a secret meeting place, under the school stage of all places and entered by a trap door behind the wings to the right of the stage. When you dropped through it you were in a situation of total privacy, an exciting darkness in which you could only crawl about. That was our den and was obviously no heinous crime by itself. What really was serious was that we were discovered, *smoking under the stage*. There were other misdemeanours, too, and I had been warned – I suppose, in fact, I was a bit of a rebel. The headmaster made it clear that, after the summer holidays, I would not be welcome to return.

I was truly shattered: I know that my form master, Bill Barrett, and at least two other masters pleaded with the headmaster on my behalf. Apart from anything else, my next role in the school play was to be Hamlet, and I had already started studying the part. I desperately wanted to do that because I hankered after a scholarship to RADA (the Royal

Academy of Dramatic Art). I wanted to be an actor even though I knew that my father didn't really approve – but I knew also that, if I got that far, he wouldn't have stood in my way.

Unfortunately, I had made a mess of it and my happy days at school ended less happily than I might have hoped. Based on that miserable experience, I have great sympathy for young people of today who, perhaps without serious thought, suddenly find themselves in similar circumstances. In my youth, 'substance abuse' would have meant using porridge to glue together two pieces of wood. My generation was in no way exposed to the hazards of life, other than the risks of war, which threaten the youth of today. Even so, I don't feel that the problems and challenges of making the transition from adolescence into adult life are really any more nor less tough today than they were in the 1930s.

I had not done too badly in what was then called 'Matric' or the General Schools' Examination – the gradings were fail, pass, credit or distinction – and I was very pleased indeed to gain a distinction in English and a reasonable sprinkling of credits in the other subjects. My two best friends, Dougan and Bobby, had taken and passed the Civil Service Entrance Examination. I took it and failed.

I can't remember exactly how it came about but I was interviewed for the position of trainee furniture buyer at Hampton's store, just off Trafalgar Square. Hampton's was one of the very top furniture stores in London. To me, the job definition sounded promising: I liked furniture and to be a buyer, as distinct from a salesman, suggested the possibility of responsibility and power. Alas, the job turned out to be little more than that of a glorified office boy. I hated every minute of it and left narrowly, I believe, before being sacked.

By that time, I was literally counting the days before, at 17 years and nine months old, I could apply to join the Royal Air Force as Voluntary UT (Under Training) Aircrew, but before I was called up I took what was to me just another 'fill-in' job. With the Metropolitan Water Board, it was not quite the Civil Service but near enough, I hoped, to relieve my father of his growing apprehension concerning my future.

Chapter 4

Training for War

War broke out. Recruits over 16 years of age were called to join the LDV – Local Defence Volunteers – the predecessor of the Home Guard. I duly joined the Metropolitan Water Board ranks of the LDV, was given a lightweight khaki battledress – gaiters and boots came later – but I also got a cap and a badge denoting that I was a soldier of the KRR, the King's Royal Rifle Brigade.

What's more, I was entrusted when on duty with a .303 Lee-Enfield, the standard issue army rifle of the First World War. The rifle and its ammunition – a clip of five .303 bullets – were handed to us at our duty post and we were given a rudimentary knowledge of rifle drill. The task of my colleagues and me was to defend the vital water supply installation of the Metropolitan Water Board in the Greater London Area and my post was a pumping station at Redbridge on the edge of Wanstead Park, a large public area mainly of unspoiled woodland. Needless to say, I cycled in uniform from home to my duties in the evenings because, like the majority of my MWB colleagues, I only undertook night duty. During the day, in our offices, we ran the business of our greatly respected employer, which from its very origin established a model in public service later to be followed throughout the world.

One night, posted alone on sentry duty at 0100 hours in a dark, quiet and somewhat unnerving environment I decided, in order to keep myself awake, to execute what I had been taught under the heading of rifle drill. One of the orders in this routine was: 'For inspection: port arms.' The rifle was brought up, smartly across the chest and the breech was opened by pulling back the bolt. Alone in the dark I did that and, after a short pause for the imaginary inspection by an officer, I slammed the bolt home, awaiting the next order: 'Ease springs.' Now that meant pulling the trigger so, after a suitable pause, I did just that; and there was the most almighty bang, which reverberated through the silent night.

As I stood there, petrified, my fellow volunteers of the Guard turned out with commendable speed, demanding the location and nature of my target. I was, beyond question, the original Stupid Boy of *Dad's Army*!

At last came the call for which I had waited so long and so impatiently. A big envelope, marked OHMS, dropped through the letterbox of our home in Wellesley Road, and I was on my way. I was ordered to report to an address in St John's Wood, the well-to-do area of north-west London. The events which followed came with such bewildering speed that, even today, I find it difficult precisely to recall. I can only sketch in what I now recognise as an extraordinary experience.

There was an inescapable irony in the fact that we, the potential aircrew of the Royal Air Force confronted with the task of sweeping the enemy from the sky, were fed in the London Zoo. We were kitted out – given our uniforms – at Lord's Cricket Ground. As new recruits we were 'Aircraftsmen, Second Class' – or 'AC Plonks' – and we therefore had no badges of rank but the eagle of the Royal Air Force at our shoulders would have been distinction enough. However, we also enjoyed the unique privilege of wearing a white flash tucked into the front of our forage caps. These denoted us as UT aircrew as distinct from any other branch of the service.

The quarters in which we were billeted were the luxury flats in tall buildings – there were no tower blocks then – which stand to this day in St John's Wood. They were stripped of all furniture but there were beautiful parquet floors and the bathrooms, in which the hot taps ran hot (the luxury of it!), were intact. We slept on what were called 'biscuits' – square mini-mattresses, stuffed with horsehair and laid on the floor. We had two or three blankets and every morning before inspection this pathetic little bundle of bedding had to be laid out according to a strictly defined pattern while we stood to one side – the order was: 'Stand by your beds' – awaiting the wrath of the corporal of the pre-war regular Royal Air Force who was responsible for our good order and discipline.

Very early on we were paraded in line, stripped to the waist, to receive our jabs, inoculations against heaven knows what. By this time I had acquired a new friend, a tall, blond ex-public schoolboy called Peter Banks. He was immediately ahead of me in the 'jab line' and as he took the needle I watched a little patch of green, between his shoulder blades, spread upwards and outwards and I caught him as he fell backwards towards me. For the few weeks we were together we became close friends, and very dependent, the one upon the other.

After ACRC – or 'Arsie-Tarsie', the Air Crew Receiving Centre – came ITW (Initial Training Wing). As at St John's Wood it was accommodation which determined location. The holiday resorts of north and south-west England offered hundreds of hotels of all shapes and sizes, and they were devoid of customers. My group was sent to 5 ITW, Torquay, to occupy what was I am sure to become later the original for *Fawlty Towers*. We slept comfortably enough on metal beds with sprung frames, crowded into every available room, with just sufficient space to walk between them.

In command was an ex-regular army senior NCO, now commissioned as a non-flying pilot officer – 'wingless wonder' to us. Obviously proud of his new rank and his uniform, he was not above teaching us how to polish our boots to the mirror finish of guardsmen. But he also kept a watchful eye on his young charges. We had an RAF chaplain to care for our spiritual being. He certainly won my confidence and, indeed, affection. But his visits to our dormitory, which often over-rode 'lights out', were not to the taste of our officer. I thought them a warming example of pastoral care. The possibility of homosexuality, of which I knew virtually nothing, never occurred to me. Such was the youthful innocence of most of us that a 25-year-old Geordie miner in our room was subjected to admiring questioning. He had had sex.

It was an energetic existence. We were not individuals, we were a flight, about 24-strong, ordered about at every minute of the day by yet another pre-war regular RAF corporal. He marched us as a squad everywhere at 110/120 paces per minute, and Torquay is a hilly little town. We marched from place to place... to eat, to learn the Morse code – read it and transmit – to listen to lectures and to strip and reassemble guns. We marched to Pay Parade where the few shillings we earned were literally placed into our caps as we held them out – hence 'cap in hand'. We also marched to march again on the parade ground – 'square-bashing'. Actually I quite liked it and when it was my turn to shout the orders I enjoyed delaying 'About Turn' to the very last yard of available space before chaos would have been gleefully exploited by my friends and comrades.

After six weeks we were 'passed out' as LACs (Leading Aircraftsmen) with our first badge of rank, a propeller badge on the upper sleeve. Far more exciting, we were issued with flying kit – a one-piece Sidcot suit, fleece-lined boots and leather helmet. That was quite something to take home on ten days' embarkation leave.

In October of 1941, the sight which greeted us at the mouth of the Clyde (the tail of the bank) is with me still. Grey ships lying almost crowded offshore, grey sky, grey mountains and a deep sense of tension and challenge, not unmixed with foreboding. We had little idea of where we were going other than Canada, South Africa or, possibly, the United States. We were taken by ferry to climb the steep gangway, kitbags on our shoulders, and board the *Louis Pasteur*, a crack French transatlantic liner.

Stripped of her finery, we were packed aboard to sleep in hammocks, slung almost touching in the 10ft space between decks. We were fed in shifts, in the dining space, eating out of our mess tins (a shallow, rectangular metal pan with a handle), with our own 'irons' (cutlery) and a mug. It may sound rough, but so was the sea.

Another image crystal clear in my memory is standing in ranks, on the deck, at 'boat stations' wearing clumsy, kapok-stuffed lifejackets over our greatcoats. We were 24 hours 'out'. The sun shone from a blue sky flanked with brilliant white clouds which matched the foam of a big sea. Clearly travelling at maximum speed – probably about 20 knots – the ship had a majestic pitch and roll (years before stabilisers). Flanking us on both sides were our 'screen' – corvettes and a destroyer – almost disappearing in spray and, no more than 300 yards astern, a capital ship of the Royal Navy in all her glory – possibly a cruiser, but maybe a battleship – slashing through 25ft waves and sending tons of white water flying back over her huge guns.

She was there because German heavy raiders were known to be on the prowl in the Atlantic, as well as the U-boats. Frankly I did not fancy my chances if it came to swimming, but the spectacle was so exhilarating that it was impossible to be afraid.

Our trans-Atlantic passage took five days to Halifax, Nova Scotia, a port which not even its proudest son could call beautiful. To us it was another world – at night, no black-out!

After a journey by special train to Moncton, New Brunswick, where the local people could not have been more hospitable, we were stuck in a holding camp, impatient to get on with it. It seemed an age, maybe three weeks, before we were issued with our grey Fifty Shilling Tailors suits with a light blue tie. The United States had yet to be forced into the war by Pearl Harbor, so we were to travel as civilians. But where? The word was Miami. Florida? No, Oklahoma. Never heard of it.

A two-day train journey via Chicago and we arrived at No 3 British Flying Training School (BFTS). This was based on an

American civilian establishment called the Spartan School of Aeronautics, taken into Royal Air Force control but retaining American flying and ground instructors, aircraft, maintenance and catering. It was the winter and early spring of 1941, bitterly cold in the open cockpits of the Fairchild PT19 on which we started (similar to the British Miles Magister), and not much warmer under the sliding canopy of the Vultee BT13 and North American AT6 (Harvard) to which we progressed. We had a little snow but I cannot remember losing a single day's flying because of the weather. Our flying instructors were American civilian pilots from a variety of backgrounds, including crop-dusting and air circuses, mostly in their late twenties, although our Chief Instructor, Bill Rogers, was 40-plus.

My *ab initio* instructor was a tall and handsome young man called Bob Swanson, only four years older than me. He sent me solo on my eighth day of flying, after six hours, 55 minutes of dual instruction – the first in our course – and he won my total confidence, respect and admiration. We learned navigation in the classroom and by flying cross-country in daylight and at night. The flat landscape of the Panhandle country made map-reading easy. All the roads and boundaries were straight lines – north/south and east/west – and the few rivers and railways were therefore prominent. Towns and cities were visible for miles, particularly at night, and airfields were identified by brightly flashing beacons. We learnt instrument flying 'under the hood', a black canopy which covered the pupil's cockpit, and on the Link Trainer – little mock-up aeroplanes, with full instrumentation, which responded to the controls – the original flight simulator.

Miami was a typical 'small town Mid-West' and its townsfolk greeted us warmly. Families welcomed us to their homes, particularly if a daughter was being dated. We were free to roam at weekends.

The father of one of the girls I met owned the local radio station at Pittsburgh, Kansas. He invited me to broadcast live a 'March of Dimes' appeal – a national wartime charity. I now realise that this was my first ever broadcast. He very kindly offered me a job, should I return, but his daughter wrote and told me she had married a sailor.

After our elementary flying training on the PT19s we got a week's leave. I took myself, by myself, to New Orleans by Greyhound bus. My purpose was to hear Louis Armstrong. Not only did I hear him, I shook his hand.

"I've travelled 4,000 miles for this," I said.

"Well, thank you, and good luck, son," he replied.

Along the highway, Route 66, there were 'diners' and 'honkytonks' with a bar, miniature dance floor and jukebox.

There were oil wells and mineral mines in the vicinity and communities centred on them were less predictable. If we went into them and the jukebox played *There'll be Bluebirds Over the White Cliffs of Dover* we knew we were welcome. If someone threw a bottle, we did not stay to argue.

We were students at a university of the air, mad keen to learn, so there were no problems with discipline. We were lucky because some others of our kind, who went to US Army or Navy flying schools, were subjected to strict discipline and tedious routines and customs. There was even a minor mutiny of British cadets at Pensacola, the famous US Navy base.

Our final flying check-out was with the RAF wing commander. Spinning in the AT6 Harvards was forbidden by the Americans. The WingCo made each of us do a spin and recovery – just to prove a point, I suppose.

The journey home in May 1942 was a re-run of our arrival but this time we wore uniform with wings on our tunics. We sailed from Halifax in the Polish liner *Battori*, in considerably greater comfort than before. But it was a high-speed dash under Naval escort, back to the Clyde. As several hundreds of trained aircrew we were, after all, a highly valuable cargo. It is a remarkable but generally overlooked achievement that not a single troopship was lost on trans-Atlantic passage to Britain, including the ever-mounting tide of United States personnel as the war progressed.

After no more than two weeks' disembarkation leave, and the

delights of reunion with family and friends, it was off to No 5 Advanced Flying Unit at Ternhill in Shropshire. I had achieved my ambition to continue single-engined flying. I was a fighter pilot in embryo.

Ternhill was a pre-war RAF station with a hard runway and permanent brick buildings. I flew Miles Masters Mks I, II, and III. I did not like any of them much. The Mk I had a Rolls-Royce Kestrel in-line engine and was underpowered; the Mk II had a Bristol radial and my preference, the Mk III, had an American Pratt & Whitney.

They were rather clumsy gull-winged, wooden trainers with two cockpits in tandem. Much more challenging was the staggering difference between flying over the 'straight-line' landscapes of the Mid-West and the apparent chaos of the English Midlands. It did not take long however to get that sorted but the black-out made night-flying, which I had quite enjoyed in America, a nightmare in England. There was still a challenging path to be followed before joining an operational squadron.

Chapter 5

Fighter Pilot

Although I never met R J Mitchell, I know his son quite well and I have a statuette, presented by the Stoke-on-Trent Engineering Society, of which he was an illustrious member. It was my reward for delivering a lecture entitled 'RJ's Brainchild' – referring to the Supermarine Spitfire which played a major role in the history of our country and became the second most important love of my life.

During my BBC Television commentary on the VJ Day celebrations on 19th August 1995, at the conclusion of the official fly-past over the Tower of London and the Royal Yacht *Britannia* with Her Majesty the Queen and members of her family on board, I tried to match words to the appearance of the lone Spitfire. Suddenly there was that beautiful and so familiar shape, silhouetted above the skyline of London towards sunset on a perfect summer evening. I said, "And now the one aircraft which has become the most symbolic of them all."

It was chosen to represent every type of aircraft of the British and Commonwealth air forces during the Second World War, the aircrews who flew them, and those 70,253 from the

Royal Air Force alone, including many of my personal friends and squadron comrades, who gave their lives in pursuit of victory.

Faced with the task of selecting that single aircraft, I am sure that those who made the decision had no difficulty. By common consent, and by that I mean the tens of thousands who lined the River Thames that night, the 8.5 million UK television viewers who watched the programme and most certainly Her Majesty, whose approval had to be gained for every item in that momentous celebration, it had to be a Spitfire. Happily it was the oldest Spitfire in the world still flying, P7350.

I write this with every respect for the other great aircraft which flew in the cause of freedom between 1939 and 1945, not least of course Sir Sydney Camm's magnificent Hawker Hurricane which, during the Battle of Britain, destroyed more enemy aircraft than the whole of the rest of the defences put together.

Nevertheless, I confess to a mischievous delight in pointing out to my friends who flew Hurricanes, that in my day at OTU (Operational Training Unit) one was required to take off and land a Hurricane before one was allowed even to step into the cockpit of a Spitfire. From that you can draw what inference you may but, I warn you, be careful and be ready to ward off a short arm jab from otherwise totally respectable elderly gentlemen who are Hurricane veterans.

In my case, the desire to fly had arrived early. As 13-year-olds, my best friend and I cycled from my paternal grandmother's birthplace, the Essex village of Little Chesterford, to the RAF airfield at Duxford. There we watched spellbound for hours the beautiful biplane fighters, Gauntlets and Gladiators, and secretly I knew that what I wanted most in the world was to fly aeroplanes like that.

My father was a man of remarkable perception and from him I learned as early as 1936, or even before, that the tragedy of another war with Germany appeared inevitable.

In that year Alan Cobham's Flying Circus came to Fairlop, a disused First World War airfield some ten miles from our home. I took a ten-shilling note and six pence from my moneybox and, without a word to anyone, cycled off alone to meet my destiny.

"You're 16, of course, aren't you lad?" said the man in the pay box.

"Yes sir," I lied, as I handed him two months' pocket money.

The ten or 15 minutes which followed could have been as many years or seconds. They have assumed the dreamlike quality of a great symphony. I remember looking down vertically at the earth below. Did the God-like figure in the leather flying coat and helmet loop me on my first flight? I shall never know.

As we skimmed over the hedge to land so unbelievably fast and so close to the ground I remember thinking, "How can I ever make myself clever and brave enough to do this?"

I cycled home, still in my dream, and in response to my parent's casual enquiry:

"And where have you been, may I ask?" I said, "I've been flying, Father. And when the war comes, that's what I'm going to do." He turned away for a moment, then he put his arm across my shoulders and said, "Then I can only wish you luck, my son, but I hope to heaven you may never have to do it." At that moment I am sure he knew, and I knew, that I would.

Thus was born my determination to become a fighter pilot in the Royal Air Force. I had thought very seriously about the Fleet Air Arm because, again from childhood, I had been fascinated by ships and boats of all shapes and sizes – and particularly warships. Seeing those great grey shapes wearing their huge White Ensigns in Portsmouth or Devonport, usually from the train while going on holiday to the Isle of Wight or Cornwall, excited me enormously. But on consideration I ruled out the Fleet Air Arm because I didn't think I could possibly be brave enough to land on the heaving deck of a carrier. It wasn't until after the war that I had the opportunity to do so and I think my initial judgement was probably right.

I also considered carefully the options available. If they wouldn't have me as a pilot, I'd go as a navigator, but that would be very much second best. I was quite clear in my mind that I wanted to be a *fighter* pilot, for reasons which now seem as juvenile as they were. It was clearly *the* Glamour Job. I reckoned that with a pair of wings and an open sports car I could enjoy the still mysterious pleasures of the company of the opposite sex. Years later when I met the American nurse who was to become my wife, I had a J2 MG, and drove around with the top button of my tunic undone – the unofficial but generally accepted presumption of the operational fighter pilot.

So I guess I got that right, but that is to jump ahead several years. My other reasons for wanting to fly single-seaters were equally quaint. I did not want to be a bomber pilot; the images on the newsreel screens of the '30s, the bombing of Guernica, Ethiopia and Manchuria and similar atrocities had shocked and angered me deeply. I wanted to attack bombers rather than fly one. I say that without the slightest criticism of those heroes, including many of my friends, who were charged with the awesome task of carrying the war to the enemy homeland – a policy which at the time and to this day I totally endorse, and a judgement which, in my opinion, applies equally to the atomic attacks on Hiroshima and Nagasaki. Once one has committed oneself to the concept of personal engagement in active warfare, the philosophical argument of academics and hindsighters can be viewed from a perspective which they did not experience.

As things turned out, the Mk XVI clipped-wing Spitfires which I flew with 602 Squadron carried up to 1,000lb of bombs – two of 250lb and a 500-pounder, and I got enormous satisfaction from dropping that little lot onto the enemy, invariably on pinpoint targets.

The third reason rattling around in my confused teenage mind was that I didn't want to be responsible for the life of anyone else in my aeroplane. In fact, of course, even flying as a junior No 2, one was responsible for guarding the tail of one's leader, and later, as a leader, the responsibility increased in direct proportion to the number of aircraft in the formation. The most proud moments of my entire life came on the very few occasions – and those by chance – when I led 36 fully-armed Spitfires into action.

Anyway, however bizarre my reasoning, it all worked out

rather well. I was first in my class to go solo, after 6 hours 55 minutes, and by then my officially recorded preference for fighters was accepted by the lords and masters who governed my destiny.

And so, at last – actually a mere matter of months since I had sworn my allegiance to my Sovereign Lord, King George VI, his heirs and successors – I met my first Spitfire. It was not love at first sight. I'd already been in love with it for ages. My earliest passions and interests – engineering, power, speed and flight – were here encapsulated in a single beautiful machine and given to me, not just to play with, but to put to the purpose for which it had been created. But now we had come to the moment of truth.

Any Spitfire pilot will never, I am sure, forget his first experience of R J Mitchell's masterpiece. It was not only the airframe which constituted the challenge, it was also the engine, the aptly named and legendary Rolls-Royce Merlin.

It was for the would-be fighter pilot a milestone, the culmination of a boyhood dream and the reward of months of demanding training – inadequate though that may appear by contemporary standards. It was also the final test. This was the aeroplane on which he must graduate in order to join a squadron, or suffer the humiliation of assignment to what seemed to him a lesser role. And if today those words read like Boys' Own jingoism, those were my feelings at the time, and they were shared by those about me.

The Great Day dawned very soon after arrival at an OTU, the last phase of formal preparation for being shot at. Here even the instructors were different. Almost all had one tour of operations behind them, and were officially 'on rest', most of them impatient to rejoin the fray. Much later, when I too became one of them, I enjoyed just about the happiest six months of my life, all the fun of operational flying, and the responsibility of leadership, without getting shot at.

For all of us, our initial assessment of a Merlin was that it was the most powerful engine we had encountered. I had come from an AFU (Advanced Flying Unit) equipped with Miles Masters, the all-wooden two-seat trainer powered by Rolls-

Royce Kestrels, Bristols or Pratt & Whitney radials. It was a short course of a mere 17 hours, but its climax and final sortie had been to fly a Hurricane. In fact the syllabus required one overshoot and two observed landings 'to approved standard'. This could be achieved in one sortie if one was lucky enough to get it right. The problem was that not only was the fledgling fighter pilot presented with his first experience of 1,000 hp, but it was an airframe of which he was totally ignorant, except in theory. He had to do it all by himself from scratch, without the luxury of the dual instruction which had accompanied his introduction to every previous aircraft in his logbook.

So, duly strapped into the unfamiliar Hurricane cockpit, as soon as one had the thing 'fired up', it became immediately apparent that here was something very different indeed. What to do, of course, was not sit there thinking about it, but get on with the job as smoothly and quickly as possible.

This experience arrived for me on 18th July 1942 and, despite the awesome power, the Merlin and the Hurricane proved a docile combination as soon as the brakes were released and cautious taxi-ing commenced, swinging the tail from side to side in order to see ahead beyond the great whale-back nose which totally obscured forward visibility while the tail was on the ground. Once the Hurricane had arrived cross-wind for the final pre-take-off checks, a further impression of power was conveyed by the engine – run up to almost full throttle in order to test for 'mag drop' and pitch control. Then, with pounding heart, the turn into wind, a deep breath, and the firm, smooth thrust forward of the throttle lever under the left hand.

It seemed to me that the armour-plate behind my head dealt me a smart blow between the ears as the Hurricane surged forward. But the hours of preparation for this moment paid off, and I have to say that nothing really took me by surprise. Everything happened in the way I had been told – only quicker. In very short order the wheels left the ground, and I was flying a Hurricane.

Then came something which was a standing joke among old hands: the 'porpoise climb', typical of everyone's first flight in a Hurricane I. The undercarriage was operated manually by a wobble-pump, and in the hands of the first-timer this led to a reflection of the movement fore and aft in the other arm and hand, holding the spade grip of the control column. Hence that 'see-saw' climb into the sky for the first 1,000ft or so, until the undercarriage was safely locked up and it became possible to relax and get sorted out.

The 'drill' was then, if possible, to execute a dummy approach and landing onto a cloud, offering a more forgiving surface than even the grass of the airfield to which one hoped to return. I was lucky. There were wisps of stratus cloud which were tailor-made for the purpose. So, wheels and flaps were down for an approach and landing at an altitude of 4,000ft. This provided the opportunity to experience the rapidity with which the air-speed fell away as the throttle was pulled back, and the pronounced change in attitude as the flaps were lowered. After this, inevitably came the business of pumping the damned wheels up again.

The requisite observed two landings and overshoot were completed to the satisfaction of my instructor, and my logbook tells me that my Merlin baptism was all over in half an hour. To my regret now, I never flew a Hurricane again.

So, off to OTU at Hawarden in Cheshire, which is today occupied by British Aerospace. There, after seven sorties on Master Is, and a map-reading and navigation exercise on a DH 86, all in only six days, on 4th August 1942 at last I flew a Spitfire.

And on that occasion when I 'opened the tap' for the first time, a single exclamation shot through my brain if not my lips. Though perhaps blasphemous, it was a cry of pure and simple ecstasy. By dusk next day I had five Spitfire hours in my logbook and I was flying in formation the day after that. So it couldn't have been that difficult. Could it?

My first operational unit was 65 Squadron, the famous 'East India Squadron' which had served with great distinction in 11 Group throughout the Battle of Britain. Of course, I had missed the Battle of Britain, so when the squadron was posted 'on rest' to Drem in East Lothian my feelings by no means for the last time in my air force career were, to say the least, mixed.

But I need not have worried about the possibility of boredom. We did 'stand-bys' and 'readiness' as part of the air defence system in our sector within 13 Group and got quite a few scrambles. We did an occasional air-sea rescue search or cover, we did convoy escorts and flew anti-intruder patrols against mine layers, and of course, being where we were, we spent a great deal of time flying over the sea.

On one occasion, in very marginal weather, I found myself alone and approaching the Scottish coast, just below cloud at about 200ft – not a comfortable situation, with visibility of about half a mile, when you're not precisely sure where you are.

Suddenly I saw right in front of me the huge grey shape of a battleship which I was pretty sure was the *King George V*, and which immediately lit up like a Christmas tree.

"Oh, how kind," I thought. "Recognition signals." But when those recognition signals started whizzing past me uncomfortably close, I realised my mistake. The Royal Navy could scarcely be blamed for taking no chances with an unidentified aircraft approaching from the east at low level, albeit I reckoned my ship recognition was better than their aircraft recognition. However, I was by no means inclined to hang about to argue the point.

There was another aspect of 65 Squadron's duties which I recalled later in a compendium of stories called *The Stars' War*. It reads: "You will rarely hear an RAF pilot speak ill of his aircraft. There are two reasons. Firstly, it is a matter of professional pride, and, secondly, one of confidence. Every experienced airman knows that an aeroplane which is unloved is far more likely to kill its pilot than one whose characteristics and temperament are treated with the consideration and tolerance of a lover towards his mistress, however trying that relationship may sometimes be."

Certainly that was true in my day and even now, when the demands of contemporary technology are a quantum leap from those of the Second World War, I discern the same sentiment between today's magnificent men and their flying machines.

Having survived, more or less unscathed, two and a half operational tours on Spitfires, I will yield to no one in my love and regard for R J Mitchell's masterpiece.

But, let's face it, the Spitfire was never a good night fighter. Only desperation could have led to its application to that role but I also admit to a personal prejudice. I never really enjoyed night-flying, for two reasons. First, the time-honoured adage that 'Only birds and fools fly, and birds don't fly at night'; secondly, my night vision was the only category in which I ever scored 'below average'. My friends of Bomber Command and others will, of course, laugh this to scorn, and rightly so. But when 65 Squadron was ordered to become 'Night Operational' I, for one, was considerably underjoyed.

At the time we were still stationed at Drem in East Lothian, the airfield which had given its name to the historic Drem System of lighting for night-flying. The 'lights' consisted of paraffin flares which looked like a two-gallon teapot with a wick in the spout, and produced a flickering, smoky yellow flare about as dim as the proverbial Toc H lamp, which they so closely resembled and from which period, I suspect, they dated. They were set out at about 25-yard intervals to mark the line of the grass runway, with a crossbar to show where you should have landed and a double flare to tell you that you had gone too far.

I had briefly experienced this primitive arrangement, flying Miles Masters at Advanced Flying Training School, and was not impressed. With a Spitfire it was clearly a different proposition altogether.

The required sequence of dusk take-offs and landings were no problem. Spitfires had no landing lights, but I could see the ground. However, my first Spitfire take-off in total darkness was very nearly my last, though I did not realise it at the time. In fact, I thought it had gone rather well, and the landing was far better than I had dared to hope.

Imagine my surprise therefore when, having taxied in without hitting anything, I was told to report immediately to the CO, a distinguished French Air Force fighter pilot.

"And what *ze* 'ell, Baxterre," he said, "do you sink you are doing? You 'ave us all under ze table in Flying Control."

Flabbergasted, it took me some time to realise what had happened – and then I was too embarrassed to explain. When I had eased the throttle forward for take-off, I remembered being impressed by the violet flames from the exhaust stubs of the Merlin. In daylight I had never seen them. At night, as the power increased and the tail came up, an intermittent stream of yellow sparks added to the fireworks display. These I had wrongly assumed to be the 'gooseneck' paraffin flares of the Drem System, flashing past as I accelerated. Following these sparks from my own exhaust stubs, I had swung right – Spitfires tended to swing left on take-off, requiring correction from the pilot – and I cleared the flying control tower by inches. I remember wondering for a millisecond why it was there.

Those who witnessed it, the CO in particular, reasonably assumed that on my first night take-off in a Spitfire, I had executed a 'split-arse' turn off the deck in order to 'beat up' Flying Control.

Blatant irresponsibility. Show off!

There is not much one can do in such circumstances. I was lucky and I never made that mistake again. There were then, and still are, those less fortunate. A few months later I volunteered for an overseas posting and in March 1943 went to the North African campaign, joined 93 Squadron and predicated the future of my life.

Daily life with 93 Squadron was quite unlike anything in my previous experience. I had come to know the meaning of the words 'on active service' – apart from anything else it meant you did not have to put stamps on your letters. Now I found myself on active service in the field, and that proved to be literally true for most of the time we followed the front line. Except for the brief, luxurious interludes when we were housed in requisitioned villas in Tunis, Malta and eventually Naples, for the rest of the time we lived under canvas – in fields.

Very soon after my arrival I was shown to my quarters. I recognised it immediately. It was the standard British Army ridge tent which had provided shelter for servicemen since before the First World War, and probably long before that. Its familiarity was due to the happy hours I had spent as a little boy studying the bound volumes of *Punch* and *The Illustrated London News*, one of the many delights of visiting my Victorian Great Aunt. I had thrilled to page after page of the brilliant drawings which illustrated the graphic accounts of the activities of 'our brave fellows' in defence of Crown and Empire across the world. Now I was to occupy the very same accommodation as that of my boyhood heroes – canvas supported by wooden poles.

But these tents were not assembled in the parade ground order of the Raj. They were scattered in olive groves, orchards, pinewoods or anywhere within easy distance of our aircraft where some element of tree cover was available. And they were dug out. The floor space was excavated to a depth of about four feet. This not only increased the headroom but also the impression of spaciousness to a remarkable degree. But this was not the primary objective of our semi-troglodyte existence. Our dug-out tents were arranged to provide maximum possible protection against aerial or other attack by the enemy, and in this they proved remarkably successful on more than one occasion.

We slept on standard service camp beds of the period – an ingenious arrangement of canvas stretched between an interlocking wooden frame supported on lattice-like legs, and each tent was shared by three pilots except for the CO who, like the adjutant and the MO, enjoyed single accommodation while the two flight commanders 'doubled up'.

A duckboard floor and single locker for each occupant completed the furnishing but ingenuity provided additional character and convenience. The vertical earthen sidewalls could be sculpted to provide shelving, whilst empty metal ammunition boxes and odd pieces of wooden planking could provide anything from a bookcase to the indispensable card-table.

Thanks to the Canadians, we played poker a lot – and these were wild games, in every sense. We used matches as chips. We gave them a nominal value and played for high stakes, but since it was a totally closed game, the theoretical money just went round and round – and no-one ever called pay day. Poker players will understand my use of the word wild – a typical Canadian game-call would be: "Seven card stud. Aces and deuces wild," ie they could be played as any card.

Really we were quite comfy for most of the time except for room temperature control. When it was hot, with every available flap open, it could be very hot, and when it was cold – and winter can be very cold in the North African hinterland – it was perishing.

Our mess was a marquee – hessian matting, wooden trestle tables, a bar to which untold ingenuity was devoted, as well as the majority of our spare time. And in the North African campaign the Royal Air Force, thanks to Air Marshal Coningham, made a break with the accepted tradition of separate messes for officers and NCOs. The aircrew mess was, as its name implies, shared by all and was the setting for some of the most hilarious parties it has ever been my good fortune to enjoy.

93 was a 'mixed squadron'. We had pilots from Canada, Australia, New Zealand, Kenya, Rhodesia, and one of our flight commanders, F/Lt Jimmy Grey, was an American, a former member of the famous Eagle Squadron of volunteers from the USA who joined the Royal Air Force before America entered the war – and were subsequently threatened with loss of citizenship if they did not abandon the RAF and don the uniform of Uncle Sam. Many, including Jimmy, declined despite the obvious advantages, including at least twice the rate of pay – and thereby won a special regard from the rest of us.

The impact of these comrades from overseas on the mess culture of the squadron – and probably its 'operational attitudes' – was significant. There was 'Screw' Rivett, for example; a tall, dark and handsome 'privileged boy' from the Australian outback. He told me, in quiet conversation about his background – during one of the rare moments of comparative peace for serious talk – that his family homestead was a good deal bigger than the Isle of Wight.

Of several Canadians, one was outstandingly bonkers. A flight lieutenant, universally known as 'Mac', he had served on the Arctic convoys as one of those incredibly brave Hurricane pilots who flew off merchant ships when their convoy was attacked. Should they be too far offshore, they had nothing to land on and either ditched or baled out, in the hope of being rescued from those icy waters.

Mac still had his black navy sou'wes'ter, from which he drank copiously if there was a piss-up in the mess. He also had a wonderful pair of Russian flying boots, with leather as soft as a Georgian ballet dancer's pumps. One day he failed to return from an Op (operational flight).

A few nights later, when the poker was in full swing, Mac's boots had joined the pile of matches in the pot, as was the custom. Suddenly the tent flaps were thrown wide and there was Mac, having walked home.

"You bastards," he yelled, grabbing his boots. "Deal me in!"

My logbook has reminded me that I flew with 93 Squadron for only nine months. That surprised me. In retrospect it seems like at least a couple of years, for so much was crammed into that short space of time – the North African Campaign, Malta, Sicily, Salerno, Naples – and I ended up in hospital back in Algiers where I'd started from. So, how fared my love affair with the Spitfire during that tumultuous period?

Well, by now, like a good marriage, ours was an affectionate working relationship, which was just as well because it was called upon to survive a trauma or two. For example, it was almost always either too hot or too cold in the cockpit. And on long sorties over Sicily from Malta, or covering the invasion at Salerno from Sicily with 90-gallon long-range tanks, the Spitfire did not provide the most comfortable accommodation ever devised.

Specific incidents spring to mind, such as my first smell of Africa when I arrived at La Senia, near Oran, from Gibraltar in a torrential downpour in which two of the section which I was leading pranged on landing – an unhappy conclusion to a ferry flight intended to bring replacement aircraft and pilots to the front line squadrons already in action.

But next day I flew to Maison Blanche just outside Algiers, then on to Setif, and within a couple of weeks joined 93 at Souk el Kemis, which was about 90 miles from nowhere.

The boss of 93 Squadron, Wilfy Sizer, was a truly great CO. A pre-war regular, he had boxed for the Royal Air Force, got a DFC in the Battle of Britain and, from the moment we met, when I reported my arrival to him in his tent, he commanded my unqualified respect, admiration and affection. I'd have followed that man anywhere and indeed I did, because after a couple of sorties, he made me his regular No 2. He was an outstanding character and fighter leader.

When the Germans broke through the American flank and began to pour through the Pass of Kasserine, he led us off in an appalling cross-wind gale after Group had left him the option to abort the mission. It was a long way out of our normal sector and in awful weather, but he found that narrow pass through high and forbidding mountains, and we shot the hell out of them, got back, and only lost one aircraft on landing.

Another time, in full view of a visiting group of American press, he chased the 'readiness section' to their aircraft, wielding a baseball bat.

"Sorry about that," he said to his stupefied audience. "Bit of a morale problem!" He saved my life at least twice and I loved him dearly.

On 10th July 1943, the Allies invaded Sicily. 93 Squadron was stationed at Luqa, a battered airfield on Malta. It was one of those brief periods when we lived in comfort in a house – a villa on the seafront at Birzebugga Bay. Churchill had spoken about "striking at the soft underbelly of Europe." We were all for that but not so sure about the softness. We knew we were to be on patrol over the invasion beaches at first light and although we turned in early I, for one, did not get much sleep. It was pitch dark and cold as we were driven up to the airfield and there was not much chat in the back of our 15cwt truck.

As we tumbled into our dispersal – a beaten-up building on the edge of the airfield – all the lights were on. Sitting alone and staring at the huge wall map in front of him was Wing Commander 'Sheep' Gilroy, our distinguished wing leader, and a pre-war farmer in New Zealand. When I asked, one of the sentries told me he'd been there "almost all night."

The briefing lived up to its name. We knew what was expected. We showed only a tail-light. There was some overcrowding at the end of the runway and I felt my wing tip touch that of another aircraft. Fearful of missing out and/or overheating, I yelled to the airmen standing by in the gloom to check for damage. I got a thumbs-up. I turned into wind and duly followed the tiny dot of white light on the tail of the aircraft in front of me. Once airborne the tension, for me at any rate, relaxed. We got ourselves into formation in R/T (radio) silence and climbed steadily on course for the invasion beaches.

At 18,000ft we were on patrol above Acid Beach, following the shoreline just north east of the southern tip of Sicily. Before it got light I saw far below what I took to be the lights of a train which then seemed to disappear into a tunnel. I thought we had really taken them by surprise. Then I thought again – there was no railway there and it was a stream of tracer fire that I had seen. We patrolled for an hour and a half without seeing any sign of enemy aircraft. The Germans had indeed been taken by surprise.

On arrival back at Luqa we said to our Intelligence Officer at the de-brief: "You might have told us about the amphibious gliders."

"What amphibious gliders?"

We said: "Oh, Christ!" We had seen the gliders carrying British soldiers dropped short by the American tug pilots. They had crash-landed into the sea and almost all failed to reach the shore.

That afternoon 93 Squadron was on patrol again and I was flying No 2 to the CO. From 13,000ft, east of Avola and south of Syracuse, on that brilliant afternoon the invasion fleet was an extraordinary sight. We had never seen so many ships – warships and landing craft – although that number was small compared to that of the ultimate D-Day off Normandy later on. We could see gunfire at sea as we were directed by the

Top left: The Lorry Driver of the Year is presented with his trophy by Mike Hawthorn in the Standard Triumph car park, Coventry 1955. Author at extreme left.

Top right: Even 'old timers' like Fangio, Kling and Stirling Moss had to practice in every detail the repairs which may be necessary to the new Mercedes-Benz 300 SLR racing car in 1955.

Middle left: RB and Mike Hawthorn, late 1950s.

Middle right: The winning Jaguar at Le Mans 1955. A vivid reminder of how close the spectators were to the action.

Bottom left: The BBC radio commentary team at Le Mans in the late 1950s. Left to right: John Bolster, Pam Guyler, Robin Richards, RB, Anthony Hopkins.

Bottom right: Graham Hill briefs RB on the minute details of his race strategy late in his career.

Top: BBC OBs and characters. Left to right clockwise, Godfrey Talbot, Rex Alston, unknown, Brian Johnston, Pat Ewing (head of OBs Radio), RB, unknown, Stewart McPherson, Wynford Vaughan-Thomas and Clifford Morgan, relaxing over lunch in the 1980s.

Middle: RB to Bernard Lee: "But M, how can a nuclear submarine be fitted into the lipstick Bond gives to agent xx??" "My dear boy – our friend on my left has already designed it!" The author in a tie befitting his position of 'Tie Man of the Year. 1975', as voted by the Tie Manufacturers Association.

Bottom, 1, 2 and 3: Ottering. On the road, launching, and in the water at the limit of navigation on the Llangollen Canal.

Top left: A radio play being performed on Egyptian State Broadcasting, Cairo 1946.

Top right: Commentating for radio at the Herne Hill cycle track with Bill Mills (left), cycling correspondent of the *News of the World*, 8th April 1955.

Above: Nancy Mitchell, leading lady rally driver, with the author at the first TV coverage of the Motor Show, RAC Country Club, Woodcote Park in the mid 1950s.

Above right: An imaginative demonstration of luggage capacity at the show with the help of some RADA members.

Right: An Austin-Healey sports car makes an early appearance watched by the author as commentator positioned underneath the camera.

Bottom left: The first flight of Concorde 001, Toulouse, 1968, as televised at the time.

Bottom right: Early TV coverage of a helicopter flying, with author dangling in mid-air.

Top left: Boarding a Red Arrows Gnat, Biggin Hill 1967.

Middle and inset: With John Farley at the Farnborough Air Show, 1978, in the BAe's unique demonstrator two-seat Harrier. The ramp was erected by 32 Field Squadron, Royal Engineers and was also used by the Sea Harrier when it made its international debut.

Bottom left: Filming a front-line RAF squadron. In a Jaguar at Laarbruch, Germany August 1976.

Bottom right: At the 1985 Castrol Segrave Trophy presentation with test pilots John Cunningham (left) and Peter Twiss.

Top left: BFN Hamburg. British Army of the Rhine team at the International Six Days Trial, 1948. Colonel Graham Oakes is on the author's left.

Top right: Production Manager and Deputy Station Director, BFN Hamburg, with his German secretary Elisabeth Depkin. Photo taken on 12th July 1949.

Middle left: Glider flying with instructor Derek Piggott at Lasham, July 1957.

Middle right: Welcome to New Zealand. Note the author's midget (!) recorder.

Bottom: The New Zealand Air Race, 1953. Crew of the BEA Viscount with John Profumo extreme right.

Top left: March 1944. J2 MG. 'English sports car used to impress an American nurse'.

Top right: Lt Sylvia K Johnson, United States Army Nursing Corps.

Middle left: With Sylvia at her hospital in Bridport on the eve of the D-Day invasion of Europe.

Middle centre: Beating the bounds of Bridport with Sylvia's closest friends. Left to right, Bonnie, RB, Doreen Baxter. Sylvia, Grace, and 'Craig'.

Middle right: The famous Spitfire. RB in 602 Squadron's Mk XV1 LOX, Sylvia K, October 1944.

Bottom left: 17th May, 1945, Allied Officers' Club, Brussels.

Bottom centre: The president of the London Motor Club and his lady at the Annual Club Dinner, Park Lane Hotel, late 1950s.

Bottom right: With Sylvia and Graham in Milan, September 1958.

Top left: Author's second tour of Ops. Operation Big Ben with 602 Squadron, the aim to attack V2 targets in Holland, September 1944-April 1945.

Top right: 'Fighter bombers smash V2 targets' said the headline. Here RB briefs his flight prior to a raid on a target in Holland with the aid of large-scale map and PR photographs.

Middle left: Max Sutherland briefing for an attack on a V2 site. Right to left: Flg Off James Farrell, 'the human barrel' from Joisey City, New Joisey, Flt Lt Wroblinski (double Whisky), unknown, and Flt Sgt 'Fanny' Farfan.

Middle right: From left to right: Flt Lt Dickie

Pertwee, 250lb bomb, Max Sutherland, 'Fanny' Farfan, Flt Lt 'Batchy' Stevenson, Spitfire XVI.

Bottom left: Flt Lt 'Fearless' Pullman, who pranged the author's Spitfire 'Sylvia K' on 17th March, 1945.

Bottom centre left: The effect of the raid on the Shell-Mex Building, The Hague, 18th March, 1945 which the author describes in his logbook.

Bottom centre right: A recent picture of the church spire narrowly missed in the Shell-Mex raid. The cockerel has been replaced by a cross or was the bird the author's imagination?

Bottom right: Max Sutherland's elevator – hit by *flak* during the raid.

Top left: Author aged four, proving beyond doubt he was the originator of the 'straight arm' driving position.

Top right: Cricket on the lawn. Uncle Albert keeps wicket.

Middle left: At the seaside, Hastings 1929, with mother and sister Doreen.

Middle right and bottom left: Early experience led to a life-long love of horses. Flower (dapple-grey) and Prince, Jevington, Sussex 1928, Blue (double-grey) and her colt Apollo, Denham, Bucks, 1978.

Bottom right: With father and sister in 1943.

Fighter Control Ship, offshore, to intercept 30-plus Ju88 bombers. Someone yelled on the R/T: "109s, up sun!"

But we were pretty well prepared for that. Wilfy called: "Break." And suddenly there were no Spitfires around me. Within a second, Wilfy's tail wheel which I had been assiduously watching, disappeared from my windscreen. He had pulled up into a vertical climb, straight into the sun. To keep up with him, effectively inverted, I went through 'the gate' – one of the rare occasions on which I did this (going through the gate meant pushing the throttle control forward to its maximum extent, which gave you total power from the engine although the time was limited to two minutes). I saw a 109 go by in the opposite direction, pretty close. We kept on climbing and climbing, into that blinding sun and I thought: "If I spin out of this, due to lack of airspeed, I shall be a dead duck."

Wilf just hung on and on, then executed what was virtually a stall turn and brought us down right into the position to attack the 88s. We both saw hits on one but were going too fast to press the attack further and could only claim a 'damaged'. Nothing we could do about it really. There were 109s and 88s all over the place, then suddenly – as it often happens after a dogfight – the sky was empty. We got ourselves sorted out and Wilfy called the boys to reform. We were still pretty high up and he asked how I was for 'gravy' (fuel). I checked the gauge and told him I was not well placed – I realised that I didn't have enough to get back to Malta. Wilfy said: "Stay with me," and sent the rest of the boys on ahead. He got us into a controlled descent and we cleared the Sicilian coast, still on a sharp lookout for hostiles. We could then see Malta and by the time we got down to 3,000ft we were only about ten miles off Gozo, still at bale-out height. I checked the fuel gauge again – there was just the merest flicker.

"It'll be all right," said Wilfy. "I'll clear you for an emergency landing at Gozo." There was an emergency strip there, covered with Sommerfeld tracking. I went straight in with a steep, closed-throttle approach and landed with just four gallons left. Wilfy flew on, telling me to fly back to base as soon as the aircraft had been tanked up. I had a cup of tea while refuelling took place, and took off 15 minutes later to rejoin the boys on Malta. By the end of D-Day of the Sicilian invasion, 93 Squadron's total was two confirmed, one probable and two damaged.

Next day we were in action again against Ju88s and 109s. Unfortunately my section was on the wrong side of the *flak* but two of our pilots got an 88 each and another hit a 109. One of our pilots went missing but later returned safely.

When the book *Spitfires Over Sicily* was published I received a complimentary copy because its author, Brian Cull, had quoted me. The dust cover depicted a dogfight between two Spitfires and two MC202s, the Italian-built 109. I showed it to Margaret Cormack, my now part-time secretary and helper, explaining that it looked as if the nearest Italian appeared safe for the moment but the Spits should be able to get onto the tail of the far one.

I then noticed that the Spitfire letters were HN, 93 Squadron, and HNH was an aircraft I frequently flew. Sure enough, my logbook recorded the encounter. I was flying No 2 to Flt Lt Jimmy Grey, an ex-American Eagle Squadron pilot. We sent one down in flames and shared the victory. The other got away because we were too short of fuel to pursue him. Spitfire pilots operating over Sicily from Malta had always to keep an eye on the fuel gauge.

That was on 13th July. In the same engagement the CO, Wilfy Sizer, got another Italian. On 14th July we landed in Sicily, to operate from a strip near Comiso, and continued to be very busy. On the 19th we rendezvoused with a formation of American Mitchells due to attack a position north of Mount Etna. We were instructed that the target, a hill, had been captured (by The Guards) and that the attack was to be aborted. But the Americans, who had taken off from North Africa, were not responding to revised orders. Wilf Sizer tried calling them on every available frequency, but they just kept going. Eventually, with the target almost in sight, the CO called us into close formation and gently slid us in until we were directly underneath them. Then, at last, the penny dropped and as we looked up from beneath them they closed their bomb doors. It was a very dodgy incident because the American bombers were notoriously trigger-happy, by reputation at least.

On the 27th a section of us was scrambled to escort a Walrus amphibian on a successful ASR (air-sea rescue) off Messina. Again my logbook reports 'Only four gallons left' when I landed at the nearest airstrip at Lentini, fifteen minutes from our home base at Comiso. We followed the 'bomb line', covering the British Army advance while the Americans were slower in the more mountainous country to the west. We moved to Lentini and operated from there and from Pachino, living in tents. It was very hot indeed and we were flying hard every day. I contracted a form of eczema on my face. The Doc thought it may have been caused by volcanic dust in my oxygen mask. I was officially 'off flying' from 29th August to 7th September.

On 6th September the squadron moved up to Falcone and our Intelligence Officer, Alan Bromley (later a well-known playwright), drove me there in his Jeep. Below my cap I was wearing a white lint mask, with holes cut for my eyes, to protect my face. When we passed through ruined villages, women crossed themselves at the sight of me. On 20th August, Wilfy Sizer had been posted off the squadron – Operational Tour Expired. There was no great send-off: he left Pachino quietly while the rest of us were doing 'readiness' with 322 Wing at Lentini West.

If I twice owed my life to Wilfy Sizer, I certainly owed it on more occasions to my Spitfire. Once was in Malta when, returning from a Sicilian sortie, I could get only one undercarriage leg down and locked, and then couldn't get it back up again.

Flying Control suggested I should fly out over Birzebugga Bay and bale out. But I did not want to lose the aircraft and, anyway, I had seen too many bale-outs go wrong. I was confident, knowing my Spit, that I could land it on one leg – and did so with only minor damage to the wing tip and prop, none to my confidence in the aeroplane.

To this day it is not generally realised that the Salerno

landings came close to disaster. The Germans nearly drove a wedge to the sea between the British and the Americans. At one point the US Commander, General Mark Clark, asked Admiral Ramsey, in command of Allied naval forces, to withdraw his troops. Without higher authority, which was not forthcoming, Ramsey declined.

The plan for 93 Squadron was that we would land on Foxes Two, a German airstrip due to be captured on D-Plus Two. It had not been. We and our fellow squadrons were doing our best to patrol the beaches from Falcone, with 90-gallon long-range tanks and even so could only manage 25 minutes over the battle area in a two-and-a-half-hour sortie. On 11th September, approaching the end of our patrol time, the American Fighter Control Ship ordered us to chase reported bandits to the north, then land and refuel on Foxes Two.

"At last!" we thought, but as we made a circuit to land we were greeted by intense fire from the ground. They blew the tail off our newly-joined CO when he was at 40ft, wheels and flaps down, approaching the end of the landing strip.

He was killed instantly, of course. At 800ft I was hit hard and realised that a wheels-up crash-landing was inevitable because I was too low to bale out. I reported that I was going down. The oil pressure had dropped to zero and the engine temperature was going off the clock. I put the flaps down and the aeroplane immediately tried to do a roll to starboard, so I put them up again very quickly. At this point I heard a Canadian voice in my headphones, saying: "Bax! Bax! Get your tank off. Get your tank off."

It was Bill Hockey who had seen what was happening and was going up-wind on the far side of the airfield. I had completely forgotten about the almost empty 90-gallon tank, immediately below my cockpit. Bill undoubtedly saved my life because had I hit the ground with that still on board there would have been a very big bang. The release lever was low, between one's legs, and very stiff; I had quite a struggle before I felt the tank go and by this time I was running out of height very quickly indeed. Ahead of me, I saw a stretch of rough ground at the edge of a vineyard. I made for it and, at the last moment, cut off the fuel and switched off the engine. I hit the ground at about 130mph-plus and, after a slight bounce thought I was doing rather well. Then I saw an olive tree which had escaped my notice. I was heading straight for it so I put in full left rudder and we skidded past it to a halt. Immediately, everything went red.

"Oh my God," I thought, "I've caught fire after all that." But it was not fire, it was red volcanic dust, stirred up by the impact of my landing. I scrambled out of the cockpit and realised I had damaged my left knee because I fell to the ground. The noise of gunfire was all around me and I could only guess that the Germans had recaptured the airstrip. But after a bit I felt something touch my shoulder. I looked up and there was an American soldier with red crosses on his helmet and both arms, holding an entrenching tool above his head.

"Are you a Hun?" he asked. I was lying within feet of the recognition roundel on the side of my Spitfire.

Then I saw a Jeep approaching, with an American colonel standing beside the driver and firing his revolver into the air. He was in tears by the time he reached me. The Americans had panicked when they saw us approaching and when they saw 90-gallon tanks hitting the ground and exploding they were even more certain that we were the enemy.

They had killed the CO. 'Andy' Anderson and I were shot down and five other of our aircraft were damaged. The colonel sent Andy and me off in a Jeep down the road towards the coast. At the intersection, where our route joined the coast road, we found an American engineer company bivouacked in a farm. The officer in charge, a young New Yorker, Captain Erskine, made us as welcome as he could. The farmyard was running with chickens and so we suggested chicken for supper.

"Oh, no," said the captain, "that would be looting."

"If we catch and kill the chickens," we said, "will you cook them?" We did. And they did.

The house, more of a villa, was we learned the property of Baron Miglia Ricardi, who was significant by his absence. As darkness fell, we asked Captain Erskine if he was posting sentries.

"Oh, no," he said, "I have told the MP (Military Policeman) on duty at the cross-roads to warn me if anything turns up." Andy and I decided that that was not good enough and resolved to keep a watch in turn ourselves from the flat roof of the house. This we did through a night during which we heard constant gunfire in the distance but, at first light, I heard the unmistakeable creak of a Tiger tank, coming down the dry river bed towards us.

I gave the alarm. We had told the Americans to park their vehicles pointing outwards and we got away just before the first shell struck. Altogether, my logbook tells me that it took Andy and me three days to cross the Hun salient to Montecorvino. We got a lift by LCM (landing craft) to Messina and then hitch-hiked to the airfield at Falcone. We got back to the squadron just in time to stop a signal informing our families that we were missing. On the 16th we flew a 2hr 35min patrol over the Salerno peninsular and I noted in my logbook: 'The position on the ground seems improved.' On the 23rd, now flying a replacement HNH, we flew from Falcone to Montecorvino and I noted succinctly: 'And so we say farewell to sunny Sicily!'

On the 28th we flew to ASA-Batipaglia, noting: 'Took off from unserviceable aerodrome after three of 111 Squadron pranged.' On 11th October the squadron moved to Capodichino, Naples. We continued active operational flying every day and by now I knew that I was physically going downhill. I was just exhausted, noting 'Jaundice again!' in my logbook, and on 23rd November I was flown from Naples to Bari. Two days later I was moved to El Alouina and installed in No 1 RAF General Hospital. I was flown on again, on 15th December, to No 2 RAF General Hospital at Maison Blanche, Algiers, so I was back to where I had started.

After ten days, the Group Captain Senior Medical Officer came and sat on my bed: "Raymond," he said, "would it break your heart if I didn't send you back to your squadron?"

"To be frank, sir," I said, "I am very tired. I would like to go home." So, on 30th December 1943, a Liberator flown by Flt Lt Duprey – in a flight lasting ten hours and 15 minutes from

Maison Blanche to Lyneham, Wiltshire – duly took me HOME AGAIN! And straight back into hospital for a couple of weeks.

Then came a wonderful six months' break 'on rest', flying as an instructor at Montford Bridge in Shropshire. Having completed one and a half operational tours in Spitfires, on 24th February 1944 I was posted to 61 OTU Rednal. Initially I had viewed this transfer, teaching others to fly and fight Spitfires, with reservation. On the other hand, I had been invalided home – I was knackered. I had been shot down, had malaria and jaundice and I was a mess. After my spell in hospital, and four weeks' sick leave, this posting arrived.

In fact I was only based at Rednal for three days before being sent on to 61 OTU's satellite aerodrome, Montford Bridge, where four of us instructors, all operational types on rest, took the pupils for their last three weeks before they were posted to a squadron. Our brief was to simulate squadron conditions so that they knew what to expect when they got there, which is more than we had ever received!

Our job involved lots of flying in formation, low flying, dogfighting, night-flying, navigation – the whole lot. It was a great life, to be honest. We worked very hard, taking the job very seriously – and that included escorting these chaps to the pub and showing them how they should behave, when to get drunk and when not to get drunk. We would visit a great fish and chip shop in Shrewsbury, plus several pubs.

A very interesting phase came when we had chaps from the Royal Indian Air Force, as it was then. This was before Partition and the Sikhs wore beautiful sky blue turbans. We kept our flying kit in tin wardrobes which were about 6ft 6in high and about 2ft 6in wide. These chaps had to get inside their wardrobes to put their flying helmets on because, for religious reasons, we could not see them without their heads covered. As they did not wear the turbans for flying, they had to conceal themselves from us in that way to don their flying helmets. After Partition, those who wore turbans became Pakistanis. They flew slightly better than their fellow Indian pilots but they still weren't very promising.

I met my future wife while at Montford Bridge. There was an American OTU quite near and at that time there was a good deal of feeling between the RAF and the United States Air Force – and it wasn't all brotherly love. Our Spitfire pupils started getting involved in unofficial dogfights with their pupils in Thunderbolts. One day their colonel rang us up and said:

"See here, you guys, we better get our heads together before somebody gets his butt accidentally shot off. We're having a party in the mess on Friday. Why not come over?"

We did, as invited, that Friday night. There were swing doors at the entrance to the mess hall, as the Americans called it, and there was a raging party going on inside. We threw open those swing doors and there we stood, the four of us, in our best blue. I said, "Duck" as an ice cream went whizzing over our heads and hit the wall behind us. Then the colonel came out of this mêlée and said:

"Say, did someone throw an ice cream at you?" The senior of our party, an Old Etonian, reacted with some *sang froid*, saying:

"No, no, no colonel, I'm sure it just slipped out of his hand." At that moment I saw this beautiful, beautiful girl standing at the bar in a full-length green evening dress. I asked her to dance. We danced. I said:

"Either you are an English girl who has spent too much time with Americans, or you are an American girl pretending to be English." She said: "I'm from Boston." So I had to marry her.

That's what I said, and that's what I did as soon as it was reasonable to do so. She was an American army nurse with the 64th Field General Hospital, stationed at Oulton Park.

I lost my wife in 1996. She was 2nd Lieutenant, later 1st Lieutenant, Sylvia Kathryn Johnson. On the favourite Spitfire which I flew with 602 Squadron, I wrote 'Sylvia K', which was the fashion at the time.

There was a wonderful pub called the Ferry Inn, near Ellesmere, and when we were both off duty we would drive there in my MG and go on into the mountains, over the border to Llangollen. We had a marvellous time. I already knew north and central Wales pretty well, having been there as a child.

At Montford Bridge, our campsite was a short bicycle ride down the feeder road and the boundary of the airfield. Each hut had its own room – so it was not like those Nissen huts which had communal sleeping arrangements. Our pleasant life was centred on an officers' mess with a snooker table, darts, and all the usual comforts, and we all played shove halfpenny in the local pubs.

As fighter pilots we were encouraged to go shooting and I'm afraid there was a certain amount of poaching. I don't think anyone really dared object, so we shot pigeons and our very good cook made excellent pigeon pies. We also shot a few rabbits but never pheasants or partridge. I think we thought that would be going too far. We had a ball. Those were my six happiest months of the war, perhaps of my entire life, despite the CO at Rednal who had been a pre-war Olympic sprinter and had flown in the Battle of Britain.

He was the only senior officer I ever served under that I really disliked. When a WAAF dance came up at Rednal, we were supposed to be on night-flying. I cancelled that because the mist was rising off the river. It was a very misty spot, Montford Bridge, and we knew it would get worse, never mind the dance at Rednal to which we all intended to go. When this CO phoned up and learned that we had cancelled night-flying he demanded to know why. Our reply, "The mist was rising, sir," prompted him to ask: "Have you done an air test?" We said, "No. It really isn't necessary." And he replied: "You can't cancel night-flying without an air test."

So, I did this blasted air test and took off all right, but it was even worse than I thought. Although I could see the runway lights when I was over the top of them, looking vertically down, they were completely invisible when I approached to land. I made three passes and in the end I was talked down by a colleague, the senior instructor at Montford Bridge, F/Lt Jimmy Devlin. Even though I was effectively blind, Jimmy could see my navigation lights (and my life was therefore entirely under his control).

That bastard of a CO had nearly killed me. In fact if I had

not made it that last time I was going to divert, probably to Rednal. Had I thought of it, I could have dressed in my blues, done the air test, said it was too foggy, landed at Rednal and then gone to the dance. Although he thought we were looking for an excuse, we were too professional for that. I was deeply insulted.

But something happened that got me into trouble. The coalfield at Wrexham, at the northern part of our sector, was in our low flying area. When the miners went on strike, I was furious and led a formation of six Spitfires, five of them pupils, towards the colliery, which was in our designated area for such training. I pulled them into close formation and dived to what was supposed to be 250ft but I think it may have been a little less.

There seemed to be a mass meeting going on and men started running in all directions. On landing I was told to report to the station commander immediately – and he really tore me off a strip. Quite correctly. He said I could be court-martialled for interference in the civil power by the military, but stopped short of giving me a bad mark on my service record. Now, of course, I realise he was quite right to read me the riot act.

I left Montford Bridge on 4th June 1944, posted to the Central Gunnery School at Catfoss, and later joined 602 City of Glasgow Squadron. Many years later, in the 1970s, Sylvia and I went back two or three times and had a look round. Driving to Shropshire and visiting the places we remembered so well was a deeply emotional experience.

One summer afternoon before I went, Sylvia and I set off in the MG. I parked in a lane and we climbed up a lovely hill with a ruined castle on top. We stayed there some time and had a cuddle and a kiss. When we came down there was a policeman waiting with his bicycle, practically with his notebook out. We were both in civvy clothes, I in my white flying sweater, grey flannel trousers and old school scarf.

"Can I see your Identity Card?" he said, and I obliged.

"Oh yes, sir," he said. "Sorry to ask you. Hope you are having a nice time, sir. Good afternoon." He got on his bike and off he went without even asking where I had got the petrol. We were given a few precious coupons but had also found two 40-gallon drums of 80-octane which was useful as three of us had sports cars. My little MG went a bomb on that 80-octane. It was all so long ago, but the memories are precious.

The posting to 602 'City of Glasgow' Squadron took me across the Channel, five weeks after D-Day. Here again I was incredibly lucky with my CO – the late, great Max Sutherland. I think he was the most dangerous man I ever met and I almost adored him. I wasn't his No 2, although we did occasional sorties together when only a pair was required. He made me his A Flight commander.

F/Lt Andy Stewart had been my flight commander at 93 Squadron. He was understanding and encouraging and soon got me 'over the hump'. When I became a flight commander myself I remembered that lesson.

We were very active above the advance and capture of the Rhine Bridge at Eindhoven, but over Arnhem the weather turned foul and our attempts at support were severely restricted. Patrolling in and out of cloud, a totally unfamiliar black shape shot straight through the middle of us. We realised later that it was our first sight of a German jet fighter – the Me 262.

After Arnhem, during which the squadron got knocked about quite badly on the ground, not least by German long-range artillery and mortar fire on our forward base, we were withdrawn to Coltishall, re-equipped with clipped wing Spitfire XVIs, and told we now had to teach ourselves to be dive-bombers. Our principal task was to respond to the mounting threat of Hitler's V2 offensive, and so Holland became our hunting ground. We dive-bombed, skip-bombed, patrolled and strafed, bust bridges, cut railway lines and generally did our best to make life as difficult as possible for the opposition.

We dived-bombed in sections of four or more. If you were leading, you flew over the target so that it passed under your wing, just inboard of the roundel. You would then count, "One and a thousand, two and a thousand", roll on your back and come down like that, with every aeroplane following doing the same thing. So, ideally it was a stream of four aeroplanes together – or following sections of four. We bombed individually but obviously did not drop bombs until the leader had pulled away. And that was the trick. It all depended on how good the leader was because if he was too far away, and his dive wasn't steep enough, then the other dives would tend to be flatter and flatter which made the bombing inaccurate and was also dangerous. The desired angle of dive was 70 to 75 degrees, which feels vertical. Ideally we would start at 8,000ft, drop the bombs at 3,000ft and then pull out, maintaining low level to clear the area. We never bombed at random, only when we were sure we had identified our pinpoint target. If there was a lot of cloud about, this was sometimes far from easy and, of course, one was always conscious of being over enemy territory.

Long after the war I compared notes with Spitfire pilots infinitely more distinguished than myself. Each has his preference. Alex Henshaw who, as Chief Production Test Pilot at the Spitfire Shadow Factory at Castle Bromwich, flew hundreds of Spits prior to delivery, is quite clear. His favourite was, surprisingly, the Mark V: "I could take off, unloaded, and do a loop from the end of the runway, which I did to the delight of The King" (George VI).

Ray Hanna, former and formative leader of The Red Arrows, preferred the Mark IX. As, in my view, the finest post-war display pilot, he said: "Given the choice, I would prefer a Mustang to fight, a Spitfire to display."

My choice was the clipped-wing Mark XVI, with the Packard-built Merlin – probably not least because I 'came good' on that aeroplane as a flight commander of 602 Squadron.

One of our ploys was to drop delayed-action bombs which would explode at varying times up to six hours after our departure, just to keep the pot boiling. And, of course, the ubiquitous Spitfire again proved its merits as a fighting aeroplane. On one occasion, when we were skip-bombing a railway embankment at about 20ft, one of my supposed 11-

second delayed-action bombs exploded on impact. The little aeroplane practically stood on its nose, but again we got away with it.

Another time, Maxy had the crazy idea of attacking at low level the Shell-Mex building on the outskirts of The Hague, the story with which this book begins. More often at that time we ran a shuttle service: take-off from base, attack the pre-determined target, patrol, land, re-arm and refuel near Ghent, then do it all again on the way back. We did that day after day, sometimes twice.

The only thing that ever stopped us was the weather, and we pushed those limits pretty hard. The codewords for deteriorating meteorological factors were 'The door is closing'. That must have really baffled the German listening service. On one occasion, when the WAAF voice conveyed the message from Sector Control, Maxy replied:

"Thank you, darling. If you ask me, some bastard has slammed it in our faces." We landed on Fido, the lines of flaming petrol on either side of the runway, at Manston.

We flew 'Jim Crow shipping reconnaissance' – low-level flights by a couple of Spitfires, to circle and observe activity – to places like Den Helder, and provided escorts to both American and RAF heavy bombers to targets such as Walcheren and Heligoland. We covered the liberation of the Channel Islands and flew our last Op two days before VE-Day.

And then, eleven days later, came the ultimate bolt from the blue: 602 Squadron was disbanded – and they even sent girls to take our aeroplanes away. These were, of course, the courageous and wonderful ladies of the ATA, like Lettice Curtis and Ann Welch, both of whom later became friends of mine, but at that time we were too brassed off and pissed to notice.

Within a month I was off to Cairo to convert to Mustangs and later Dakotas. But that was the end of my official love affair with R J Mitchell's brainchild, although by good fortune, and with a little help from our friends, we have been able to indulge in one or two flirtations together since that unforgettable period of our romance.

RAYMOND BAXTER

YEAR 1945		AIRCRAFT		PILOT, OR 1ST PILOT	2ND PILOT, PUPIL OR PASSENGER	DUTY (INCLUDING RESULTS AND REMARKS)
MONTH	DATE	Type	No.			
—	—	—	—	—	—	TOTALS BROUGHT FORWARD
Feb.	14	Spit XVI	X	self	⟋	armed recce
,,	20	,,	X	,,		armed weather recce. 6 a/c
,,	21	,,	X	,,		Dive bombed Hazulvsche & recce.
,,	,,	,,	X	,,		,, ,,
,,	22	,,	X	,,		D.B Hazuelvsche: strafed Edenburg
,,	23	,,	X	,,		Coltishall – Ludham
,,	24	,,	L	,,		D.B Bridge & rlwy S.F Ijmuiden
,,	,,	,,	P	,,		D.B. road bridge northern area
,,	25	,,	X	,,		D.B Hazuelvoche & recce N. Amsterdam
,,	,,	,,	X	,,		,, ,, & recce.
,,	26	,,	X	,,		,, ,, ,, up to Katwick
,,	,,	,,	X	,,		,, ,, ,, E area
,,	27	,,	X	,,		armed weather recce
,,	,,	,,	X	,,		D. B & strafed Hazuelvsche
,,	,,	,,	X	,,		,, ,,
,,	,,	,,	X	,,		,, ,,
				Summary	Feb '45	
				Unit	602 Sqdn.	A/C Types │ Spit XVI
				Date	28/2/45	
				Sig	R.J. Baxter	

GRAND TOTAL [Cols. (1) to (10)] 753 Hrs. 05 Mins.   TOTALS CARRIED FORWARD

YEAR 1945		AIRCRAFT		PILOT, OR 1ST PILOT	2ND PILOT, PUPIL OR PASSENGER	DUTY (INCLUDING RESULTS AND REMARKS)
MONTH	DATE	Type	No.			
—	—	—	—	—	—	TOTALS BROUGHT FORWARD
Mar	18	Spit 16	P	Self	⟋	Skip bombed road bridge N. Gouda
,,	,,	,,	Y	,,		,, ,, Bautascher – Mex building
,,	,,	,,	Y	,,		Rlwy interdict: Delft – Rotterdam

Two entries in the author's logbook. Reading across the page, the first shows how busy he was in February; the second, on March 18, details The Shell-Mex raid.

SINGLE-ENGINE AIRCRAFT				MULTI-ENGINE AIRCRAFT						PASS-ENGER	INSTR/CLOUD FLYING [incl. in cols. (1) to (10)]		LINK TRAINER
DAY		NIGHT		DAY			NIGHT						
DUAL	PILOT	DUAL	PILOT	DUAL	1ST PILOT	2ND PILOT	DUAL	1ST PILOT	2ND PILOT		DUAL	PILOT	
(1)	(2)	(3)	(4)	(5)	(6)	(7)	(8)	(9)	(10)	(11)	(12)	(13)	(14)
95:25	612:55	12:00	7:25							40:05	23:55	2:25	
	1:20			Turned back just after cross in. Oil leak.									
	1:35			Very bad weather. Now deputy F/c to gerk									
	1:35			Strafing seems to keep light flak down									
	1:30			Roads appear empty in area Fire start									
	1:35			"House in Wood" beginning to show signs of wear									
	:20			Decent station again									
	1:45			Hague obscured but found alternative through gap									
	1:45			gock loading bombed alternative Rlwy cut &									
				bridge damage Strafed troop carrier, flamer & I brols									
	1:45			With Barrell. Got I truck flame, I damaged. Section got 7 in all									
	1:40			Broke cloud over Hague at 4 shou! Fearless lost re, found train									
	1:55			Strafed I small staff car - smoker									
	1:35			Utch Boss, but no joy.									
	1:35			Above 10s all the way, but lovely sunrise									
	1:45			Cloud base 6,000' but bombing good.									
	1:40			Recc'd past Rotterdam but no joy									
	2:00			Nice bombing over 6,000'. I tractor-trailer, & tipper fir o									
										Month's Ops			
	47:30			[signature]			F/Lt (B Flt) 38:40						
				J. A. Sutherland S/L (C.O 603 Sqdn).									
95:25	638:15	12:00	7:25							40:05	23:55	2:25	
(1)	(2)	(3)	(4)	(5)	(6)	(7)	(8)	(9)	(10)	(11)	(12)	(13)	(14)

SINGLE-ENGINE AIRCRAFT				MULTI-ENGINE AIRCRAFT						PASS-ENGER	INSTR/CLOUD FLYING [incl. in cols. (1) to (10)]		LINK TRAINER
DAY		NIGHT		DAY			NIGHT						
DUAL	PILOT	DUAL	PILOT	DUAL	1ST PILOT	2ND PILOT	DUAL	1ST PILOT	2ND PILOT		DUAL	PILOT	
(1)	(2)	(3)	(4)	(5)	(6)	(7)	(8)	(9)	(10)	(11)	(12)	(13)	(14)
95:25	667:40	12:00	7:25							40:05	23:55		
	1:40			Bombs burst instantaneously. Fair shook up.									
	1:40			6 up tight vic at deck level. Boss had rudder torn, & Zuber pinged wing. Best show ever									

In September 2003 the post-war 602 Squadron Spitfire, restored to as-new condition, was presented to the City of Glasgow Transport Museum. All ex-members of the squadron were invited. I went along to the ceremony, not seriously expecting to see any of my old flying mates, although I have kept in touch with one or two as well as the 602 Museum Association.

Imagine my astonishment when a lady confronted me and said: "Hello, Bax. Do you remember me? I'm Babs, and here's Jock." My fellow flight commander on 602 was Iain 'Jock' Sutherland. He was not a relative of the boss, although he married Maxy's young sister, Barbara ('Babs') after VE-Day.

I had neither seen nor heard of Jock and Babs since that black day back in 1945 when the wartime 602 was disbanded. There had never been any shadow of jealousy between Jock and me, as was sometimes the case. Indeed once or twice when a pair was called for – to do a 'Jim Crow' – we did it together, although risking both flight commanders on that sort of operation may have been considered irresponsible. We had been truly brothers in arms and after 58 years it was one of the most memorable reunions of my life.

Chapter 6

Love and Marriage

A few weeks before D-Day, Sylvia's hospital moved to Bridport in readiness for the invasion. I drove there in my MG, scrounging petrol from warm-hearted garage owners who liked the look of the wings on my uniform. Knowing what lay ahead, Sylvia and I had become engaged. Although deeply in love, we had decided not to marry until people stopped shooting at us, particularly me, although in ensuing months Sylvia's hospital was deliberately attacked three times.

When I had joined 602 Squadron, shortly after Sylvia had gone to France, for the first couple of weeks I found it hard to get going again on ops (operational flying). I now had so much more to live for.

Thanks to my boss, Squadron Leader Max Sutherland, I was able to snatch a couple of brief visits to the 16th General Hospital 'in the field'. This astonished the Americans, who always thought their whereabouts were secret.

When I joined 602, it was doing exactly the same job as 93 had been in North Africa. We were a Forward Fighter Squadron, based as close behind the front line as reasonable, with the task of defending and supporting the ground forces.

Second TAF (the 2nd Tactical Air Force) to which we belonged was aptly named and we considered ourselves a crack outfit. Also, the actual manner of my joining 602 was an echo of my experience with 93. I was a replacement pilot, joining a squadron already in action and taking the place of someone missed by his comrades and with whom one would inevitably be compared. This, on top of my recent engagement to Sylvia, made getting back into the swing of ops on a daily basis harder than I had expected. However, such was the spirit and morale of the squadron that it was simply not possible to avoid being welded into its comradeship and common purpose. From the outset I knew that once again I was in great company, and the one thing to be avoided at all costs was to let the side down.

I had told Max that I was engaged to an American army nurse. "You can't get married without your CO's permission," he said with a grin. "I want to meet her!" And in November 1944 he did.

My logbook in 1944-45 contains many cryptic notes, some so cryptic as now to be meaningless. One reads, 'You'll never forget this one.' I have. Completely. A few other examples, taken totally at random, are more explicit:-

'4th October. Delighted to find train near Zwolle. Strikes on five wagons.'

'15th January. Ten tenths (cloud) over whole area. Brought bombs back.' (It was possible to land a Spitfire with a thousand pounds of bombs on board but one had to be extra careful.)

'18th February. ASR (air sea rescue) scramble off Skegness. No luck.' (Obviously, a little tragedy there.)

'4th December. Bombed through gap in cloud. Got train on recce.'

'4th February. DB (dive-bombed) hotel promenade, Hague. Bombs hung up.' (This only happened occasionally!)

'14th February. Squadron show (twelve aircraft). Pretty good bombing on Hague Bosche. Lots of light *flak*, then went in again. Hole in cockpit.'

On the same day, 'Strafed hotel promenade. Engine cut over beach. Yike!' (The engine re-started as soon as I closed the throttle and reopened it. Just as well, because I was at about 20ft.)

But my logbook entry on 21st November 1944 reads, 'Armed recce: Egmond – Hague – 1hr 20min – emergency landing Antwerp, with CO. Most memorable.'

We flew back to our base at Matlaske in Norfolk next day but what happened meantime was that Max, always with an eye for opportunity, said, "Let's grab a Jeep and go and see your fiancée, Bax."

I knew only roughly where Sylvia's hospital was but after about an hour and a half, driving back towards the Franco-Belgian frontier through a countryside ravaged by war, we found it. The sentries had never seen RAF aircrew in battledress and flying boots before. They described us as "a couple of guys looking like cinema attendants". Lt Johnson was playing bridge, we were told. She would join us as soon as she had played her hand.

Maxy took a real shine to Sylvia and remained very fond of her until his death. Later, I knew that the 64th General Hospital had moved up to Liège. Hitler openly declared his intention to destroy the city with V-weapons, and Max appreciated my anxiety.

On 10th March 1945 twelve aircraft, led by the boss, were tasked to destroy a road/railway bridge near Amsterdam. Our intended route back passed close to Liège, and I noticed on the map a landing strip called B56 on the edge of the city. I asked Max, in confidence, if it would be OK for me to experience a sudden drop in oil pressure, requiring an emergency landing at B56. He agreed, on the understanding that I should return next day.

All went according to plan. We did a good job on the target despite a lot of *flak* but, after reforming, I confess to paying more attention than usual to detailed map-reading. Sure enough, from about 7,000ft, B56 was not difficult to spot.

"Tarbrush Leader. This is Blue One. I have a sudden drop in oil pressure."

"Blue One. Precautionary landing at B56. Good luck, Bax."

I peeled off from the formation, only to see that my faithful and regular number two, Warrant Officer Jack Amies, was coming with me. Fortunately Max spotted it and called him to rejoin the squadron. As I got lower and closer to B56 I saw that the strip was surrounded by slagheaps, chimneys and pit-head gear. It was in the middle of the coalfield.

A quick look at the signal square, always laid out close to Flying Control (in this case, a caravan) told me the direction in which to land on the single runway – and in I went. Having parked by the caravan, a group of 'erks' (ground crew) came to enquire the reason for my unexpected visit. I told them to check the oil pressure gauge and change the oil, booked in to Flying Control and said I'd be back in the morning. By amazing good fortune, a tramway ran on the road beside the strip, and I was soon in the centre of the city. There I was told that there was an American military hospital in the grounds of a château, another short tram ride out of town.

There was no room in Spitfires for personal luggage but I had put my service cap in the tiny locker behind the cockpit, so I was a properly dressed British officer and recognised as such.

"Le château," said the tram conductor. I had no money. RAF crew were forbidden to take any money on ops for fear of being accused of spying if captured. However, my uniform and wings seemed to open all doors. This time Sylvia was not playing bridge but she was not on ward duty and in no time, uniform or no uniform, she was in my arms.

The château itself was the Nurses' Home. Sylvia herself shared a room with her dear friends, Bonnie and Grace Larrabee. The hospital was an extensive canvas sprawl marked with huge red crosses, which did not deter marauding German aircaft on three occasions. Sylvia's fellow nurses were as pleased and excited to see me as I was to be there. I ate with them in the mess hall. Sylvia and I took a stroll together, hand in hand, through the château's gardens and in the evening we had a few drinks in the ubiquitous Officers' Club.

We could not sleep together even had we intended to. Although we were engaged, in those days it wasn't done, at least not by us. After we eventually kissed goodnight, I slept under a blanket on a settee in the nurses' dayroom. When I queued with the girls for breakfast in the mess hall, it may have raised an eyebrow or two but no-one made any comment. Sylvia took me to see an injured RAF sergeant in one of the wards. He was terrified that I had come to take him away!

I left at about noon, returning to the landing strip as I had come, by tram. The erks reported that no fault had been found in the oil system of my Spitfire. The apparent loss of pressure was put down as 'just one of those things', which did happen occasionally, even on Merlins. I had thought carefully about my flight back to Matlaske. A Spitfire on its own was still not very good news in those parts. I decided low and fast was the way. That evening Max and I had a quiet drink together, on me.

Next day my logbook reads, 'Squadron show, Dwindicht. 1hr 30. A lovely attack with 6hr delay in 500-pounders. Re-bombed at Ursahl (to attack a different target on the way home). Took my section at *flak*. Revenge!'

After VE-Day I was desperate to be with Sylvia again and on 13th May – my lucky number – I got a lift to Liège in an Anson, of all aircraft. Sylvia and I spent three blissful days together in Brussels.

The city was celebrating victory *en masse* and everyone was smiling. I was not allowed in the American Officers' Club and Sylvia was not allowed in the British but we found that the Allied Officers' Club was more fun anyway. Also, it had acquired more than its fair share of the trainload of champagne captured from the Germans in the last few weeks of the fighting. When 602 Squadron was formally disbanded, as from 9th May 1945, we had all been sent on indefinite leave.

Sylvia got some UK leave, too. We were together for a few days and went to stay with my father and sister in Monmouthshire; and later had a few more days together in London. But although peace had come to Europe, the war had yet to be won in the Far East – and I was posted to Cairo. For us, that parting was the hardest to date but we promised each other it would not be for long, and tried hard to hold back the tears and smile.

Cairo in July 1945 was extraordinary. It reminded me of Gibraltar just before the North African invasion. Thousands of service personnel were stuck in Egypt, waiting for the next move in a game over which they had no control. There were a lot of Australians, more or less on the loose. Their delight was to hire a 'garry' – an open, horse-drawn taxi and bribe the driver to relinquish his reins. Garry chariot races were not uncommon in the city centre.

There was a tramway from Cairo to its outer suburb, Heliopolis. On more than one occasion I took part in a friendly hi-jack of the controls while the driver, clutching a fistful of Egyptian currency, watched nervously but without intervention.

Posted to 5 Ferry Unit, with five of my old mates from 602, the first task was to convert from Spitfires to Mustangs. Despite what American pilots said, we did not find the P51 a 'hot ship'. Slightly quicker on the final approach to land – 120mph against 95 – we found it, however, a delight to fly. Not quite as nimble as a Spitfire, more stable 'hands off', and infinitely more comfortable, it had more than twice the maximum range.

Our ferry trips from Cairo to Jodhpur in India (now Pakistan) were unforgettable. Led by a Blenheim or Hudson, with a navigator on board, we crossed the Great Arabian Desert, saw the green confluence of the Tigris and the Euphrates – the Garden of Eden – and flew back in the luxury of an Imperial Airways C-class flying boat. It was unbelievable. Furthermore, we moved out of our tents and lived in a boarding house in the centre of Cairo, run by a slightly mad but very friendly Hungarian lady. The apartment had a balcony on the third floor and an Egyptian policeman would occasionally stand in its shade. We aimed water-filled balloons at him. We never scored a direct hit but the game was typical of that time.

My logbook tells me that on 13th September (note that number again) I flew Mustang, registration number 469, from

Sharjah to Cairo West via Shaibah in 8hrs 15mins. I suspect that was some sort of single-engine, single-seat record at the time, and I was certainly in a hurry. Sylvia had written to say that she was going to a US Army Leave Center at Mulhouse, prior to returning to the States to be demobilised. Selfishly, perhaps, I desperately wanted us to be married before she left.

On the 14th I got a lift in a Dakota from Cairo Almaza to Istres, near Marseilles, in 12hrs exactly. It took me a day to hitch a ride on the next leg but on the 16th a Flying Fortress, flown by 1st Lt Scott of the 92nd Group US Air Force, flew me to Villa Coublai and I arrived at Mulhouse to be told that 1st Lt Johnson was in Switzerland with her two close friends, Bonnie and Grace, on an American leave party. I managed to send a signal saying: "Please come back and marry me." She replied that it would take her two or three days to complete her trip.

The people at the Leave Center could not have been more kind – in fact they were clearly tickled pink at the prospect of staging a wedding in such romantic circumstances. I had packed my 'Best Blue' in the empty parachute bag which was literally my hold-all. The American Red Cross girls took care of my laundry. They also took care of Sylvia's wedding dress, made I was told from parachute silk and sugar bags. I thought it was beautiful, and so did Sylvia.

The wedding ring was made from an English half crown, an American silver dollar and a German mark, by a German POW who was a silversmith.

At the bar of the Officers' Club I got chatting to a chap who looked about my age: "Doing anything particular the day after tomorrow?" I asked.

"Don't think so," he said.

"I'm getting married. How would you like to be my best man?"

Sylvia returned on the 19th but we scarcely had time to say hello before she was whisked away to have her dress fitted. In the late afternoon of 20th September 1945, we were married by an American army chaplain, on the stage of the cinema in the Leave Center, complete with organ music. There were 500 people at my wedding and I only knew three: Sylvia and her closest friends, Bonnie and Grace, who were her bridesmaids in uniform. There was a party at the Officers' Club and Sylvia, still in her wedding dress, and I danced and danced into the night.

The following afternoon, at 3pm, we were married again, this time by the mayor, wearing his tricolour sash, in the Hotel de Ville. He was very cross because we were a bit late! Both our children have visited Mulhouse to check the register, in case we had made it all up. The colonel commanding the Leave Center lent us his staff car, and I drove us into the beautiful and unspoilt countryside of France.

But on the 25th came yet another cruel parting, as I began to hitch my way by air back to Cairo. Another friendly Fortress pilot, 1st Lt May, flew me from Villa Coublai to Istres and from there it was plain sailing, or rather flying, to Cairo.

After the Japanese surrender, ferrying Mustangs to India went out of fashion and we were posted to 1330 Conversion Unit, near the Suez Canal, to learn to fly Dakotas. I quickly came to love that aeroplane, foreign as it was to any of my flying experience, and after only 18 hours in five days we joined 78 Squadron, who had flown Lancasters in the UK.

Our base was Cairo West where there was a proper mess, and little terraces of adjoining single rooms with a covered pathway in front, like a verandah. There was no air conditioning, of course, but it was sheer luxury compared with what we had endured elsewhere.

Our flying 'parish' covered the whole Mediterranean area from Istres to Suez, and down to Lagos in Nigeria. We flew passengers and freight, with a crew of three on long distances – two pilots and a navigator/wireless operator – and I loved it. Taxi-ing up to the Control Tower on Malta, with my headphones on over my cap, James Stewart had nothing on me.

But it was time to think seriously about the future. My close friend from 602, Wyn 'Robbie' Roberts, and I applied for permanent commissions. Within a matter of days we were informed that they were only to be awarded to Volunteer

Reserve and Auxiliary Officers above the rank of Squadron Leader. We were offered four years' Regular Service, and seven on the Reserve. I thought, in four years' time I should be an unemployed old man of 27 – and married. Not on!

Robbie took the Short Service Commission and retired as an Air Commodore. Each thinks the other made the better choice. Later I came to realise that Sylvia would not have been happy with life centred on a peace-time RAF officers' mess.

In early March, 1946 I walked into the Forces Broadcasting studios in Cairo and asked if they had any jobs.

"Read this," I was told. It was the NAAFI News, I remember. After a bit of to-ing and fro-ing, on their advice I applied for a posting. It took about three weeks to come through. The CO of 78 Squadron, a wing commander with a distinguished record as a bomber pilot, sent for me.

"Got a posting here for you," he said, "to HQ MEDME (Middle East and Mediterranean) Welfare. Something about broadcasting. Not thinking of making that a career, are you?"

"Well, yes, sir," I said, "I thought I'd give it a go."

"Hmmmm. Scarcely a job for a man, I should have thought." I should have loved to have met him again in later years.

How we managed it between us, I do not know. The British Consul in Boston was a great help, and a letter arrived from Sylvia saying she was booked aboard a Liberty ship from the USA which was due to arrive at Alexandria – the approximate date and time was given. Although I had stopped flying, I was floating on air. I had settled into the broadcasting job and because I was the only officer, they made me the CO although the Station was really run by an Army NCO who had been the chief announcer at Radio Luxembourg before the war.

I had the nerve to apply for an official officers' married quarter and after a blissful ten days' holiday at 'Alex', in the sun by the sea, Sylvia and I set up our first marital household, in a slightly bizarre furnished flat on the Soliman Pasha, the Bond Street of Cairo, complete with a Sudanese servant.

Talk about 'Summertime, and the Living was Easy'! The

studios were a ten-minute walk from our flat, and because we were on air from 6am to midnight we worked in shifts. I became an occasional newsreader on the English Service of Egyptian State Radio, and also read parts in some of their radio plays, for which I was paid.

There was sufficient time to explore the antiquities, to Sylvia's delight, to enjoy the country club and to dance through jasmine-scented evenings at the open-air nightclubs. Small wonder that I postponed my release from the service for six months.

Unfortunately, but not surprisingly, we both fell victim to a vicious throat infection, which was rampant, and went to Cyprus by ship to recuperate. To our surprise, the Leave Center accommodation was under canvas, high in the hills of the pine-clad Troodos – it was just what we needed.

Sylvia would have nothing to do with the tradition by which officers' wives left the shopping to the servants, and she enjoyed the bustle and the bargaining, assisted by her regular 'shopping boy' – a street urchin who looked about eleven. When we returned from Cyprus he had vanished. The other kids told Sylvia he had joined the army. We hoped nothing more sinister may have been the truth.

It was all too good to last, of course. When the time came to leave, our huge young Sudanese servant begged us to take him with us.

"But Tahar," I said "What about your wife?"

"She come later," he said.

"But Tahar," I said, "when I get to England, I shall not have a job. Perhaps I would not be able to pay you."

"You get job, sah. Pay me later." I have often wondered what would have happened, had I joined the BBC with a Sudanese servant in tow. Perhaps I would have been Director General before I was 30. The last thing Tahar did for us before our final handshake was to carry Sylvia's full-size cabin trunk, on his back, down three flights of stairs. It was too big for the lift.

RMS *Andes*, built as a luxury liner, had been a troopship throughout the war. Interestingly, during the '60s she carried thousands of British schoolchildren, including one of my honorary god-daughters, on educational cruises. But she won a special place in the affection of Sylvia and me. It was a five-day voyage from Alexandria and, although we were unable to share a cabin, nights were warm on deck, and the days relaxed. We each shared a same-sex cabin with three others. The company was very different from Sylvia's fellow travellers on the Liberty ship, many of whom were pregnant Jewish-American wives determined to have their babies in Palestine or, as they called it, Israel.

The Solent never looked lovelier, although I have seen it often enough in a score of different contexts, and when *Andes* turned to steam slowly up Southampton Water, with the low shores closing in on either side, it was as if Mother England was extending her arms to welcome Sylvia to her new home. However the Customs men impounded her little fur coat which her mother had insisted she brought with her when she left America.

Getting 'de-mobbed' – ie leaving the Royal Air Force – was a curiously mixed experience. It was as if six years of my life were being stripped from me. They took my battledress but, as an officer, I retained my uniforms. After all, I had had them made at my own expense, and they are still in my wardrobe. But everyone was issued with a civilian suit. From what was available I chose a brown chalk-stripe, which was pretty awful, but the Harris Tweed jacket which I was also entitled to was very nice indeed. I wore it for years.

We rented a little cottage at Bigsweir, at the Monmouth end of the Wye valley. It was the gate lodge to a large estate belonging to the Brook family, of White Rajah fame.

We decided we would retire on my demob pay before we started work. Tintern Abbey was just a couple of miles down one of the most beautiful valleys in England, and the ancient Forest of Dean lay close. Our old haunts in the mountains of Wales were within sight of my father's house on the ridge of high land which separates the valleys of the Wye and the Usk. My schoolfriend, Dougan, came to stay with us and we made new friends.

The future remained a challenge which had soon to be faced. I had an idea of growing lettuces under the newly-invented glass cloches and we looked at a few smallholdings. Until the bridge was built the Aust Ferry, crossing the Severn from Chepstow, avoided Gloucester and saved almost two hours on the drive to London. I considered it inefficient and offered my services to the managing director. He was not impressed.

After my experiences in Forces Broadcasting in Cairo, I had my eye on the BBC – although Sylvia and I had assured each other that we would go to work anywhere in the world but provided we were together. It was not to be. The chance of a job duly came but with a snag – the offer of a two-year contract with BFN in Hamburg. Another separation. On the strict understanding that it would only be for a couple of months or so, Sylvia bravely agreed. From my point of view, the only factor that made it acceptable was that the cottage was within easy distance of my father and sister, and Sylvia had the MG, but to this day I am lost in love and admiration for her courage and loyalty.

Chapter 7

Life in Germany with BFN

When Sylvia and I went to live in Hamburg in the winter of 1946/47 we were launched into an experience remarkable by any standards. Despite being only 24 years of age we were both experienced veterans of war. We had seen things and done things in our respective ways which could perhaps have made us old for our years, but this is not to say that we were embittered, disillusioned or cynical. Far from it. We looked forward to the challenges which our future together would inevitably bring. Bear in mind that Sylvia had left her beloved country, her loving family and the society in which she had been born and raised, and was now married to a foreigner convinced that the world was our oyster but with very little evidence to prove it.

What we found when we got to our new home in Germany – albeit a temporary one – could only be described as shocking. Ruined villages and towns were all too familiar but in Hamburg, in that cruel winter less than a year since the last bombs fell, people were dropping in the streets from deprivation, hunger and exposure. They were not left to die where they lay. Aided by the British CCG (Control

Commission for Germany) and the occupying forces in the British Zone, there were hospitals and a police and ambulance service which worked. But ruination, death and defeat formed the inescapable image of Hamburg that winter.

I shall make no bones about it. I hated the Germans during the war, although I respected, even admired, their fighting capability, especially that of the Luftwaffe. The Italians, on the other hand, I simply despised. They had bombed defenceless tribesmen in Ethiopia and Libya prior to 1939, including using mustard gas. And when, defeated, they hung their so recently revered leader, Mussolini, upside down from a lamp-post in Rome with his mistress, my disgust was profound. Now we were living in Germany and Italy appeared to offer a sunny haven of escape, south of the Alps.

At first I had had to leave Sylvia in the peace and safety of the Wye valley, close to the watchful eyes of my father and sister. I lived in the kind of officers' mess, in commandeered houses, with which I was familiar. The only difference was that I was not now wearing uniform. But within a couple of months, as promised, I was offered a place in married quarters in which Sylvia could join me. It was a charming little detached house in the well-to-do suburb of Blankenesee, close to the Elbe, fully furnished with brand new standard equipment and, unlike our cottage in the West Country, it even had coal-fired central heating!

Seemingly remote from the devastation of the port and the industrial area, 14 Moltkestrasse was in fact barely fifteen minutes by Volkswagen from my office at BFN (the British Forces Network). This was in the famous Musikhalle, the Albert Hall of Hamburg, which had miraculously escaped serious damage. The baroque interior of the handsome building had been easily adapted to provide studios and control rooms of various sizes, from a small 'continuity suite' to the vast auditorium of the concert hall itself.

My job was Production Manager and Deputy Station Director, so I had only one boss. Originally, when I arrived, he was a charming ex-actor and BBC man serving as a major in the British Army, but the policy was to civilianise BFN and about six months after my arrival John Humphreys left to be demobilised and was replaced by Alec Sutherland. He was a dynamic Glaswegian who had already established himself as a high-flying programme executive in the BBC. He was in his early forties and, from our first meeting, we formed a good partnership. And when Alec's wife and little four-year-old daughter joined him, Sylvia and I and the Sutherlands became close friends. Alec was proud of the fact that his father had been a policeman in the tough quarters of Glasgow who, having opened a bottle of whisky with his teeth, would throw the cork into the fire.

We had about us a remarkably talented group of young people, all in service uniform and happy to exchange humdrum military duties for the exciting world of radio. Squadron Leader Cliff Michelmore, an RAF engineer who had trained as an apprentice before the war, became our Head of Entertainment. Amongst his other activities he presented the Hamburg end of the weekly BBC hit request programme, *Two-Way Family Favourites*. At the London end was Jean Metcalfe. Sylvia and I were delighted to attend their wedding and Cliff and I are still in touch, having lost the loves of our lives.

As head of presentation I was responsible for our announcers – nowadays called newsreaders or presenters. Among them were Bob Boyle and Jimmy Kingsbury, both to become household names with the BBC. The actor, Nigel Davenport, remembers me giving him a microphone audition and a job. Derek Jones became one of the BBC's first wildlife pundits on radio and our classical music department was run by Geraint Evans, who was later knighted in recognition of his international acclaim as an opera singer.

Bryan Forbes and Roger Moore, both to become big names in film, were members of the BFN Players. Trevor Hill and Margaret Potter, army and WAAF respectively, became an extraordinarily creative drama team and went on to fame, if not fortune, with the BBC Children's Department. Another young soldier amongst our technicians, Ron Chown, became a cameraman and was later the senior outside broadcast engineer at the BBC. I worked with him often on many major shows, including Farnborough.

We had our own concert orchestra of German musicians and a 28-piece dance band, headed by a slippery Spaniard called Juan Llosas, who was already well established in Germany before the end of the war. We relayed programmes direct from the BBC, of course, but originated at least 50 per cent of our output and enjoyed two-way traffic with both Danish and Swedish state radio.

I made several reports direct into BBC News, one of the most harrowing of which was a live, eyewitness description of a tragic incident typical of those troubled times. A ship, overcrowded with Jewish refugees bound for Palestine, was intercepted by the Royal Navy and returned to Hamburg, as required by International Law. Palestine at that time was a British Protectorate and Israel had yet to be born. The refugees, including women and children, refused to leave the ship. I

219 metres (1366 kcs.)   274 metres (1095 kcs.)

BFN PROGRAMMES

29 May to 4 June

BRITISH FORCES NETWORK IN GERMANY · WELFARE BRITISH ARMY OF THE RHINE

ISSUE No. 22-1949

WHAT'S ON BFN

The Inter-Services Quiz this week—No. 6 in round one—will be a contest between two teams, A and B, from HQ 7th Armoured Division. Friendly rivalry is keen and the encounter should be spirited and lively—good listening at 8.30 p.m. on Wednesday!

How real is the unreal? How unreal is the real? Suppose that you saw a man, spoke to him—and then discovered that he wasn't there, that he never had been, really. That is the theme of 'The Man Who Wasn't There', a mystery play written by Victor Andrews. It is produced by Martyn C. Webster, with a strong cast drawn from B.B.C. Repertory Players and will be on the air at 8 o'clock on Wednesday evening.

Saturday is Derby Day. Millions of British people who have no interest in other horse races have a 'flutter' on the Derby. This

Raymond Baxter's office door bears the legend 'Production Manager', but he is probably best known to BFN listeners as editor of Poets Corner. He is responsible for our Drama and

Sunday Afternoon's Concert from our Concert Hall will be given by NWDR Symphony Orchestra, which will play Mozart's famous 'Linz' Symphony K.425, in C Major. This programme, which begins at 3.15, will also afford listeners an opportunity of hearing the celebrated French pianist Monique Haas who is the guest artist and who will play the Mozart piano concerto in C Major.

Sporting calendar for this week: Rex Alston and E. W. Swanton will be commentators on the English Test Trial (North v. South), and there is also the New Zealanders' game against Glamorgan. See programme for times of broadcasts.

One of the first principles of British Justice is that the law presumes a man to be innocent until he has been proved guilty—unlike that of the French legal code

Early media exposure for the author.

watched and reported the agonising task of British soldiers, tin-hatted and armed with long staves, and their iron self-discipline, as they urged, cajoled and, as was necessary, forcibly removed those poor people to further detainment in a DP (displaced persons) camp.

DPs in Germany at that time were not only a humanitarian problem but also a potential menace. At around noon one day, Sylvia telephoned me in my office – yes, we had a domestic telephone system which worked – to say that some men in uniform, claiming to be Yugoslav partisans, were in our house saying that they were looking for something, and one was lying on our bed with his boots on.

Shouting to someone to phone the British Military Police, I jumped into one of our Volkswagens without waiting for a driver and got there before they did. I had a little black Biretta automatic which I had not handed in with my .38 service revolver when I was demobbed. I honestly cannot remember how or where I acquired it. I knew it was tucked away in the chest of drawers in our bedroom. It might just as well have been on another planet – fortunately perhaps because I knew I was in a killing mode, the white-hot rage which I had experienced occasionally during the war.

So, unarmed and in civilian clothes I simply burst into my house, shouting at them in English-cum-German: "Raus! Get out! Jetst! Now! You understand me? Raus! Jetzt!" And they did, but it was by no means a pleasant experience. Sylvia was extremely cool about the whole thing but an elderly German had been recently shot dead in his house nearby. I wonder if what those Yugoslavs were looking for was the murder weapon.

As well as our musicians we employed a considerable number of Germans. Each department had a trained, English-speaking secretary: the senior of them, who carried considerable authority and responsibility, was a tall, charming and handsome girl in her late twenties called Brünne Depkin. She became a good friend of Sylvia and came to our house to teach us German. Her sister, Elisabeth, became my secretary and we

RAYMOND BAXTER

were invited to take *kaffee und kuchen* – coffee and cakes –
with their parents. They were an English-speaking middle-aged
couple whose warmth survived the rigid formality of their
hospitality in their clearly expensively furnished flat.

Key components of our civilian staff were the four or five
recording engineers who operated the German-invented
Magnetophone tape recorders. We had inherited these from
our predecessors, the Nazi radio station infamous for the
propaganda broadcasts of the traitor William Joyce, or 'Lord
Haw Haw'. Our engineers found a tape of his last broadcast.
Although extremely primitive by today's standards, the desk-
high machines produced faultless quality and the capability of
being cut and edited. They became fundamental to our
operation.

When I returned to the BBC in London I extolled the virtues
of magnetic tape recording and was instructed to present a
paper on the subject. Some weeks later I was told that after a
serious study it had been decided that the requirements of BBC
News editing could not be met by tape. The preferred medium
was acetate discs, as used before and during the war. I could
scarcely believe such blindness and in fact it was some time
before the BBC actually started to use tape.

Another very important element in our efficiency, and
certainly our lifestyle, was our German drivers – and three in
particular. Fritz, probably in his mid to late forties, had been a
sergeant-major in the *Panzerkorps* (tanks) and told me he had
seen the skyline of Moscow. Muller was tall, fair-haired and
blue-eyed, a typical young, junior officer in the German army.
Peter was so young he might even have missed active military
service. They were at our beck and call, uncomplaining,
efficient, and they became very good friends of Sylvia and me
as well as the Sutherlands. On one occasion when we had gone
over to their house for drinks, Alec and I switched from a few
Gordon's gins to Steinhager, the local brew, and both of us
suddenly and ingloriously passed out!

Fritz picked me up over his shoulder, drove us home and
dropped me onto my bed. Sylvia and I very much appreciated
the absolute loyalty and friendship Fritz displayed towards us.

Another outstanding character in our BFN scenario was Sergeant 'Moosh' Cousens, of REME (the Royal Electrical & Mechanical Engineers). He was in charge of our outside broadcasting equipment but had the uncanny knack of making the best of any situation, which is the hallmark of the best type of NCO in the British Army. Moosh knew everybody and everything. He was even responsible for our invitation to shoot wild boar on a huge estate half way to Hanover. Armed with .303 service rifles, we made a party of six or eight. The gamekeepers wore the traditional dress of the estate servants, and to our considerable astonishment they used little *dachshunds* to flush out the game in the thick forest. With my back to a tree, and Sylvia behind me, I got a good shot at a very big animal as he broke cover about 30 yards away across a small clearing. I knew I had hit him but he pitched forward out of sight over a bank. I ran forward at once to finish him off but although his hindquarters were paralysed he struggled to get at me, not to escape. He was a really big tusker and made very good eating for all present, including the delighted Germans who were forbidden guns and ammunition.

Moosh had already found for us one of the most beloved dogs in our lives. He was a *munsterlaende*, then unrecognised by the Kennel Club but now valued as game dogs. At the time of the shoot he was still little more than a puppy. While the hunters were grouped around the kill and the big dogs were licking at the blood, Ricky (pedigree name, Sir Richard of Agincourt) remained outside the circle begging for sandwiches. He died with us in England, aged only 11, having survived six months of cruelly enforced quarantine. He is remembered with love by my family to this day.

In his historic Missouri speech in March 1946, Winston Churchill had defined the Iron Curtain. When we first went to Hamburg, Sylvia and I realised that we were going to live very close to its sinister shadow, but this did not worry us unduly. Indeed, wandering deep in the forests of the Hartz Mountains, there was a curious fascination in the knowledge that the frontier between East and West might well be across the next valley or just over that skyline. But I was careful to avoid stumbling into trouble which could be – and occasionally was – done quite accidentally. The proximity of an unfriendly force was never more apparent than when driving along the autobahn to Berlin. This I did several times on BFN business. The first time, I chose our Humber 4x4 staff car, for the sake of prestige. The second time I chose a Volkswagen because it was snowing. On another occasion I went in a Halifax bomber, flown by the RAF and full of coal.

In 1948, when Stalin closed the rail link and only road to Berlin, he galvanised the British in Germany – as well as the Germans – into full realisation of the threat confronting us all. The Germans and the occupying forces of the Western allies found themselves on the same side in a potential war. West Berlin was suddenly cut off and, in the rest of West Germany, the mood of defiance was tangible. The speed with which the Berlin Airlift was built up was remarkable. It was a fantastic achievement in co-operation and organisation. Within weeks, two unbroken streams of aircraft were landing at Berlin's two airports. British and American aircraft, service and civilian, all took part while operators large and small were quick to get in on the act.

I made another trip, this time in a Dakota, and as an airman I was hugely impressed by the standards and discipline of the flying. There was simply no margin for error, nor did the crews enjoy the luxury of today's satellite navigation and other aids, although there were at that time radio beacons and beams. Regardless of the weather, if you missed your landing slot by more than 90 seconds, you'd had it. There was no going round again. It was back to base, and no argument. The Germans loading and unloading the daily requirements of an entire city worked with the dogged energy which they had devoted to rebuilding their country. No-one could say for sure if it could work but gradually the Russians were forced to back down. If my memory serves, only one aircraft was lost – an American. It crashed in appalling weather in those same Hartz Mountains which had fascinated Sylvia and me.

At BFN our job was 'business as usual'. Of course, we

reported on every aspect of the operation, devoid of censorship other than our own self-imposed sense of responsibility. I went to Germany to earn my living and embark on a professional career. In fact my wife and I had played our tiny part, on the spot, in the history of the second half of the 20th century and when we left Hamburg we had a monumental party.

Chapter 8

Fab Flying

What will probably go down in aviation history as the last of its kind was the New Zealand Air Race from London to Christchurch in October 1953. Peter Masefield (later Sir Peter) was Chief Executive of British European Airways, under the chairmanship of Sir Sholto Douglas, distinguished former RAF Air Chief Marshal. Both were dyed-in-the-wool aviation enthusiasts.

Led by Sir George Edwards, Vickers Aviation – nationalised to become the British Aircraft Corporation – built Britain's first nuclear deterrent V-bomber, the Valiant, and also the world's first prop-jet civil transport, the Vickers Viscount, powered by four Rolls-Royce Dart gas-turbine-driven propellers – again the world's first of their kind.

The then boss of Rolls-Royce was Lord Hives, and he was The Boss in every sense. These four outstanding men, intent on assuring Britain's place in world aviation, agreed that the proposed NZ Air Race offered a unique opportunity to demonstrate their purpose and capability. They also secured the assent of the Treasury, since public money was involved.

Charles Gardner, friend and former colleague as Air Correspondent of the BBC, had accepted an invitation to join

Vickers as Personal Assistant, Public Affairs, reporting directly to Sir George Edwards – or 'GRE', as he was known.

That was the background to my invitation to fly as a member of the crew in the specially named Vickers Viscount *Endeavour*, entered for the race. I was the acting, unpaid, part-time co-pilot, and the official BBC commentator. In command was Captain Bill Bailey, with two other senior BEA captains, A S Johnson and Stanley Jones. Peter Masefield was team manager, flying aboard, and other crew members were Ron Chadwick, BEA navigator, a couple of radio operators and two engineers, one from Vickers and one from Rolls-Royce, neither of whom were called upon to be very busy during the race.

John Profumo, Parliamentary Secretary to the Ministry of Transport and Civil Aviation, which actually owned the aircraft, was our flight steward, complete with bob-tail white jacket and brass buttons. He took the job seriously, did it faultlessly, and thereby won the friendship and admiration of us all; which survived the scandal that subsequently blighted his career.

In readiness for the start, we assembled in what was then called Heathrow's Central Area, a vast empty concrete space surrounded by the steel frames of buildings yet to be constructed. Surprisingly there was no Valiant, no Comet and no competitors from the United States. The only jets were two Canberras, from the RAF and the Royal Australian Air Force. Since these were by far the fastest aircraft, the only question was which would get there first. In fact, it was the RAF Canberra, in just under 24 hours, this being long before in-flight refuelling.

But it was also a handicap race, based on payload, and our Viscount stood alongside a Douglas DC6A four-engined conventional airliner, entered by the Royal Dutch Airlines, KLM. That, with 69 young emigrants aboard, stood every chance of winning the handicap, and duly did so. The Viscount's payload had been sacrificed for fuel. Most of the passenger seats had been replaced by big rectangular fuel tanks, on which we slept, increasing the fuel capacity to 2,900 gallons, offering an estimated range of 3,500 miles at 365mph.

The aircraft was also cleared for take-off, even in the Tropics, at 65,000lb – well above the original 48,000lb. Our actual experience of that, just after a tropical storm at Negombo in Ceylon (Sri Lanka), proved somewhat nail-biting. We cleared the palm trees at the end of the runway by about 20 feet!

The race atmosphere was intensified by the fact that each aircraft was to be flagged off at the start, and racing remained the watchword by the way the Viscount was handled throughout. Only four refuelling stops were made – Bahrain, Ceylon, The Cocos Islands and Melbourne. The aircraft was taxied at about 50mph to and from every runway, and the actual refuelling was more like Formula 1 than commercial aviation practice. For the record, we completed 12,490 miles in a flight time of 39 hours, 36 minutes; and total elapsed time of 40 hours, 43 minutes – only one hour and seven minutes on the ground for all four stops.

Our average speed was 316mph, fuel consumption 290 gallons per hour. Those statistics may seem almost pathetic today but they were of enormous significance in the world of aviation in 1953. They proved the commercial potential of the prop-jet, boosted the names of Rolls-Royce and Vickers/BAC, and secured orders for Viscounts, most significantly in the United States and Canada.

Later I flew on a Viscount delivery flight to Capitol Airlines of Washington, DC. The refuelling point for the trans-Atlantic leg was bang on the point of no return – the American base and former wartime staging airfield at Bluey West One in Southern Greenland. I made a radio programme about that, called 'The White Land on the Way', having got trapped by a white-out when visiting an Eskimo community and having to live with them for six days – but that, as they say, is another story.

So too is the fact that Captain Stanley Jones and I shared watches on the flight deck of the Viscount on that New Zealand flight. During the war, as an RAF Lancaster bomber pilot, his aircraft had been so badly damaged in a raid on Milan that he realised he could not fly back across the Alps. So he crash-landed in the sea, so close to the Portuguese coast that the crew almost paddled onto the beach. They were interned in a villa near Lisbon and the gate was left unlocked until the German Embassy protested in no mean terms. So the Portuguese commandant gave Stanley the key.

He won a DFM, then a DFC and he and his wife, Joyce, became close friends of Sylvia and me as our children grew up. After the Viscount, Stanley pioneered BEA's operation of the Comet 4, including all the political hassle with the Russians of opening up the route to Moscow. I flew with him a lot as his guest in the sharp end, in those happy days before terrorism took the fun out of commercial flying.

Another master pilot of my time was John Cunningham, CBE, DSO and two bars, DFC and bar. During the war the press christened him 'Cat's Eyes' Cunningham because of his phenomenal success as Britain's leading night-fighter pilot. But his deadly ability was not due to his night vision. He was the first pilot entrusted with the newly invented and highly secret airborne radar. He rose to the rank of Group Captain, was heavily decorated and he and his faithful radar observer developed a brand new element in air warfare.

After the war he became acknowledged by his peers as the leading display pilot of large civil aircraft. But much more important, as Chief Test Pilot at de Havilland he piloted the maiden flight of the world's first jet airliner, the Comet, at Hatfield on 27th July, 1949. I flew with him in the Comet's display at Farnborough in 1953. Less than a year later, three of the 22 production Mark 1 Comets had broken up in mid-air. These tragic examples of structural failure, due to unprecedented stress of speed and altitude which caused metal fatigue in the pressurised fuselage, snuffed out the Comet's potential commercial world leadership. In a remarkable programme of investigation at Farnborough, the precise cause of the disasters was identified – to the enormous advantage of the Boeing Corporation of America, whose 707s scooped the infant jet world market. By the time the modified Comet 4 came into service, excellent though it was, Britain had lost the lead.

Looking back, there is no doubt that the 1950s were vintage years in the story of the Farnborough Air Display. As the Jet

Age came into its stride, 'breaking the sound barrier' became an everyday phrase to people in the streets of Britain. Many became familiar with the sound, and display pilots at Farnborough competed to produce the best sonic boom. We saw an unofficial air speed record duel between pilots representing the well-known companies which made up the British aviation industry. Star pilots such as Neville Duke and Peter Twiss became celebrities and were household names.

The intense excitement and fierce rivalry of those early years of trans-sonic flight made that decade unforgettable. Designers and pilots were pushing at the frontiers of their knowledge, and in this lay the roots of the most tragic disaster ever to mar the Farnborough display. I have never ceased to thank my stars that I did not see it. In fact I was driving home when I heard the news on my car radio. It was during the Saturday public show in 1952. Having completed my broadcasting commitments and watched the show throughout the week, I left the airfield some 40 minutes before the end of the display to avoid the traffic jams. It was estimated that the record crowd exceeded 140,000 people. John Derry was flying de Havilland's successor to the Vampire and 108, the DH 110 in the unofficial high-speed stakes. After his dive from altitude to generate the anticipated sonic boom, he pulled out and was turning behind the Control Tower when the aircraft started to break up. One of the engines fell into the crowd not far from 'The Hill', causing death and injury to spectators. John Derry and his flight-test observer Tony Richards were both killed. Within minutes Neville Duke was continuing the display with his own spectacular booming dive, precisely as John Derry would have wished.

Another Farnborough tragedy occurred during the 1968 show. On the Friday I was watching from my commentary box high above 'The Hill'. The French maritime reconnaissance Bréguet Atlantique appeared to me poorly placed for a spectacularly tight turn to land, particularly as one engine was feathered. To my horror I saw the wing drop and the aircraft instantly plunged into the old RFC hangars near the main gate. All five of the crew and an RAE employee were killed in the crash. The immediate fire was controlled with amazing speed by the ever vigilant Farnborough fire crews. New regulations concerning asymmetric flying during the display were introduced forthwith. A cruel irony was that the Nimrod, BAC's super long-range maritime reconnaissance jet was making its debut at the same show. Was the pilot of the Bréguet trying too hard to defend the honour of France? Either way, I felt sympathy for him.

Countless prototypes were put through their paces at Farnborough. One never seen in public was the 'Flying Bedstead', a piece of inspired research begun by Rolls-Royce in 1953. Flown tethered, it led eventually to the Harrier, the world's first single-engined vertical take-off and landing (VTOL) combat aircraft. In my book, *Raymond Baxter's Farnborough Commentary*, published in 1980, the triumphs, the lost causes and the occasional tragedies of those days are recorded in some depth. Now is the time to look back on some special memories of those three decades.

Beginning as very much the junior assistant to the BBC's then Air Correspondent, Charles Gardner, I was to attend the Farnborough Air Display on behalf of the Corporation for 30 unbroken years. In the early days of the BBC's radio and television coverage of Farnborough, everything was done live. Radio was first to enjoy the advantages of the tape recorder and, provided that the problems of background noise could be overcome, the sky was no longer the limit.

When the advent of videotape began to revolutionise television, it became the practice at air shows to record the television rehearsal in case bad weather interfered with the intended live coverage on the day of transmission. The next step was to record certain important items which could not be fitted into that section of the flying programme covered by the live transmission.

Finally, as the technique for editing videotape on site became available to the Outside Broadcast Units, it was clear that the best way to give the viewing public the widest possible coverage was to abandon almost entirely the purists' concept of the 'live OB'. I choose deliberately the words 'almost entirely'. The limited time available to record and edit the video tape with its accompanying sound effects meant that, as often as not, I had to do my commentary live as the recorded and edited pictures were transmitted. As will be appreciated this could be a somewhat nerve-racking task since the margin for error is precisely zero. It is much more difficult than doing a live commentary to live pictures, during which there is a dynamic relationship between the producer directing the cameras and his commentator, to whose words he is listening and, hopefully, responding.

On one such occasion, in 1972, my friend John Blake was sitting in during my ordeal. His brilliant public address commentaries once enlivened almost every air show in the country, including Farnborough. Although he never admitted it, I am sure that Dennis Monger, the BBC producer responsible – and also an old friend and colleague of many television adventures – had thoughtfully invited John to be present against the possibility of his ever having to replace me at the microphone, for whatever reason. From my point of view, having John Blake within earshot was invaluable since, however meticulous one's preparation, a last minute question often arises in the pressure of the moment – and his knowledge seemed encyclopaedic.

Concentration is fundamental to success in a broadcast of this kind and within minutes of starting that 1972 commentary I had completely forgotten my guest. But as I embarked upon the Harrier sequence, I noticed out of the corner of my eye that John Blake was very busy with his felt pen on a card identical to those on which I make my notes for each aircraft in the display. When he tentatively pushed the card towards me I snatched it with the sinking feeling that he may have spotted some error in what I had been saying. Not a bit of it. Beneath a delightful cartoon of the aircraft John had composed one of his instant limericks:

> "A remarkable beast is the Harrier;
> It takes off very close to the barrier.

It can lift enough stores
To start several wars,
From a wood or a beach or a carrier."

I instantly read it aloud, of course, and had the satisfaction of watching John's jaw drop.

In the daunting task of preparation for air show commentaries I was singularly blessed. From 1970 I enjoyed the unfailing assistance of a fellow enthusiast, Andy Tallack. Then a stage manager with the BBC's Outside Broadcasts team, he was the most willing and generous collaborator ever to walk miles in the rain to find the answer to a question. Fortunately our interests coincided. He too was a lover of aeroplanes and motor cars – preferably old ones. Himself a would-be amateur pilot who ran out of money before his first solo, he was totally unflappable and a delightful companion as well as being super-lative at his job. We shared many notable assignments, from the last homecoming of *Ark Royal* to the Festival of Remembrance, as well as Farnborough, and I believe every air show covered by the BBC since he joined its staff.

Broadcasting to the public from an aeroplane in flight presented considerable difficulties in those days. Add the problem of matching television pictures to the commentary and you were in for headaches. As the years went by the technical problems were steadily solved but, to be perfectly frank, it was never an easy job.

In 1962 I flew again with John Cunningham in his display of the de Havilland Trident. This 100-seater, three-engined jet was the first in the world to be equipped with an automatic hands-off landing system, in the development of which John Cunningham played a leading role. His technical knowledge, as well as his display skills made him an excellent salesman and he succeeded in selling Tridents to Maoist China. In confidence he told me that the Chinese had asked him about the possibility of a downward-looking transparent panel in the nose – "for a bomb aimer"! John Cunningham was a huge figure in British aviation. By common consent in informed circles it was scandalous that he was not knighted before his death in 2003.

I was also a guest in the sharp end of an interesting assortment of RAF and other aircraft, in order to make both live and recorded broadcasts for the BBC. All were, for me, unforgettable – not least several trips in the confined space of the immortal Avro Lancaster *City of Lincoln*, operated by the Battle of Britain Memorial Flight. Apart from the inescapable sense of proximity to the heroic past, I was fascinated by the crew. Like all who fly with the Memorial Flight, they are contemporary front-line officers on modern aircraft who fly the 'Historics' in their spare time. But their complete professionalism is apparent every second as they bring the old aeroplane to life, and delight millions of spectators of all ages.

Like me, the modern aircrew marvel at the performance achieved by Sir Arnold Hall's design, with its astonishing range and ever-increasing bomb load – up to the 16,000lb 'Blockbuster'. And the ice-cold and confined spaces in which the crews fought and died are redolent with heroism to an almost sacred degree.

Equally loved by air show enthusiasts for the past 40 years are the RAF Formation Display Team, The Red Arrows. I first flew with them at The Biggin Hill Air Show, when they had the Folland Gnat. Commentary was recorded on tape and their engineering officer, 'Chalky' White, had a tricky job installing the then clumsy BBC equipment. But when the 'Reds' were re-equipped with the Hawker/British Aerospace Hawk they entered a new era of display capability in terms of range as well as pure performance.

Happily my technical ability to broadcast from the air was also enhanced immeasurably, thanks to John Farley. John was the test pilot who put the Harrier on the map, following Bill Bedford's pioneering work on the historic Flying Bedstead and the Kestrel prototypes. Bill, by the way, had broken his leg in a car accident in Germany, but nonetheless bullied the doctors into issuing him with a certificate at his medical back in the 1950s. It read, 'Fit experimental test pilot – tethered hovering only'.

Prior to our Harrier flight in 1974, John Farley had discovered that the newly invented Sony micro-cassette recorder was unaffected by the g forces inseparable from his work. So he used it as an airborne electronic notebook. With an additional microphone inserted into my oxygen mask, it enabled me to record commentary in the cockpit. Contemporary technology has improved sound quality beyond measure since then and it eventually became possible for me to talk to a television camera in the back of a Hawk. That was in 1993 when the 75th Jubilee of the Royal Air Force was celebrated by a formation of Hawks from RAF Valley, forming the figures 75: the seven was easy, the five rather more difficult.

In fact, I flew with the Red Arrows when they first received their Hawks. Squadron Leader Brian Hoskins saw them through that difficult transition and I flew with him in their original Hawk display at Farnborough. Sent out to get strapped in before the pilots got aboard their aircraft, I was left with the canopy open and there was a short, sharp shower of rain. I had the display sequence written in ink on a pad attached to the right knee of my flying suit. The rain transformed my painstaking notes into an indecipherable blue smudge, but afterwards Brian Hoskins was complimentary about my commentary – and that was all that mattered to me.

I had had to have an RAF medical at Valley before being allowed to fly with the Reds. But later, in 1996, I was truly honoured by an invitation to deliver the annual Andrew Humphrey Memorial Lecture to the Air League. This is an event of major prestige, and the superbly illustrated presentation was to be a joint effort with Air Commodore Simon Bostock, the Deputy Commandant of the Central Flying School at RAF Cranwell. The Queen Mother was the Commandant. The subject was 'The Red Arrows', and Simon invited me to get up to speed via a flying visit. For that I had to have another full RAF medical, and emerged from it with a qualification which only the Royal Air Force could have invented: 'Pilot, Fast Jets – Fit to fly – Passenger in control'. Simon made me live up to it, and my first attempt at a slow roll prompted his laughing comment: "That's the biggest barrel-roll

I've ever done!"

But after a few more aerobatic efforts he said: "Look at that beautiful big cu-nimb over there." (A cu-nimb is a towering white cloud). "Let's go and play!" Only those who have done it can know the sheer joy of swooping, climbing and diving a high performance aeroplane in the elaborate contours of such a cloud. It is a truly heavenly experience.

Returned to the airfield, after several passes under Simon's guidance, I got the Hawk firmly and safely down onto the runway, and my day was made. And so it should have been. Air Commodore Simon Bostock was, after all, the Chief Instructor of the Royal Air Force. The lecture was also considered a success.

Flying a Harrier

Few non-service people have ever got to fly a Harrier, but this great privilege came my way first at the 1974 Farnborough Air Show, sharing Hawker Siddeley's two-seater demonstrator with the company's then Deputy Chief Test Pilot, John Farley.

Until my first visit to Peking in March 1973, the expression 'culture shock' had little meaning. It was just another overworked American buzz-phrase. For the professional observer, having done his homework, total surprises should be rare. They should certainly not constitute anything approaching a traumatic experience. I was wrong, of course.

So, having done my homework on the Harrier, and indeed commentated on all its BBC Television air show appearances, I fancied I understood what the aeroplane was all about. Wrong again! If it is possible to experience culture shock in aviation, it is just that which the Harrier has in store for any pilot flying it for the first time. It is, quite simply, something else.

I know now why those pilots fortunate enough to fly Harriers tend to strike in the mouth anyone who dares criticise their aircraft. After a mere four flights in the two-seater, that may seem presumptuous but since my first joy rides were at Farnborough '74, and my pilot was John Farley, I may perhaps at least be allowed to join in their support.

For me, it all started a long time ago – but so did the Harrier.

The two-seater made its first public appearance at Le Bourget in 1969. As soon as I saw it I resolved to make some professional excuse for a ride, and Bill Bedford instantly agreed. It wasn't his fault that it took five years to make good the promise.

Even my suggestion to include a sequence of commentary from the aircraft in the televised coverage of Farnborough '74 didn't seem to set fire to Television Centre. This itself may say something about the curious lack of enthusiasm which the Harrier unjustly suffered. It was not until after the Sunday press show that the first practical steps were taken.

There were, of course, difficulties. Ironically, they beset the audio rather than the video aspects of communication. It was not difficult to record the pictures. A mobile video tape recording suite is essential to a modern television outside broadcasting unit. Pressure on the availability of channels precluded our old technique of simply using the aircraft's R/T for the commentary. When I flew with the Red Arrows originally, we overcame this difficulty by securing a Uher tape recorder in the Gnat's cockpit. But securing is the appropriate word, and in the Harrier there is not much internal space unoccupied.

It took John Farley about nine seconds to offer a solution once the problem was explained. The two-seater has a built-in voice recorder using a standard cassette tape. Determining whether it would run at the correct speed to enable the subsequent synchronisation of recorded commentary to recorded pictures was an excellent reason to get airborne without further delay.

Control gave us a slot at 6.20pm after Monday's display. John said he'd pick me up at the Hawker Siddeley chalet at 5pm. For the following 45 minutes we just chatted. It was not until later that I realised that, in that time, I had been given the most detailed and succinct pre-flight briefing it has ever been my privilege to hear.

In his quiet, earnest but informal way, this distinguished test pilot explained precisely what was different about the theory of flight in a swivel-jet VTOL aircraft. He included many aspects of close-to-the-ground flying which simply had not occurred to me. For instance, the vital importance of differentiating between drift induced normally by wind and that produced by aircraft attitude.

As John puts it, demonstrating with the long fingers of both hands: "At the hover, think of the aircraft as being balanced on top of a pencil of air. It is the pilot's job to keep that column vertical to the ground regardless of the attitude of the aircraft, or what it may be trying to do. He does this with the vector control or nozzle lever which gives him fore and aft angular control of the main jet all the way back towards the tail, to 17° forward of vertical to the fore and aft axis of the aircraft.

"Control in the other planes is achieved in the normal way with stick and rudder – except instead of the control surfaces (which are, of course, ineffective at below normal flying speed) we have little puffer jets under the nose and tail for the elevators, in the wings for the ailerons, and on either side of the fuselage below the fin for the rudder. They are perfectly adequate, and it's perfectly simple – it really is – provided you remember at all times what you are asking them to do." Could any complex and unorthodox system be expressed in fewer words?

Much later in our conversation, when we were getting to the subject of harness and ejector seats, John Farley added, "The Harrier is an easy aeroplane to fly – but it is also an easy aeroplane to have an accident in. Most of the time, if anything should go wrong, I'd – you know – set it all up, and tell you exactly what to do. But in the actual display, because we're trying to show the aeroplane off as well as we can, and make it look good for the people and everything, there are one or two places where we wouldn't have a lot of time – like none – if the fire went out. And then, Raymond, I wouldn't say anything. Nothing at all, I'd just go. And if you see me go, you go too."

It could not have been said less dramatically. It could not have been more reassuring.

Nor could the attitude of the ground crew. It was not at all surprising to find an air of quiet efficiency about the men tending an aircraft displaying at Farnborough. What was impressive was their ill-concealed admiration and respect for the test pilot, his total confidence in them, and the scrupulous attention to every minute detail. My loaned overalls, boots and helmet fitted perfectly – and that wasn't by accident. And there was tolerance and kindness in the way my clumsy and unfamiliar attempts to get the gear on were eased by expert hands.

The view from the rear cockpit of the two-seat Harrier is fabulous. The seat can be elevated until one's helmet touches the canopy. It's a 360° arc of visibility, and the forward vision is remarkable, with the comforting white top of John's helmet just showing.

We did a short take-off down the runway – in perhaps 80 yards. It seemed so normal it was almost an anti-climax, except for unfamiliar accelerations which were a foretaste of things to come.

Clear of the circuit, John pointed us in the general direction of Dunsfold. It was fairly rough and there was a big storm in our path. "Dash it," said John. "I think we'll go round that beggar" – or words to that effect. A steep turn, an increase in throttle, and we skirted a fair chunk of the Hampshire border-country fast.

"It's a very responsive aeroplane," said John. "OK. You fly it." I took the pole and did the usual tentative things.

"If you aim for that patch of sunshine, we'll be over Dunsfold." I turned – the controls were light, marvellously positive.

"Try a roll," said John.

"What, now?" I heard myself say. We were at 280 knots (320mph), and about 2,000ft. "Sure," he said. "Just bring the nose up and whang her over." So I did – and if he cheated I didn't feel it, and it didn't seem to me a bad roll at all.

"Told you it was easy," he said. We called the Tower, entered the circuit, and got down to serious business. He showed me exactly how the speed was reduced; bringing the thrust forward with the vector control, accelerating again, turning, manoeuvring at low air speed. We came to the hover at about 40ft, with the vector control at the 'hover stop'.

"Now just ease the throttle gently back a little." I did so and it was remarkable. Exactly like working the lever of a lift – we just went down. "Now open it again." And up we went. "Now just try the stick – remember it's perfectly normal." I applied a whisker of forward stick – the nose dropped and we went forward – check, and we stopped; back – and we backed. A feel on the rudder, and we turned, and lined up again.

It really was easy – and I understood exactly what John meant about being balanced on top of a vertical column of air. That is precisely how it felt. Different, and much more available than the knack of hovering a helicopter.

The end of the runway at Dunsfold was marked out to the dimensions of a 'through-deck cruiser' – effectively 550ft by 70ft. Farley demonstrated the margins the Harrier has to short-land in that space, overshoot, or taxi round and take off again, with two-way traffic between the island and the port edge of the flight deck. I could understand the enthusiasm of the US Marine Corps but was even more puzzled by the negative response of Whitehall at that time. We took off and flew back to Farnborough.

"Now I'll show you the display sequence," said John, and we taxied on to the take-off pad. I had seen the display that afternoon; I had been taken through it verbally in that original briefing. But ten seconds later, if it hadn't been for the Dunsfold sequence of familiarisation, I think I would have screamed. No sooner had the Harrier lifted off the pad than the nose reared up to a crazy angle, and from zero speed we clawed our way into the sky.

Once upon a time, over Holland, I saw a V2 rocket unbelievably come up off the ground – those V2s, which the Germans fired at London during the last year of World War Two, climbed slowly off their launch pads at first but then the acceleration was astonishing. Since then I've seen many rocket lift-offs and I can only say that there is nothing else to which that display climb by John Farley can be compared.

Then nose down (thank God!) to just over the horizon – we had over 1,000ft already – and forward acceleration so violent that it forced my head back. That was the transition to normal

116

flight. At the Laffan's Plain end of the runway we were doing over 350 knots at about 1,500ft. Steep turn in a gentle dive with the speed and the g building up to bring us back up the display line of the runway towards the Tower. Right down to the deck, at around 500mph, I was ready for the nose-up and two quick rolls to the right, but their speed and violence shook me. And then all hell broke loose. A break left, very steep turn with the g-meter up to 6, and then the ASI going down like an altimeter in a dive. I couldn't believe my eyes, even though I knew this was 'viffing', the evasive manoeuvre invented by the US Marines in which the vectored thrust is used to drive the aircraft into a turn which will escape a missile attack.

Suddenly everything seemed to stop – for indeed we had – at about 1,500ft over the perimeter track just past the famous Black Sheds. And then down went the nose so that we pointed like a dart straight at the landing pad. But no dive this – the airspeed scarcely increased in this 40° plus descent.

So to level off at about 40ft, and then crab in at the hover for the smoothest of smooth touchdowns. An immediate lift-off again – transition forward – stop – bow – and STOL landing on the runway. Total time: 3 minutes, 40 seconds.

I was quite glad that we had all kinds of petty problems with the voice recorder, because it gave me the excuse to fly with John Farley three times more in the display itself. By the Thursday I was better equipped to try to make verbal sense during that little lot than I had been able to do that first Monday evening – and John had thoughtfully tried to take it a bit gently during my baptism.

All in all it was for me the aviation experience of a lifetime. But that is a subjective comment about what was, after all, little more than a stunt for television. In view of the subsequent history of the Harrier it is interesting to recall my comments, written in 1975, when the future of the aircraft was by no means secure.

The two-seat Harrier in which I flew over 30 years ago, G-VTOL, is now in the Brooklands Museum. The important thing, it seemed to me at the time, was what it said about the character and capabilities of the Harrier – admittedly in the hands of a master. John Farley did in that display things which are not standard squadron practice – but only by a degree or so. He was flying the two-seater with an all-up weight equivalent to a squadron aeroplane carrying a full war load.

I then wrote: "Much is made, by some, of the Harrier's fuel consumption. Yet it can hover for a full minute using less fuel than a Phantom on a single overshoot. Think what that means in tactical approach-and-landing terms, remembering that 12 seconds would be an exceptionally long operational hover.

"Much is made of the complexity of the supply train necessary, it is claimed, to support Harriers in the field. I am no expert in logistics, but surely the whole point is that you fly this aeroplane to where the stores are. What's wrong with the forecourt of a filling station, with a nice hot meal and a kip for the pilot in the proprietor's house?

"Finally, though I am no commentator in political affairs, could it be anything less than a stark screeching tragedy if this aircraft, designed, built, developed and flown in Britain, and still a generation ahead of anything the rest of the world has been able to produce, should be allowed to wither on its native vine."

That was my view in 1975. In 1978 the Harrier was again a major star of the Farnborough Air Display. But it was not only the aircraft which grabbed the attention. It was a curious structure of scaffolding supporting a narrow ramp. This was the experimental prototype for the now familiar upward sweep of deck in the bows of Britain's three current aircraft carriers, HMS *Ark Royal*, *Illustrious* and *Invincible*. It replaces the steam catapult previously employed to launch aircraft off a flight deck, but can only be used in conjunction with variable thrust such as the Harrier enjoys – and as will, to a limited extent, the next generation of Joint Strike Fighter.

Thanks to my previous experience with John Farley, and perhaps his of me, it was agreed that in our TV coverage of the show I would fly with him again. But, first, careful preparation was necessary – and no man better to provide that than John himself.

The difficulty from my point of view was to explain what

was going on during the take-off in the time available – 3.5 seconds from 'brakes off' to clear of the ramp.

I still have the tapes from G-VTOL's on-board voice recorder. The following is a transcript from the first of the recordings. The sequence starts with John Farley in the front cockpit as we start taxi-ing out towards my introduction to the art of ski-jumping by Harrier. The rising and falling whine of the Pegasus provides background music interspersed with occasional percussive intrusions from harshly distorted R/T between Farnborough Tower and aircraft in the circuit at the end of the Wednesday display. Our breathing is audible via the oxygen mask microphones:

John Farley We'll just have to put up with it. (R/T break-in). After all, the object of the exercise tonight is for you just to get the feel of it. We'll try to make a recording over the top of it all, just to see what it's like. But you know how difficult it is to talk sensibly over someone else's conversation, don't you?
Raymond Baxter Yes, it's called television.
JF (chuckles) I know what you mean... Well you get a good view of the jump there.
RB Yeah. It's getting bigger and bigger.
JF (laughs) I like it... Standing on the right over there in that group of people by the ramp we have got John Fozzard, the erstwhile chief designer of the aeroplane – now a salesman.
RB Yeah?
JF And in front of us we've got Dick Ball who is going to marshal us to the correct run-distance because... ooops! I see. OK, round again. (Farley turns the Harrier in its own length on the pad.) I wasn't watching him. I was watching the Dash 78 out of the corner of me eye... He's going to marshal us to the correct run-distance because it is by setting the run-distance that you set your end speed – the speed at which we'll get airborne of course.
RB I see.
JF We have no control over the speed we get airborne at, do we, other than the distance we allow ourselves to accelerate on the ground?

RB Right.

JF Do you understand?

RB Yes.

JF So he has to put us at the right place... Well he don't give me the slowdown signal, you see; he just gives me the gone too far signal which is... (Laugh – pause as Farley turns the Harrier a second time. R/T break-in.)

RB It's that critical?

JF Well, only if we want to play the game for real; you know, and get it in the right place.

RB Yes, yes.

JF Right (in the swift monotone of pre-flight checks). The voice recorder is on and running. Full flap is down. The throttle stop is at 97. I haven't done any 'accel' checks – so we'll just do a couple of them (R/T break in). Engine accel checks are OK. STO stop going into 35°... and checking... showing 31... that's OK. Trim going to 5%... Setting the altimeter to nought. That's lovely. My pins are out. I took your pins out. The water I'm not using... (sing song). We're ready for take-off... I'll just talk to Air Traffic and see what they've got to say... Tower – Harrier for take-off?

Farnborough Tower Roger. Is this the same as the last sortie?

JF A-firmative – to re-land zero seven, sir.

Farnborough Tower (typical swift, slightly distorted R/T) Roger. You want to watch for the chopper at low level on your right. When you have him in sight you are clear to take off; the wind light and variable.

JF Roger Harrier... OK, Raymond. I'm going up to 55 per cent rpm on the brakes which is all we can hold at that stage... Now I'm engaging the nose-wheel steering ready to keep straight up the ramp... Brakes off and full throttle... And 'way we go (talking fast) and as we run up the ramp...

RB Jesus!

JF (talking continuously and very fast) I've got me hand on the nozzle lever and as we get to the end (the Harrier shoots off the ramp) bingo, we put the nozzles down, and it's coasting its way through the sky, slowly building up speed. We're going now from 55, we've increased to 105. There the thing will fly away

– so I'm pushing the nozzle lever slowly forward now and as we get to 150 knots we're fully flying on the wing. (One second pause.) Well, there we are. There was no great pain to that, was there?

RB That's amazing. It still took me by surprise.

JF Did it, yeah?

RB Yeah, I agree no great pain but the jump off the top of the ski jump is just unbelievable.

JF (laughs)

RB You know, you'd never think it possible, would you?

JF OK. Well, let's put the jet back on the ground and try it again, and this time you follow me through on the controls. OK?

RB Not 'arf!

That, I repeat, was a recording of the first rehearsal. When we did it for real, the combination of recorded commentary and pictures from the ground television cameras continued throughout John Farley's 3½-minute demonstration: from the ski-jump take-off and steep climbing turn right to 1,500 feet; steep wing-over left and dive to the Display Line; low-level pass up the runway (50 feet, nearly 500 knots – or 600mph); steep pull up and two quick rolls; 'viff' left; Tu 144 with recovery; vertical landing on pad.

After the conflict in 1982, the British people had reason to be thankful that scepticism in Government and Whitehall was overcome just in time. Harriers flown by Royal Naval and RAF pilots played a key role in the liberation of the Falklands, providing the only air-to-air opposition to the Argentine Air Force.

Display pilots of John Farley's calibre are rare individuals indeed. Strange to relate, I may be able to claim credit for the return to Farnborough display flying of another master of the art – on the eve of his retirement, when in his own words, he "really had decided not to perform again."

Having first displayed at Farnborough in 1956, Duncan Simpson's last great professional achievement was his leading role in the flight development of the Hawker Siddeley Hawk.

He displayed it at Farnborough in 1974 within days of his maiden flight in the prototype. In fact, the trip to Farnborough was only the Hawk's ninth flight. At the end of the show it had completed 25 sorties and never missed a day – a remarkable achievement for a brand new aeroplane. Just before the Farnborough Show of 1976, two years after its debut, I rather cheekily asked Hawker Siddeley if I could ride in the Hawk. Since it was intended to put the aeroplane through its paces, with the spectacle demanded by its performance, the test pilot originally allocated the task apparently and not unreasonably expressed no uncertain reservations, *viz* "Not bloody likely"!

It was at this point that Duncan moved in. He was, after all, Chief Test Pilot and whether or not I flew in the Hawk was therefore ultimately his responsibility. Being the gentleman he is, he tactfully suggested "a little fly around, Raymond, so that you can get the feel of the thing." I realised, of course, that his true objective was to determine whether I was capable of coherent speech during high-speed, low-level aerobatics. We took off immediately after the press preview at Farnborough and after a tentative wingover or two and a few minutes following those wonderful words, "You have control" we re-entered the Farnborough circuit with permission to perform the display routine. It was every bit as exciting and impressive as I had known it would be. The aircraft clearly had all the character of its thoroughbred lineage. After landing, Duncan said casually: "You'll find I might tighten up a bit when we do it for real, Raymond. You know how it is in the heat of the moment, but I don't expect we'll be pulling very much more g." I had noticed five-plus on the meter already.

In fact when, on the following day, we did it for real we pulled well over 6g and had it not been for Duncan's previous meticulous briefing and introduction I'm sure my commentary would never have caught up with the action. I wanted to describe the amazing view of Farnborough through the beautiful canopy of the Hawk, inverted. Duncan immediately suggested and duly executed an additional inverted fly-past up the whole length of the runway. That was the first of many happy experiences in the Hawk which remains an outstanding success of post-war British aviation.

But it was another aircraft which got me out on the only political demo I've ever attended. I went with my colleague John Blake, the public address commentator at the Farnborough Air Show and a splendid fellow who had suffered the misfortune of having his hand blown off by a German grenade at Eindhoven. He fell on it to save his comrades. We agreed that we would go to Parliament Square to demonstrate in favour of saving the greatest of all the V-bombers, the Avro Vulcan, but John was uncertain as to the propriety of taking part in any kind of protest demonstration. He stipulated: "We shall march but neither of us will chant."

The last Vulcan bomber squadron was disbanded in 1982 but the aircraft continued to fly at air shows for another decade. Despite more than 200,000 signatures on our petition, including John Blake's and mine, our political demo failed to sway those in power and the last official Vulcan demonstration flight took place at Cranfield in 1992. It's good to know that, as I write, one is now being restored privately at Bruntingthorpe.

Flying an airship

Certainly the most unusual flight I had out of Farnborough was in an airship. In the early '60s a group of enthusiasts had got design and money together to build at Cardington – the traditional home of British airships – a rigid-framed dirigible filled with helium. It was intended to provide a very large radar scanner within the envelope. I asked the protagonists of this remarkable project about the potential vulnerability of such an aircraft in the face of enemy action.

"No problem," they said. "Bullets and cannon shells would go straight through without causing serious damage." I confess I would not have been prepared to put that to the test myself. The airship was powered by two specially adapted Porsche car engines, driving propellers, and once we were safely off the ground and flying at about 1,500 to 2,000ft I was invited to take the controls. These consist of a wheel and rudder bar and the elevator control is operated by pushing or pulling, forward or backwards, the steering column. But flying an airship is infinitely more complicated. My initial experience was to pull the nose up by pulling back on the control column. Nothing happened for an immense period and then, although the nose came up, the altimeter did not appear to show any significant increase of height.

Similarly, when I wished to descend, the same rather disturbing slowness of reaction was apparent. Turning was however more respondent. The captain, a delightful young enthusiast and one of the few certified airship captains in Britain at that time, or indeed today, explained that in addition to response to the normal flight controls an airship is strongly influenced by change of temperature, even to the extent of going in and out of bright sunshine because of cloud. If the temperature of the envelope increases, the machine rises. Therefore, in addition to operating the conventional controls, the captain of an airship has to juggle with elaborate trim problems related to fore and aft balance, and the degree of lift resulting from the helium.

Airships are today not all that uncommon but they are used essentially for demonstration purposes and for providing flying camera positions at sports and other events. Their military capability, however, has been abandoned presumably because of their total vulnerability to missile attack.

Concorde

From the outset in the 1960s I was a passionate supporter of the Concorde project. Whether it would be cancelled by a Labour government was anxiously debated at Farnborough and wherever else those in the know were gathered. At long last our anxiety was dispelled despite vociferous criticism and protest, including that from Mary Goldring, a respected newspaper economist.

A tentative date for the maiden flight of Concorde was announced. Two pre-production prototypes had been built – one at Bristol, the other at Toulouse. The French won the political argument as to which should fly first and needless to say the event was to be televised live by RTF (Radio-Télévision

Française). The BBC planned to relay the French pictures and I was to provide the on-site commentary. My number two (commentator's assistant) was to be Andy Wiseman, a remarkable character of Polish-German-Jewish origin, who also spoke fluent French. I had worked with him on *Tomorrow's World* (see later) and elsewhere, and despite and maybe because of his tendency towards deliberately outrageous behaviour – mostly verbal – we were good friends and colleagues.

Even more important, I had known Brian Trubshaw, the British Concorde test pilot, and his co-pilot and deputy, John Cochrane, from way back. John was to share the commentary with me. Off we went to Toulouse, hotel booked in, arrangements made with Aérospatiale and French television, and day after day the weather was awful. For reasons known only to themselves, the French posted gendarmes at 200-metre intervals on the spectator side of the runway.

John invented the technique of measuring the visibility by counting the number of gendarmes which we could see. But, at long last, on 2nd March 1969, it was all systems go. André Turcat, the French Chief Test Pilot, taxied Concorde 001 to the far end of the runway. Thanks to John at my side, by reference to a stopwatch I was able to call the speeds as she accelerated towards us: "Rotate ... lift-off ... and she flies. Concorde flies at last." My jubilant words have been repeated over and over again, sadly most recently at the time of the final flight which I also covered on television at Heathrow.

The following month, Brian Trubshaw and John Cochrane flew the British Concorde 002 for the first time, out of Filton to land at Fairford. BBC TV gave it full live coverage and I was able to interview Sir George Edwards, who not only headed the British end of the project, but without whose masterful and diplomatic contribution I firmly believe Concorde may never have flown.

I flew on several proving flights with 'Trubby' and John. A memorable one was to Tangier with Douglas Bader and Air Chief Marshal Sir Harry Broadhurst, my former AOC (Air Officer Commanding). As John Cunningham was the world's first certified captain of a passenger jet, Brian Trubshaw was the world's first certified captain of a supersonic passenger jet. I opened the BBC TV coverage of Farnborough, 1972, from the flight deck of Concorde with John Cochrane in command. Yet again, the weather was marginal, with a lot of low cloud. We flew in from Fairford and once more I was privileged to watch closely a master pilot at work. In his own words John flew "exactly like displaying a large military aircraft." He certainly pulled 3g in three or four spectacular climbing turns from low level. At one point he said: "Christ, I've lost the runway." It was somewhere round below his right shoulder. I could see it, and said so. He reefed over the pride of British aviation to swoop straight down the length of the runway in a low-level pass. Brian Trubshaw died before Concorde's last flight, as did Sir George Edwards. But Sue Macgregor invited John Cochrane, Mary Goldring, Tony Benn (the minister then responsible) and me to a BBC Radio discussion to mark the end of an era. Mary Goldring did not withdraw her original condemnation of the Concorde project. Our roles had been different, yet we parted friends.

But my favourite memory of Concorde is more personal. In the late 1970s BBC Radio Schools invited me to originate a programme in the Master Work series. To their surprise, I think, I nominated Concorde. It was agreed and Geoff Sherlock, their producer, told me to get on with it. I wrote and recorded a script including the technological challenge of Concorde in terms which, I hoped, would be comprehensible to a junior audience – generation of heat at supersonic speeds which expanded the structure, major alteration of stability involving the transfer of fuel carried aboard, relatively small passenger space and so on.

But the climax had to be personal experience. The BBC Schools budget was sparse to say the least but the publicity was welcomed, particularly at that level, and Sylvia and I were booked onto a transatlantic flight. As we went supersonic, with my microphone plugged into my recorder, I said:

"Sitting beside me is a lady with considerable transatlantic air experience." (Sylvia had flown in piston-engined Boeing Stratocrusiers, Lockheed Constellations and DC-6s to Boston

126

on many occasions.)

"What, madam, do you think of Concorde?"

"Oh," she said. "I think it is quite the nicest airplane I have flown in since the Comet."

"You have control"

Keeping up to the minute, and sometimes actually flying the latest aircraft myself, has always had a strong appeal but an occasional return to older machines has proved pleasing in a different way. This is from a flight in 1996: "Just maintain the climb at 55 miles an hour, turn 30° right out of the circuit and level off at 2,000 feet. OK Raymond? You have control."

The voice in the headphones of my cloth flyingcap was that of Len Clayton, managing director of company car specialists, Hertz Leasing. We were at about 70 feet above the brown grass runway of the historic Headcorn airfield in Kent. Our aircraft was equally historic – the oldest Tiger Moth in the world still flying, built in 1933 and No 3 off the production line – or what passed for a production line in the days of hand-built craftsmanship – at de Havilland.

Len had gone through the meticulous and time-honoured procedure of the 'hand-swung-prop-start'; the pre-flight checks and the cautious taxi-ing, swinging the nose from side to side in order to overcome the Tiger's total lack of forward visibility on the ground. Lined up into wind, he had opened the throttle, eased the tail off the ground, and bounced us into the air with the confidence of 200 hours flying on Tiger Moths.

That may sound easy. Believe me, it is not. It had been many years since I last flew a Tiger, and I had forgotten what a challenge it is. I was quickly reminded. After a few minutes with the uneasy feeling that I might be flying with the controls 'crossed up' – an easy mistake in an unfamiliar light aircraft – I followed the normal procedure and took my feet off the rudder bar. The Tiger immediately leapt into a pronounced nose-up right turn.

"I think, Raymond," chuckled the voice in my ears, "that you will need rather more rudder than on that Hawk you were flying last month." Some fifteen to twenty minutes later, after a few gentle manoeuvres, changes of course, and so on, another chuckle:

"Fine! I reckon you've got the hang of it again, haven't you? Isn't it marvellous?" Of course, it was, but also I was reminded that it is hard work. Flying a Tiger, like ski-ing, requires sixty seconds of concentration in every minute. After about forty-five minutes we both agreed we were getting cold. Light flyingsuits over T-shirts had been a mistake, even at a mere 2,000 feet. Under precise instruction, I made the descent to rejoin the airfield circuit at 85mph – the fastest airspeed of the trip. A notice in the cockpit says, 'This aircraft may never exceed 130 mph'.

"That straight line at two o'clock is the railway. Turn right to it.... You see the airfield at 11 o'clock?.... You see three black towers. If you cross them at right angles to the runway, you have a good base leg.... Continue the descent to 750 feet.... Turn now to line-up with the runway.... Fine.... OK Raymond, I have control."

"You have control."

We were clearly too high. Len immediately embarked us into a steep slide-slip – a low-level manoeuvre which has killed more pilots than enough. I said "Whoopee" into the intercom. He bounced once in an otherwise perfect three point landing and, mildly annoyed with himself, apologised.

Open tandem cockpits are not conducive to serious conversation – but the environment certainly focuses the mind on the essentials of communication. In that, I have no doubt, Len Clayton is a master. His patter in the air could have been spoken by a QFI (Qualified Flying Instructor), but it went further than that. Here was a man who very much wanted me, a stranger, to enjoy to the full a shared experience, dear to himself. So why does he do this? Why should he snatch – with, I sense, some feeling of self-indulgence – every available moment away from his total commitment to his family and his job to indulge his love of flying? And flying the hard way in ancient aircraft or else his own modern state-of-the-art high performance glider. Simply, for the challenge – and the sheer pleasure of being a competent pilot.

Chapter 9

Commentary Box

To the outside broadcaster the commentary box is his cockpit, as to the professional pilot – the place where he earns his daily bread. The most spectacular one I ever occupied projected from the upper clerestory gallery, high above the nave in Westminster Abbey. My distinguished colleague, Audrey Russell, flatly refused to step into it and I confess it was no place for anyone without a head for heights. The view was as if suspended in space. Magnificent.

Fear of heights is a funny thing, probably not based on logical reaction to any situation. One day at Silverstone, for example, I had invited my old RAF CO, Max Sutherland, along as my guest but he was unable to climb the nearly vertical ladder up into the commentary box, then high above the circuit, which rather blew my theory about RAF types being immune to vertigo.

The most hallowed commentary position I ever occupied was the so-called Dimbleby Box, named after Richard who had demanded it for his television commentary on The Royal British Legion Festival of Remembrance. It had glass at the front and on two sides, a shelf, space for two chairs and was designed to fit into a box at the Royal Albert Hall.

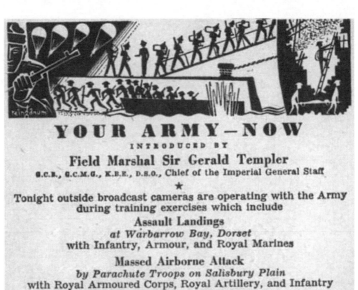

A 16th August 1957 advert for a typical event covered by the author on television.

It offered a side view of the Royal Box and an unobstructed
view of the arena and the great dais leading up to the organ. I
occupied it every year for 33 consecutive years, until 1996.
More seriously, to return to the Festival of Remembrance there
is only one full dress rehearsal on the Saturday morning,
followed by an afternoon show and then the royal performance
in the presence of the Queen and members of the Royal Family
in the evening. It is a tough nut to crack for all concerned but
thanks to the succession of BBC producers responsible I look
back upon it with pleasure as well as pride. After Sylvia's death
that September, I could not trust myself to cope with what was
always an emotionally demanding experience. During those
years I had watched the festival, and its television coverage,
mature. It was started with *Daily Express* sponsorship before

the war. In 1944 Beaverbrook and Churchill decided it should be revived. Ralph Reader, of pre-war Boy Scout Gang Show fame, was recalled from Burma to produce it – and did so from 1944 to 1956. He was joined by his son, Bob, for a further 20 years. Then Bob produced it from 1977 to 1999, to be succeeded by Tim Marshall, who had directed the BBC coverage. It is a story of remarkable continuity and dedication, which is reflected by the very nature of the festival itself. My long association with it was rewarded with many lasting friendships among colleagues, by no means least Bob and Tim.

My first involvement in a State occasion was the funeral of King George VI, to whom I had sworn allegiance when I joined the Royal Air Force, and for whom I had enormous admiration. My job on that day, 15th February 1952, was to act as number two (assistant) to Godfrey Talbot, on a roof overlooking Whitehall. It was the first of my many close co-operations with that splendid broadcaster.

I was in Trafalgar Square, on radio, for the wedding of Princess Margaret and at the far corner, where The Strand crosses Northumberland Avenue to join Whitehall, for the State funeral of Sir Winston Churchill on 30th January 1965. The gun carriage bearing the coffin was drawn by young bluejackets of The Royal Navy, gaitered and chinstraps down. As they controlled the change of gradient with the discipline and precision of a team in the Field Gun Challenge of The Royal Tournament, I remember saying of them: "He was our man. We have him safe; and all is well."

I then had to scamper across the river to Waterloo Station for the departure of the funeral train to Blenheim and was not on the air for the moment which BBC Television missed. ITV, tipped off by the unions, had this wonderful shot when all the riverside cranes lowered their jibs in salute as the coffin passed aboard the PLA launch, *Havengore*.

The ceremonial funeral of Lord Mountbatten, on 5th September 1979, hit me unexpectedly. My position was overlooking Whitehall, just past the Cenotaph. I had done my homework, and watched the pre-dawn rehearsal. But when I saw his horse, led with stirrups reversed, carrying his empty riding boots, I momentarily choked up. Years later, at the unveiling of his memorial by the Queen, I shared the TV commentary with Godfrey Talbot.

Far happier are the memories of the state visits made by Her Majesty in the early years of her reign. They were preceded by the return from Her Commonwealth Tour, aboard the Royal Yacht, *Britannia*, on 15th May 1954. As was the right of the Brethren of Trinity House, their yacht, *Patricia*, preceded the Queen up the Thames and I was aboard.

In those days the BBC covered, with live and news reports, virtually every royal occasion. I was very lucky to be a member of the radio team – with Godfrey Talbot (Court Correspondent), Audrey Russell and Wynford Vaughan Thomas. We covered the state visits to Holland, Denmark, Portugal and Canada. In Rotterdam, crossing the *Rembrandtsplan*, Wynford and I were riveted by theatre bills advertising *Under Het Milchvoud van Dylan Thomas* at the state theatre. We both knew the play word for word, not to mention the author. At the theatre we were told that every seat and box were taken for the royal performance but we could watch discreetly from the wings. The director had realised that the Welsh 'Milkwood' matched precisely similar communities on the remote coastline of northern Holland. So the play was not only spoken in Dutch but also dressed in Dutch traditional costume. Magic!

Wynford and I also shared another very Dutch experience. In a bar full of businessmen one lunchtime we ordered *halb und halb Bols* gins. Two small tulip glasses appeared, so full that the meniscus stood proud of the lip. Very carefully we prepared to raise glass to lip when we were stopped in mid-tremor by the barman: "No, gentlemen, please. Not that way. Like this." And he brought his head down to take the first sip from the unlifted glass.

"In the 18th century," he explained, "there was a quarrel here concerning short measure. Six men were killed in the ensuing swordplay." As we looked around, there were all these stockbrokers observing the tradition by bending forward to take the first sip from their unlifted glasses.

Everyone in Britain over the age of 55 will have their own memories of the Coronation in 1953. Mine are encapsulated in this letter to my father:

Westerly, the day after

Dear Pa,
Just to say a very sincere thank you for both your note and your telegram. I appreciated them both very much – the former came when I was just beginning to get frightened and the latter when I was just beginning to get my breath back.

Despite the fact that 12 hours in a narrow space with no roof, in that weather, was scarcely comfortable I wouldn't have missed that day for almost anything.

It was quite unforgettable. Sylvia was down on the Middlesex Guildhall stand, bang opposite the Abbey, with a BBC pass. Mrs Elvidge had charge of Graham. We went up together on the Monday night, she to stay at the Newcombes, our former flatmates, and travel by Tube at 0530, me to sleep at the office – 55, Portland Place – and start walking at the same time.

Sylvia was home at about six, I followed seven and a half hours later. I wonder if you heard our piece from the Square – that's Trafalgar Square – at 25 past midnight, after the failure at the fireworks. I was livid about that technical hitch. I fought my way through about 15,000 people to get down Northumberland Avenue, and the show was superb.

As I looked out across the vast throng from our shelf on King Charles's statue and saw one or two little fellows on their fathers' shoulders, I remembered our trip to the Trooping, and your bowler hat. What year could that have been?

There were so many things which you would have appreciated, but for which there wasn't time to talk. The mounted Chief Inspector, with the fine hawk face, on duty at Our Corner. At one time a section of the crowd was in trouble and it began to look really serious. Our man just rode into that swaying mass of people, gently, coolly, and of course everybody was so busy patting the horse that they forgot to be angry at being moved.

And the touchingly paternal gesture of an elderly cop during the long wait of the Abbey service. The sailors lining our section of the route were only boys. The cold rain fell on their absurdly inadequate uniform and the whiting from their caps was trickling in chilling fingers down their naked necks. The bobby put his hands on one boy's shoulders as he moved up close behind him, extending his cape in a protective mantle. And soon dozens of sailors had similar temporary comfort from the Law, until duty again demanded the rigid line of unfeeling blue and white.

And there were the three young Australians I first met on Sunday afternoon on the Northumberland Avenue corner. They had a cheerful system of watchkeeping. One guarded their pitch, one went in search of food, the other was off looking for a job.

By them was a woman from Royston, lean with hard work, and with her a boy of nine and a girl of four. This with over 50 hours to go. I saw them on Monday twice. They were the first thing I looked for in the six o'clock drizzle of Tuesday morning.

The little girl, a tiny green huddle, was quietly sobbing with misery as she nibbled from a paper bag. I discovered later that they had slept under cover. The Aussies had seen to that, and assumed guard of their tiny space.

The little pinched face watched the opening phases in sullen unhappiness. The mother's expression became literally radiant, the little boy came to life.

But when that indescribable moment came, with the golden coach, that tiny green figure glowed in the warmth of a Royal smile, direct and I am sure deliberate.

And with that and the previous glance down Whitehall, and thence to Philip, I felt a lump in my throat and, but for the microphone, I believe I might have wept. It's all so emotional that there's no accounting for it. I saw quite a bit of the television (we had a set rigged at our site) and turning from the real thing to the screen was such an anticlimax that it shook me (remember that those pictures were in black and white). The pictures were splendid, obviously, but about as vivid to the living scene as a muddy river is to the Mediterranean on a spring morning.

See you soon, meantime love from us all.

Ray

PS Graham saw the TV and told us all about "the Queen lady" and "Princess procession" and "donkeys come out of church"!

It is sad to realise that, today, that policeman's kindly gesture would certainly cause a snigger, if not worse.

I did not enjoy the luxury of a commentary box on that occasion, which would have been unusually welcome in view of that weather. Instead my position was a small open stand, almost under the equestrian statue of King Charles in Trafalgar Square. My commentator's assistant was James Pestridge who was in charge of outside broadcasts, Birmingham – it was all hands to the pumps. As the excitement mounted, our colleagues of the press, who were supposed to occupy a shelf behind us, pushed forward. The only way I could maintain my view of Admiralty Arch was by leaning forward, full length across the low parapet, with James hanging onto my legs to secure my balance. But the moment the magical burst of colour came into view, James's patriotic fervour overtook him and, throwing his hat into the air, he let go of my legs. I very nearly ended up interviewing the lead pair of Windsor Greys.

The BBC, particularly in my early time, was rich in character and characters: Richard Dimbleby, the patrician of broadcasters who never signed a contract – all his engagements were by gentleman's agreements arranged by his wife, Dilys; Wynford Vaughan Thomas, the bubbling Welsh commentator with an endless fund of outrageous stories and an irrepressible sense of humour; my boss in radio OBs, Charles Max-Muller, a gentleman of the old school who had fought as a Territorial officer in the disastrous Norwegian campaign; Seymour de Lotbinière, head of, first, radio then TV OBs, who virtually invented the technique of outside broadcast commentary; John

ADMIRALTY Arch	London	AD-mǐ-răl-ti	
AGINCOURT	France	AJ-in-kort	(-j as in 'jet')

This is the historical English pronunciation.

ALANBROOKE, Viscount		AL-ăn-brŏok	(-a as in 'man')
ALBANY	Scottish Herald	AWL-bă-ni	
AMBULATORY	Cloister	AM-bew-lay-tŏ-ri	
AMPULLA	Vessel containing anointing oil	am-POOL-ă	
ANCASTER, Earl of		ANG-kă-ster	
ANNULUS	Ring	AN-yŏo-lŭss	
ARGENT	Heraldic term for 'silver'	AAR-jĕnt	(-j as in 'jet')
ARMILL (or ARMILLA)	Bracelet	AAR-mill	
ARMILLA		aar-MILL-ă	
ARUNDEL	Herald of Arms Extraordinary	ARR-ŭn-dĕl	(-a as in 'marry')
BACULUS (or BACULUM)	Sceptre	BACK-yŏo-lŭss	
BACULUM		BACK-yŏo-lŭm	
BEAUFORT, Duke of		BŌ-fŏrt	
BELLEW, Sir George	Garter King of Arms	BELL-ew	(ew as in 'few')
BLUEMANTLE	Pursuivant	BLOO-man-tĕl	
BOTHA	South African General	BŌ-tă	
BOWER, Dr. J. DYKES	Organist of St. Paul's Cathedral	DĪKS BOW-er	(-ī as in 'high') (-ow as in 'now')
British HONDURAS		hon-DEW-răss	(-ow as in 'few')

Please note stress on middle syllable.

BROUGHAM	Closed carriage	BROO-ăm	
		or BROOM	
BRUNEI, State of		BROO-nī	(-ī as in 'high')
BUCCLEUCH and QUEENSBERRY, Duke of		bŭ-KLOO ănd KWEENZ-bĕri	
CAP-A-PIE	'fully armed'	KAP-ă-PEE	
CAPARISONED	'bedecked'	kă-PARR-ĭ-sŏnd	(-a as in 'marry')

The next three pages show excerpts from BBC 'notes for commentators' given to the author for his Coronation commentary. Firstly, on pronunciation; secondly, what he was to eat on the day; thirdly, helpful information.

CORONATION DAY HAMPER

PACK FOR ONE PERSON

3 rounds	Sandwiches	a) Cream Cheese & Gherkin b) Ham & Sweet Pickle c) Tongue
2	Finger Rolls	a) Creamed Chicken b) Creamed Ham
1	Meat Pie - Individual	
1	Buttered Bap	
1 portion	Fruit Cake	
1	Hard Boiled Egg	
2	Tomatoes	
1	Apple	
1	Pear	
1	Banana	
1 portion	Gruyere or Demi Sel	
1 bar	Chocolate	
1	Penguin Biscuit	
2	Kia-Oras	
2	Straws	
1 squill	Salt	
2	Paper Serviettes	
2	Paper Cups	

TOPOGRAPHICAL NOTES FOR RAYMOND BAXTER AND JAMES PESTRIDGE
AT TRAFALGAR SQUARE   (PRÉCIS OF NEWS INFORMATION SERVICE NOTES)

CHARING CROSS

One of 12 crosses erected to commemorate resting places of
Edward Ist's Queen, Eleanor of Castile, on her journey from
Harby near Lincoln, to Westminster, November 1290.
(Over 660 years ago).
Actual site is our broadcasting position - Cross destroyed
during the Great Rebellion, 1647.

STATUE OF CHARLES I
Erected on this site 1675 by Charles II after purchase from
Countess of Portland.   Statue made in 1633 by the Huguenot
sculptor, Hubert le Sueur, commissioned by Lord Weston
to stand in his garden at Roehampton, but originally erected
in St. Paul's church yard.
Sold by Cromwell's agents as old brass to a brazier, one John Rivett,
to be broken up.   Rivett, however, hid the statue and
flogged brass mementos allegedly made therefrom (original spiv).
After Restoration, second Earl of Portland, traced statue to
Rivett, and sold by his widow to Charles II.

Mentioned in street vendors' cry "I cry my matches at Charing
Cross where sits a black man upon a black 'oss".

Charing Cross is one of the sites where Heralds proclaim the
Accession of English sovereigns.   Her Majesty's Accession
proclaimed here.

Snagge, another perfect gentleman, famous for his *In, Out*
rowing commentaries and one of the most beautiful speaking
voices ever to broadcast – his radio commentary from inside
the Abbey during the Coronation was every bit as brilliant as
Richard Dimbleby's was on television.

Frank Anderson was a proud product of Rugby School who

had installed the telephone networks of Brazil and Chile before becoming manager of the Radio OB Department. His brother was the Bishop of Salisbury and one day he visited us clad in full day dress, complete with top hat and gaiters, and Frank brought him into my office. In no time he was explaining to me how the bomb-dropping mechanism he used as a pilot in the First World War would occasionally jam. For some reason, which now escapes me, this resulted in us both being on our hands and knees, in curious attitudes, when Charles entered unexpectedly. I had yet to learn the expression 'gobsmacked' but that 'Charlie Max' most certainly was.

Frank Anderson had a fund of classic limericks, including:

Said the gloomy old Dean of St Paul's
While inspecting the cracks in the walls,
"Quite the best thing to do
Is to fill them with glue."
But the Bishop of London said: "This would do no good whatsoever and the mere fact that he should put forward such a preposterous suggestion demonstrated beyond peradventure that not only had he grossly overestimated the adhesive qualities of glue but had also completely failed to grasp both the magnitude and gravity of the situation."

Soon after my arrival in the department, Wynford Vaughan Thomas took me to the Bolivar, much-frequented by BBC people and later to become the BBC Club. It was across the road, behind the Langham Hotel, then requisitioned as BBC offices and studios. There Wynford introduced me to the great Gilbert Harding. Clad in coat and muffler, he was about to depart to conduct the next contest in *The Round Britain Quiz*.

"Mr Harding," I said lightly, "I hope you're not going to be as beastly to the team this week as you were last time." Gilbert inflated like an angry bullfrog, and:

"Boy," he thundered, for all to hear in the Bolivar, "if you persist in making these spurious allegations against my professional integrity, I shall be obliged to revise my attitude towards you, which has I may say up to now been one of benign interest, into one of implacable hostility." And he swept out of the bar.

Poor Gilbert. Despite or because of his fame – indeed notoriety – he was a lonely man and in some small ways I was able to befriend him. He invited me to lunch one day in his nearby flat: "The tomatoes were flown in from Jersey for me this morning, dear boy, and do try this cheese: I found it in Shropshire."

Gilbert accepted an invitation to be interviewed on Television in the *Face to Face* series. John Freeman deliberately humiliated and deeply offended this gentle soul, reducing him to tears. In my view it was a shameful thing to have done to someone who had brought so much pleasure and colour into so many programmes.

As a child, thanks to my mother, I thought St Paul's Cathedral was the most beautiful building in the world and, at school, I did a project on ecclesiastical architecture. Since then I have never missed the opportunity to visit a cathedral. Consequently I was very happy in my work at the Dedications of both Guildford and Coventry Cathedrals and the Re-dedication of St Clement Dane, the church of The Royal Air Force, all of which were attended by Her Majesty.

The Queen was also present at the Review of the RAF at Finningley. Prior to the major BBC outside broadcast feature, 'This is Your Royal Air Force', the producer, Denis Monger and I visited the Commander-in-Chief, RAF Strike Command, to secure his co-operation. From that first meeting, Air Chief Marshal Sir Denis ("Call me 'Splinters'") Smallwood, and later his wife Jean, became family friends. But he had also proved himself an excellent broadcaster. Immediately following his retirement, Denis Monger invited him to be my fellow commentator at the Finningley Review. At the end of a day-long rehearsal, Splinters and I were walking through the static aircraft display park when we were stopped by a rather pompous, non-flying wing commander who told us we were 'Off Limits'.

"Are we?" said Splinters. "We're from the BBC."

"From BBC West?" asked our interrogator.

"No," said Splinters. "From BBC London, as a matter of fact."

"That's funny," said the man. "I thought you looked familiar."

"I should bloody well hope so," said Splinters. "Until a couple of months ago I was your Commander-in-Chief."

Each D-Day celebration – in 1974, 1984 and 1994 – was a wonderful broadcasting experience for all the BBC Television team, of which I was one. But for me the proudest and most touching moment of all came at the Pegasus Bridge in '94. Major Howard, who commanded the heroic glider assault which captured the bridge at 1am on D-Day, led the march past of veterans and The Parachute Brigade. As he beat time to the music, his wheelchair was pushed across the bridge by the pilot who had flown his glider on that epic day.

Of the state visits, my favourite moments came when the Queen and Prince Philip travelled coast to coast across Canada from June to August, 1959. Keeping up with the royal progress in the heat of summer was testing and I fell victim to a gippy tummy. A Canadian colleague recommended Chinese food and, remarkable as it may seem today, that was my first taste of it. It did the trick.

But the highlight of the Queen's engagements was the opening of the St Lawrence Seaway, an engineering feat of monumental and commercial significance. The ceremony was followed by a cocktail party on the deck of The Royal Yacht. Sylvia, who had flown over to visit her mother in Boston, joined me in Quebec and we were both invited. We suddenly found ourselves face to face with the Queen. She was charmingly interested to learn how we had met, and that Sylvia was half-Canadian. On that warm summer evening aboard *Britannia*, no cool champagne ever tasted more delicious.

Chapter 10

Live and Let Live

When television started it was all live. Well into the late 1950s, major dramas as well as serials such as *Dixon of Dock Green* and *Z Cars* – the BBC's first cops and robbers – were acted and transmitted live in the studio. There was a sort of purist attitude which considered recording, when it became available, as a sort of cheating – "It doesn't have the same impact, you know."

To some extent I believe that still to be true but I confess to bias since the majority of my work on television has been live. In any case the ability to transmit film and later magnetic tape swept aside such conservatism in the overwhelming tide of technical progress and all that it offered to the increased enjoyment of the viewer. Even during the last few years digital techniques have made possible ever more brilliant visual tricks of which instant replay is but one example. It is interesting therefore to recall an intermittent series of BBC outside broadcasts called *Now* which obtained good audience response more than 40 years ago.

Three men made it possible – Peter Webber, Jimmy Moon and Peter Dimmock. Webber was a former journalist, in his late thirties, whose passionate belief in the impact of live telly, together with boundless ambition and vivid imagination threatened to explode within him. Moon was a young engineer whose speciality was establishing links – the connection between the cameras on site and the transmitters. Jimmy reckoned he could create a link from just about anywhere to anywhere, and did. Peter Dimmock was the dynamic head of BBC Television Outside Broadcasts. Like many members of his department, a former RAF pilot, he had established his reputation with the coverage of the Coronation, for which he had overall responsibility. He encouraged his producers to be as adventurous as he was and the result was television created by an exceptional team of which I was more than happy to be a member. We considered ourselves to be the Light Cavalry of the BBC.

Peter Dimmock was one of the very few if not the only British television executive to be snapped up by an American network. On one of his innumerable New York shuttle flights by Concorde he found himself sitting beside Lord King, the aggressive saviour of British Airways. Dimmock complained that the Concorde menus, though good, were too repetitive.

From this background came *Now*. Peter Webber would conjure up a hitherto unexplored environment and challenge Jimmy Moon to establish a link. Bob Danvers-Walker's voice was well known for his commentaries to newsreels, then a popular cinema attraction. He and I were given the task of matching the live words to the live pictures. Consequently, our presence was required on site, wherever that may have been. The most bizarre of these was the Royal Navy's 90ft-deep submarine escape tank at Gosport. Without rehearsal I was to open the programme by breaking the surface from the 60ft level. This was an air-filled compartment like a diving bell at the side of the circular tank, just big enough to contain two men. Self-evidently the air pressure inside the compartment was sufficient to keep out the water – ie the pressure experienced by a diver at 60ft. The Royal Navy invented the inviolable and world-recognised rules which protect deep-sea divers from injury, such as the bends. The rules are all based on time and pressure.

The programme preceding *Now* that time was coverage of the Queen's visit to a gala performance in Paris. The commentator of that was Richard Dimbleby and, as we all feared, he and the proceedings over-ran. Trapped in my tiny space without breathing equipment, I could only wait and wait for my cue to get out, knowing that my safe minutes were rapidly running out.

At last, a firm push from my hefty guardian – an RN Petty Officer Instructor – and I was on my way. The instruction was to take a deep breath before exit and then blow out the whole way to the surface. This is to avoid serious damage to the lungs as the pressure decreases and the air inside them expands.

I thought I was doing OK until I discerned the eerie shape of a masked frogman approaching me. He grabbed me, pointed at my lips and punched me positively in the solar plexus. Thus encouraged to blow even harder, I broke surface into the floodlights and said, in what I hoped was the direction of the camera: "Good evening, and welcome to *Now*."

Equally unlikely was a live TV transmission from a submerged submarine at sea. This is theoretically impossible because radio waves do not penetrate water. Jimmy Moon's solution was to rig a small TV transmitting aerial to the top of the submarine's periscope. Thus 'up periscope' meant 'up aerial'. At periscope depth, secret at that time, viewers found themselves with the cameraman and me in the confines of a submarine of the Royal Navy in exercise action. On 16th June 1956, the submarine was HMS *Tapir* and Richard Dimbleby was aboard the frigate *Granville*. At one point I was addressing the then hand-held camera, supported on a sling in front of the operator, when the captain called, "Dive, dive, dive!" Immediately the deck assumed a steep angle, and gravity propelled the cameraman swiftly past me until he fetched up on the next bulkhead. But he never lost focus and I never stopped talking, so it could have been seen as a brilliant change of perspective. The cameraman was Bill Wright, who became the founder producer of *Mastermind*.

I did my first glider solo live at Lasham, taught by the legendary chief instructor, Derek Piggott, but although exciting for me, and I hope for the viewers, it was a bit of cheat because I was already an experienced powered-flight pilot – but we made no pretence to the contrary.

Not exclusively in the *Now* series, I was involved in a number of television firsts. The first live air-to-air pictures were particularly memorable because of the weather. The purpose was to demonstrate the then new GCA – Ground Controlled Approach. Using radar the ground controller in the tower on the airfield was able to talk down any pilot regardless of visibility to a minimum of 150ft above the runway. Nowadays the process is completely automatic for modern jet liners at all major international airports. But in those days neither the pictures nor the landing techniques had been seen before. The site chosen was RAF Watten and the aircraft chosen was a Vickers Varsity twin piston-engined trainer. It had a fixed television camera, looking down through the bomb-aimer's window in the nose, and one manned which looked forward over the pilot's shoulder. I was to its right.

It was the only occasion when, as commentator, I had control of the picture. A two-way switch enabled me to select either the bomb-aimer's view or that from the cockpit. The coverage was planned in three separate transmission slots – pre-flight briefing and take-off, air-to-air pictures of other aircraft and the GCA landing with pictures from the air, plus the control tower where Peter Dimmock was commentator. The weather was ghastly and what was intended to be a clear visibility demonstration turned into a GCA for real. As we flew above ten tenths cloud, at about 3,500ft towards the end our of second transmission, I said, "Frankly, I doubt if we are going to be able to get down again."

At least, I had real doubts about whether we could land at Watten and I hoped that viewers would be drawn in to see if the new GCA really could defeat the conditions. There were several other airfields available so there was no question of danger. Unfortunately the wife of our on-board cameraman was watching us live at home - and feared the worst. She did not forgive me for several years. He was Ron Chown who, as I mentioned earlier, had been a National Service soldier when we met at Hamburg. I can add now that he was known as 'The Bishop' and was able to take unusual events in his stride.

Our descent through cloud was reported almost foot by foot. I cut between the flight deck shot of the pilot's instruments and the opaque grey of the bomb-aimer's window, with rain drops racing across it. The pilot, a F/Lt Bell, did brilliantly. We had a glimpse of the last lead-in light and then the first runway light, followed almost immediately by an immaculate touchdown. Throughout my career I have seized every opportunity to praise the men and women of Her Majesty's forces. I have never lacked material.

Other television firsts included pictures from a ship at sea – *The Queen Mary* – and a yacht under canvas, *Bloodhound*, which formerly had been owned by the Duke of Edinburgh. Peter Webber wanted to televise live from a coalface but the authorities would not permit that, so we went into an iron mine instead and watched, at arm's length, the explosives being laid for the next blast.

We broke a lot of new ground, live in *Tomorrow's World*, including proving that light apparently does not have to travel in straight lines. A 3ft cable, made of strands of transparent optical glass, was attached to a television camera with a lens at the other end. The camera duly reported the image at which the lens was pointed. I then tied a loose knot in the cable and that did not distort the image on the screen. When I rotated the lens past various objects in the studio they all appeared on the screen. It was a dramatic demonstration of the huge potential of the newly discovered glass fibre optics.

It was *Eye on Research*, however, which confronted me with a couple of unusual challenges. A Welsh university acquired a Cobalt 90 source and they were using it to research food preservation. So, at Aubrey Singer's suggestion, I ate an irradiated breakfast of bacon and eggs and tomato, which may well have glowed in the dark, but I declined personal participation in another of his experiments. The programme concerned was called 'The Magic Mushrooms'. A Swiss pharmaceutical company had isolated and then synthesised the effective ingredients of a type of mushroom known for centuries to primitive tribes to produce hallucinations. They called the chemical LSD and Aubrey suggested I should take a small dose so that viewers could see the effect. I was not disappointed when our family doctor and dear friend, Dr Derek Roper, advised me against it, saying, "The possible long-term effect of these behavioural drugs is not yet known."

We went to Switzerland to do the programme and a local artist was invited to draw a cockerel, using red and green pens, before taking the drug. We then recorded three more drawings at half-hour intervals. The result was spectacularly dramatic. His drawings became progressively more grotesque and flamboyant, although still just remaining recognisable. If you consider this to have been gross irresponsibility on our part, at that time LSD was being considered as a potential treatment for a variety of psychiatric disorders, including manic depression and schizophrenia.

I wonder if its subsequent abuse as a so-called recreational drug might have been checked had its actual effects been demonstrated in a massive publicity campaign although, of course, that equally might have produced entirely the wrong result.

Chapter 11

Ottering

In the 1950s, the special promotions manager of the *Daily Express* was a delightfully unassuming but very influential man called Albert Asher. The promotions for which he was responsible reflected the tastes and indeed hobbies of his proprietor-in-chief, Max Aitken. He was the son of Lord Beaverbrook, and at the end of the war returned to civilian life as an extremely distinguished pilot in the Royal Air Force with the rank of wing commander.

Not surprisingly perhaps therefore, his tastes ran to motor racing, powerboat racing and flying. The *Daily Express* sponsored its own one-day meeting at Silverstone which rivalled, in prestige and interest, the British Grand Prix meeting itself. It also ran the *Daily Express* 1,000 miles trial which was a round-Britain motor rally, the south coast air race and the Cowes-Torquay power boat race and all of these were subject to my professional interest in the Outside Broadcast Department of the BBC.

Consequently I got to know Albert Asher quite well, indeed he became a good business and personal friend. He was a truly remarkable man. I seem to remember him telling me that his mother was a gypsy and he certainly had, shall we say, shadows of that kind of unconventional background.

His opposite number and I suppose rival on the *Daily Mail*, was a man called Frank Coven, with whom I also became professionally involved as well as being friends. One of the wilder projects in which he was involved, I remember, was when we posted Brian Johnston, wrapped up as a parcel, in pursuit of some charitable objective or another.

Frank Coven was also responsible for the *Daily Mail* Ideal Home Exhibition, on which Brian Johnston and I reported for BBC radio for many successive years and this was an extremely rewarding experience in more ways than one. After one exhibition I returned home with a mechanical potato peeler, much to Sylvia's surprise. It wasn't really all that practical. You put the potatoes in a pot, with a rotating platform in its base on which were carborundum studs. It was a very abrasive surface and when you turned the handle the spuds bounced around and were progressively peeled. It was a rather laborious process and Sylvia reckoned it was much easier to peel the potatoes the conventional way.

One day, when we had arranged a meeting to discuss some *Daily Express* project or another, I was somewhat taken aback when Albert Asher said, in response to my enquiry, "How are things going at the office, old man?"

"Very difficult. My boss has gone off his rocker."

"Oh really," I said, "in what way?"

"He intends," replied Albert, "to run a boat show in London in the middle of winter. Now I ask you . . . who on earth is going to come to Earl's Court in January in order to buy a boat?"

"Thousands," I said.

"I don't believe you," Albert replied.

"I don't mean they'll be there to buy a boat," I said, "but they'll come in their thousands to *dream* about buying a boat."

And thus was born the London boat show, an instant success which continued for many years and from which I was very happy to broadcast for many years.

And that was really how I first got my family into boating,

although we called it "ottering" at the time.

It was at the boat show in 1955 or '56 that I discovered, tucked away in a corner almost in the background, an unusual shape. My enquiry revealed that its manufacturers described it as an amphibious caravan and instantly my curiosity was aroused, although I little dreamed of the various and extensive pleasure which this little device would bring into my life and the lives of my family.

On the stand I met the builder of the Otter – for that's what it was called – Ron Sams, who became a very good friend. He ran a joinery business inherited from his father, at Hoddesdon, in Hertfordshire. But with the assistance of his friend, Alan Eckford, a distinguished naval architect, they had decided to embark upon this extremely adventurous project.

Offering more than six feet of headroom throughout her length, the Otter was 16ft 6in overall, 6ft 6in beam and, fully laden with all the clobber inseparable from family life afloat, she drew about eighteen inches of water.

The purpose of the design was to provide practical four-berth accommodation ashore or afloat and in that the Otter undoubtedly succeeded. But this leads me to a curious point. My family loved living in the Otter on water, but we did not particularly like living in exactly the same box on land. I hasten to add, however, with all the attendant risks of abuse from outraged caravaners, that we never particularly enjoyed caravanning, as such, anyway.

But this was different. Very different.

From this you will have gathered that, after a short demonstration on the River Lea near Ron Sams' joinery works, I bought one.

The cost, I believe, was some £384. And that was a not inconsiderable sum in those days, bearing in mind I had only recently achieved my secret ambition of earning £1,000 a year.

Readers with experience of boating will already have raised a suspicious eyebrow at my mention of Otter's shallow draft in relation to her evidently enormous freeboard. And I am prepared to admit that she was not the easiest boat to handle in a stiff crosswind, particularly when the air currents were bedevilled by the towering sides of a 12-foot deep lock. There was a conventional wooden rudder and tiller which provided responsive control right down to very low water speeds.

After starting on craft borrowed from Ron Sams, with a 3.5hp outboard engine, we worked up to 5 and 7 horsepower units and eventually to an Evinrude 10, an engine for which I had unqualified admiration.

The engine was mounted without any remote control attachments on the removable transom (removable to permit easy access when the Otter was being used in her shore role). I normally steered standing on one or both of the cockpit lockers. The engine's tiller, therefore, was always in easy toe reach and consequently with ease and a certain amount of dexterity I was able to employ power steering as required merely by swinging the Evinrude tiller with my foot.

A unique quality of the Otter was the generous internal accommodation provided, which was quite exceptional in a craft of her size. This enabled my family to pass their time in complete comfort without getting into each other's hair, while I suffered whatever the elements may have cared to throw at me, in the cockpit manning the tiller. Narrowboat owners will appreciate this situation.

But the overriding advantage of the Otter was in her mobility. Here we had a practical four-berth boat with generous headroom throughout, her accommodation in which we could cruise for indefinite periods on any stretch of sheltered water which took our fancy.

I use the word sheltered advisedly because Ron Sams and I had a long shared ambition to cross the Channel in one; but it would be unrealistic to pretend the Otter was a good sea boat. Nevertheless, my licence from the Inland Waterways branch of the Transport Commission, as it was then, offered me 2,000 miles of assorted going within the United Kingdom for £8-10s (£8.50) a year. I got a rebate on her footage because the Otter lived in the garden and that accounted for what could be then, and still are, expensive mooring fees and very considerable maintenance costs.

All this was achieved by a brilliantly simple applied design, boatbuilding not only to a budget but also to a specific purpose clearly defined in the mind of the designer. As you will see from the photographs, the hull was pontoon-shaped to economise her overall length. But do not be deceived by that apparently brutally squared bow. Properly trimmed, fore and aft, her shearwater fell well below the front face of a shoebox shape. Her bottom was curved from bow to stern, and was also tapered sharply inwards from her vertical side members. Under power, therefore, the bows lifted prettily and presented a planing surface to the water. Her performance, at better than 5mph, was evidence of her efficiency.

On land, Otter lived on her trailer. This was a very simple tapered rectangle with small independently suspended wheels, high-pressure tyres and three pairs of rollers mounted outboard of the main longitudinal members. The launching procedure was simplicity itself: back trailer to the water's edge, undo rope, out pins, lift the trailer front end – that is to say the shoreward end – and off the trailer runs the Otter, stern first, onto the water. Average time: five minutes from arrival.

The recovery technique was even more ingenious: a winch and wire simply pulled the Otter back onto the trailer. We could complete this process unaided in less than 15 minutes. And this was just me, Sylvia, who was not a particularly strong person, and our two quite small children.

Boat and trailer together scaled a mere 13cwt (660kg), and with excellent towing characteristics long overland journeys presented no problem. Indeed, we tackled some pretty forbidding lanes and tracks in search of a good launching site in places like Scotland and the Lake District. On one occasion, hurrying to get home in time to return to my BBC duties, I was stopped by a police car and accused of driving at more than 55mph with my caravan in tow. I didn't argue the point but I did say to the policeman: "Did it look steady?"

"Extremely steady, sir," he said, "but you'll be reported anyway." And so I was, and duly fined, but not a fortune.

We lived in the little village of Horton in Buckinghamshire at the time, about three miles from Datchet and the River Thames, and indeed only just outside the 1947 flood area. But we preferred to launch on the Slough arm of the Grand Union Canal, which may not sound very attractive but anyone with experience of the long stretch of wooded banks by Denham, and the quiet beauty of Black Jack's Lock on the way to Rickmansworth, will know that despite its name it alone was a delightful little waterway.

I discovered a splendid launching place on the banks of the Oxford & Banbury Canal near Kidlington and that became one of Sylvia's favourites. On one occasion, arriving on a Friday evening after work, we'd launched and set off on our way. Unbeknownst to us, someone driving past had seen what they reported to the police as "people pushing a caravan into the canal, with children in it". By the time the police car arrived, assuming that it did, all that they would have found was a deserted stretch of water, and a parked and locked, legally licensed car. By that time we would have chugged several miles, happily on our way, but we heard the story at the local pub on our return.

The Otter was an all-wooden structure – mahogany marine ply on an ash frame with twin-sledge keels of oak – but despite its apparent flimsiness it was very stiff, both as a boat and as a caravan. In the forward section two berths ran fore and aft, on which the children slept although those berths were capable of sleeping adults more than six feet long. In the after section a double bed could be contrived, lying athwart ships. Light and heating were by Calor gas – I remember with great affection the friendly light of the little gas mantles surrounded by pink and transparent glass globes.

Sleeping bags had yet to come into fashion, so Sylvia stowed the necessary bedding for the three beds in the lockers at head height. It was a really very cosy arrangement, which enabled us to remain warm and snug and happy despite the worst that the weather could throw at us, which it did.

I still marvel at the way Sylvia was able to cope, getting everything stowed, cooking and caring for us – a task considerably heightened after Jenny had joined us – a small baby in a caravan is no mean undertaking but a small baby in an amphibious caravan afloat is another matter. But Sylvia took it all in very good part to say the least and, to my shame, I confess that I took her very much for granted.

After a couple of preliminary demonstrations, Ron Sams joined us on our first proper cruise. This was on Ullswater, in the Lake District. I drove up with Sylvia and Graham – this was before Jenny had arrived – and Ron met us at a pre-arranged rendezvous at the head of the lake. In company with him we drove down the western shore and ran out of daylight, parked the 'van in a wide spot, and turned in for the night – Ron retiring to a hotel. It rained very heavily that night and in the morning we discovered that we had parked virtually underneath a waterfall, but this was our first test of the Otter's waterproofness. A couple of miles down the road we discovered a little bit of beach onto which, with care, I could drive both car and caravan.

With Ron Sams' experienced assistance I got the car and trailer lined up for an easy launch into the shallow water at the edge of the lake. All was set to go when a passing AA man on his motorcycle combination spotted the situation and without hesitation called to me: "Hang on, sir, we'll get you out of there in a jiffy," little realising that that was the furthest from our intentions.

Leaving Ron ashore, we set out for the wide-open spaces of Ullswater and I must confess to a certain amount of trepidation. It was after all an entirely new experience with a completely new piece of kit. I have no doubt whatsoever that Sylvia shared my misgivings, probably to an even greater extent, but she concealed her feelings – as she did subsequently on so many occasions.

We later travelled from Weybridge to Haslemere via Guildford, though our waterways licence didn't cover us there and we had to pay. We also wound our way round the outskirts of London to one of the early rallies of the Inland Waterways Association at Little Venice.

On our trip up the Severn waterway we saw Worcester Cathedral for the first time from the river and that alone would have made the whole exercise worthwhile. For that, we launched on the canal just above Sharpness, on the Friday evening. We turned some 2¹/₂ miles north of Stourport on the Sunday afternoon and were back home on Monday night. We logged 116 miles for that exciting cruise and, after coping with the Severn's current, the wind and the deep sea craft which we encountered we were more than ever full of confidence and prepared to go anywhere.

This led to a bit of an adventure on Lake Windermere. For an overnight stop I ran the Otter ashore on the beach of an island, with the sledge keels just touching the ground – and I ran the two lines, which I normally used, from the bow, tethered to a couple of trees. Unfortunately, during the night the wind got up and by morning it was blowing a full gale. My attempts to get off that island against the wind, going backwards, were to no avail, and I was over the side, fending us off rocks when fortunately we were observed from a passing workboat. I can remember little Graham jumping up and down with excitement and shouting: "The towers are coming, Daddy, the towers are coming."

But years later Jenny was telling her friends that her father had shipwrecked her while she was still in her baby basket – for so indeed she was. We visited the Llangollen Canal and crossed the famous high aqueduct (Pontcysyllte) which was a very interesting experience and excited the children no end.

We launched on the rivers Avon and the Trent and went far across the Fens to reach the Boston Sea Lock. There the lock-keeper advised us very strongly not to proceed further but I went some distance towards the river mouth before the water in any way became rough – just for the hell of it.

We did encounter a problem in the famous Blisworth Tunnel – 3,076 yards of inky blackness with a tiny circle of light at the far end. The shearpin holding the propeller sheared and we had no drive. Consequently I remembered the way in which the narrowboats had gone through that tunnel in the early days: it was known as 'legging' and this was not difficult on the Otter because Graham and I were able to lie full length on the roof and propel us towards daylight and salvation simply by effectively walking the distance.

Another time, we crossed the border into Scotland and

explored the delightful little Loch Ken in Dumfriesshire and later went further north along the road to the isles to launch in Loch Shiel. On that loch there is a statue marking the embarkation point of the Young Pretender and I sensed that his ghost must have resented our presence because we were storm-bound there for three days. The deep, dark peat water of the river into which I ran for shelter turned overnight into a foaming torrent. I woke at first light, uneasy about the movement of the boat and tottered out into the pouring rain, clad only in my pyjamas, to make sure that the clothes lines which I used as mooring ropes were secure, as indeed they were. Returning, soaked, Sylvia remarked that it was just as well that we were so far from the beaten track: had a passer-by observed this mad man, struggling with a caravan in the river while soaked to the skin, he would probably have sent for the ambulance from the asylum.

Probably our finest sortie of all was our conquest of the Caledonian Canal. Launching at Fort William, we proceeded via Loch Lochy and Loch Oich into Loch Ness, the three joined by a beautiful, silver ribbon of water. At one point there was a very considerable flight of locks which was quite beyond the capability of my crew. Fortunately the locks were manned by a team of lock-keepers who emerged in the pouring rain in their oilskins, and their resentment at having to work this stricken shoebox through the flight of locks was quite apparent, only assuaged by the bottle of warming liquid which I presented to them at the bottom end.

Loch Ness can be a forbidding environment at the best of times and, for our first overnight mooring, I beached on what appeared to be an agreeable and isolated stretch of the bank. We were approached, however, by some men in monks' habits who pointed out that I was on the property of their monastery and, since I had women aboard – that is to say, Sylvia and little Jenny – would I please go elsewhere? This was accomplished without difficulty and we had a nice, quiet, cosy evening together; and a good night's sleep.

The following day the weather was much better and I cruised down Loch Ness towards the far end, beaching at about lunchtime on the eastern side, which is miles and miles from any road. After lunch the children and I went ashore to scramble up a very exciting-looking waterfall nearby. Having got as far up as I intended to go, I happened to look over my shoulder to see that the Otter was being washed much further ashore by an unexpected and unexplained series of waves on a perfectly still afternoon. To this day, I wonder if that was not the wake of the Loch Ness monster.

Towards the end of one little trip on the Grand Union Canal I moored to the bank overnight near Heath and Reach, where the mainline railway to Scotland runs very close to the canal. We intended to leave early in the morning and, looking towards the railway line, I was astonished to see a long, stationary train which just stayed where it was. Little did I know that this was the morning following The Great Train Robbery of 1966 and we were within less than half a mile of the scene. Later I was approached by the police and asked if I knew the whereabouts of Roy James, whom I had known as a young racing driver at Brands Hatch. I knew also that he was a silversmith but was able to convince the police that I knew nothing about it. They were rather more curious, however, when I told them where I had been that night.

It may not have been everybody's cup of tea, the Otter, yet we were really rather glad that it wasn't. Sadly, it was years ahead of its time and only a handful were produced. Interestingly, some were exported to Canada but during all our time on British waterways I think I never saw more than four or five of her kind. Today there are some modified, glass fibre imitations floating about but not, I am quite sure, enjoying the same degree of mobility as our amphibious caravan. But when the metaphorical gin pennant was flying, my son was on the helm, my little daughter off watch, singing happily to herself, a delicious whiff of soup coming from the galley, and the glories of rural Britain went gliding by in an endless waterside panorama, I was well content that I had discovered the Otter and all the happiness it brought into our lives.

Chapter 12

Lap Chart

The phenomenal success of the Goodwood Revival Meeting and the Festival of Speed is due to the determination, style and major investment of Lord March. It has given pleasure to hundreds of thousands – not least me, and this for two reasons. I was delighted to be asked to do the PA commentary on the flying there in 2003 and 2004 and it was at Goodwood that I did my first motor racing commentary for the BBC, at the British Automobile Racing Club Easter Meeting 1950.

Until then, in what little BBC coverage there had been, the principal commentators were Raymond Glendenning, who did everything from horse racing to football and boxing, and Max Robertson whose expertise was tennis. John Morgan, the unassuming but brilliant secretary of the BARC since pre-war Brooklands, was surprised when I asked him for a list of runners and riders two weeks before the event. My purpose was to memorise names and numbers, but no one seems to have made that request before. I asked my friend from Hamburg motoring days, Tom Walkerley, to keep the lap charts for me. I made contact with as many drivers as possible, enjoyed the event immensely, and was the BBC's principal motor racing commentator for the next 23 years.

Although I did not know it, Robin Richards had written to the BBC just before that, complaining about the lack of good motor racing coverage. He was an ex-regular officer then running a London motor business, having been invalided out of the army following a motor racing crash which seriously injured his legs. We became very good friends and colleagues and were soon joined by John Bolster, who had suffered a terrible accident driving an ERA in the 1949 British GP at Silverstone. Eric Tobitt was working in the scientific civil service at Malvern. A motor sport enthusiast, Eric had done several broadcasts in the Midland region, including for *Children's Hour*, and he completed what proved to be a happy and long-lasting team.

Eric Tobitt tells me we first met at the Metropole Hotel in Llandrindod Wells. It was the first control after the Glasgow start of the Monte Carlo Rally in 1951. He was there to report for the Midland Region of the BBC.

Eric was never on the staff of the Corporation, nor had a long-term contract, but I never worked with anyone with a more professional attitude and application to the job. He was a natural broadcaster who first spoke into a microphone in 1939, in an under-20s programme introduced by the great Howard Marshall. His active interest in motor sport drew us together and he was a regular member of our commentary team from the early 1950s.

In case a famous name seems to be missing here, perhaps I should explain. Today, of course, Murray Walker is celebrated as the voice of Formula 1 motor racing of the past, whose commentating career stretches back to the 1950s. Although that is completely correct, neither Tobitt, nor Robin Richards nor I ever met him at a circuit while we were the BBC's motor sport A-team, that is until 1973. Although Murray did broadcast once from a Goodwood motor race, he joined his ex-TT rider father, Graham, to cover motorcycle racing and that took him out of our orbit in those days.

Actually, one of my very first BBC jobs was as number two to Graham, whom I greatly admired, at the start/finish line of the Isle of Man TT. Murray was out in the country, as we used to say, stationed at a point far round the course. My boss had briefed me to try to stop Graham talking when the time allocated to live radio commentary ended and believe I told that story when I was invited to take part in Murray's *This Is Your Life* programme.

Only five years ago I was introduced at the Classic Car Show in the NEC as, "Raymond Baxter, BMW."

"No, no," I protested, "I never drove for BMW."

"Not BMW, the cars," said this witty chap. "Raymond Baxter, Before Murray Walker." It got a good laugh.

Initially on radio, I occupied the commentary box at the start/finish line, Robin would be 'in the country' – ie Stowe Corner at Silverstone – and John was a roving reporter in the pits. When the BBC televised its first motor race, the British Grand Prix at Silverstone, in 1953, I did the television commentary while Robin took my place on radio, with Eric Tobitt at Stowe.

Before electronic information direct from Race Control became available, the only way in which a pit manager, let alone a commentator, could keep up-to-the-minute track of a race was by means of a lap chart. This was a pencil and paper operation, demanding concentration, a quick brain and a cool head.

When I persuaded the BBC to send me to Monte Carlo for its first coverage of a continental motor race, the European Grand Prix in 1955, I took Sylvia with me as my lap-charter. We drove there in my beloved, tuned Standard 8 drophead and my knowledge of the principality enabled me to pre-book a room with a balcony in the modest, but delightful, Hotel Bristol.

This provided an excellent view of the Gasworks Hairpin and a long stretch up the hill towards Rosie's Bar. Rosie's was something of a British institution. Although Rosie herself was Monegasque, her impeccable little establishment was a favourite watering hole for British racing and rally people, as well as sailors from visiting British and American warships. When re-development, which was never-ending in Monte

Full House – plaques commemorating Dunkirk Returns 1965-2005. Unique to *L'Orage*.

Top: First Return to Dunkirk 1965. Crew of *L'Orage*. Left to right, Dr Derek Roper, Peter Garnier, Jenny and Graham Baxter, RB, Sylvia.

*Opposite page, top:*1990 over. HRH the Duke of Edinburgh aboard *L'Orage*. In the background are Paul ?, RB's son-in-law, and son Graham. Captain Bryan Salwey, RN, NRO Eastern England is at right. Prince Philip also visited Little Ships prior to departure in 2000.

Below: Leading section of Little Ships mid-channel, 1990. *Wanda, L'Orage, Firefly* and *Daphne*.

Top: Monte Carlo Rally stage on the Monaco Grand Prix circuit. Author on the limit at the station hairpin, 1964.

Middle: On site briefing during the London Motor Club versus British Army autopoint, late 1960s.

Bottom: Fairley Spoke, Shelsley Walsh, July 1968

Top: A Rootes promotion for the 1961 Motor Show with Jack Brabham (left) and Peter Harper.

Bottom: Monte Carlo Rally, January 1962, approaching the summit of the Col du Turini with Peter Harper in their works-entered Sunbeam Rapier.

Top: At the Monte Carlo Rally prize-giving. Third overall and a class win, with Peter Harper in the Rapier, 1960.

Bottom left: An RAC Rally class win in a Humber Super Snipe with navigator Leonard Miller, 1961.

Bottom right: Relaxing with Jackie Reece in Monte Carlo.

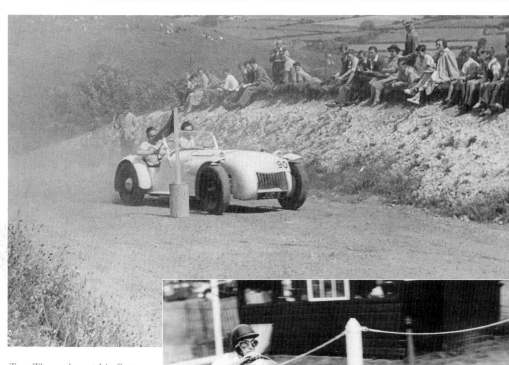

Top: The author at his first international event, the Lisbon Rally, 1950, with his co-driver and owner of the Allard, Goff Imhoff.

Middle: At the RAC Eastbourne Rally, again with Imhoff in the re-bodied Allard.

Bottom: In Fairley Special V8 Mercury built by Reg Phillips at Prescott Hill.

Top left: Eye on Research title sequences. A precursor to *Tomorrow's World*.

Top right: 'The Spiral of Life'. Francis Crick with a model of the DNA molecule.

Above: Telstar, the first TV satellite antenna dish.

Above right: A scene from *Tomorrow's World*. Alternative energy, 1974.

Right: Christmas edition 1974. RB as 'Willy Wonka'?

Bottom left: The author makes his point with James Burke.

Bottom centre: Health and Safety at work. Demonstrating fire protection material made from silicon platelets.

Bottom right: Cover of the *Radio Times*, 7th November 1970.

Carlo, threatened the place, I was one of the organisers of a huge petition to Prince Rainier, which was successful. But that's by the way.

Sylvia and I settled into our exciting surroundings and, as arranged, an engineer from French radio turned up, smoking a Gauloise, and joined wires to a microphone and headphones. At the appointed hour, and after some muttering to and fro, he handed me the microphone and headphones and said, "Monsieur, ici Londres," and there left me to get on with it. It was a terrific race, snatches of which we broadcast, and despite many changes of places and pit stops, Sylvia's lap chart was a model of its kind. After 80 of the 100 laps, Stirling Moss (Mercedes-Benz) had built a commanding lead over the distinguished Italian, Alberto Ascari (Lancia).

Moss then pulled into the pits, to retire in a cloud of smoke, and seconds later Ascari plunged into the harbour on the exit from the tunnel. All hell broke loose but despite the confusion Sylvia remained in total control. We got the result right – Trintignant won in a Ferrari – and broadcast it live while most people were wondering what had happened. When I got back to the office and submitted my expenses, my boss, Charles Max-Muller, told me I could not claim for my wife. I protested that without Sylvia to keep the lap chart, my commentary could not have been possible. "Then you must teach your secretary how to do it," he said. Sylvia's New England sense of justice was outraged and she never again accompanied me to a motor race.

At the Nine-Hours Race at Goodwood, I had two of the secretaries from the Outside Broadcast Department, Pam Guyler and Pru Hindle, 'driving' the lap chart. A major fire broke out during the pit-stop in the Aston Martin pit, which was about ten yards up wind of our wooden commentary position above Race Control. "Just keep the lap chart going, girls," I said, "I'll tell you when we get out," and they did, and we didn't. I'm sure that the war had given me an almost detached attitude towards fire and other emergencies, indeed tragedies, which in those days were all too common in motor racing. But in that, I was not alone. Like many of his

161

contemporaries, Duncan Hamilton had been a pilot. He had served in the Fleet Air Arm. His Jaguar partner at Le Mans in 1953, when they won the race, was Tony Rolt, an army officer who wound up as a prisoner in the notorious Colditz castle. There he had been involved in building the escape glider, and complained bitterly to me about the BBC's dramatised version and the film.

In the small hours I visited the Jaguar pit. The race was in the balance, the conditions, including rising mist and drizzle, dangerous. Lois Rolt, with Angela Hamilton standing beside her, said, "Oh, good morning Raymond, would you like a cup of tea?" Talk about courage!

For my commentary on the British Empire Trophy Race in the Isle of Man, I had John Bolster with me but, for some reason or another, I had no lap-charter. It was a comparatively short-distance sports car race, round the houses at Douglas, a far cry from the motorcycle TT course, which was forbidden to cars. My friend, Cliff Davis, was driving a Cooper MG variant and I asked his wife – also named Sylvia – to keep my lap chart. I told her that she would get a better view of the race from my commentary box – and I knew she could do the job.

Unfortunately, at about three quarters distance Cliff went missing but his wife's lap chart remained faultless although it was a short while before we learned that Cliff hadn't hit anything, but had just broken down somewhere out in the back. In later years, Bette Hill always kept the lap chart in Graham's pit.

For me, the fascination and pleasure of motor racing was centred as much on the people as the machinery. Both were equally incorporated by John Cooper of Cooper Cars and Colin Chapman of Lotus. Both could have been first rank drivers but, of far greater importance, between them they changed entirely the shape and size of the single-seater racing car. The large and beautiful classics from Maserati, Lancia and Ferrari, little changed from their pre-war predecessors, not to mention the 4.5 litre Lago-Talbots and the gothic perpendicular 1.5-litre ERAs became outdated and outclassed almost overnight. Diminutive by comparison and, in the

Coopers, invariably rear-engined, they owed much in their relative simplicity to the 500s and even more to Coventry Climax Engines Ltd.

That celebrated firm of Midlands engineers had produced a magnificent four-cylinder engine to power the fire pumps which fought the Blitz. Its managing director, Leonard P Lee, was more than man enough to take in his stride this totally unexpected demand on his company's product and, indeed, he delighted in it. His only concern was that journalists and broadcasters should refrain from dropping the word 'Coventry' when the names Cooper-Climax or Lotus-Climax became famous. He was a major connoisseur and collector of art. His Regency house in central Coventry was literally littered with masterpieces – unhung because there simply was insufficient wall space. A little Rubens could be propped up in a corner, as I saw for myself.

He commissioned a beautiful, bronze equestrian Lady Godiva, replicas of which he presented to John Cooper, Colin Chapman, Peter Garnier of *The Autocar* and me "for services to British motor racing". Mine was stolen from our mantelpiece and dumped in a nearby roadside hedge, presumably because the thieves realised it was too recognisable. Six months later, following a major road accident on that very spot, my beautiful statue literally dropped from the hedge to be caught undamaged by my neighbour. With my daughter, who had also gone out to investigate the incident, she was picking up the pieces to clear the road. "Good gracious," she cried, "Do you think I can keep this?" "No, you may not," said my daughter firmly, "it's ours." I had to repay my insurance claim!

John Cooper and Colin Chapman were both gifted designers, but whereas John's remained a small-scale but extremely successful business, Colin created Lotus which, in its heyday, produced and ran a Grand Prix racing team, built trend-setting sports cars, motor yachts and even a diesel outboard engine – his only failure. One winter's day, when he invited me to his works in Norfolk, he took his leave apologetically, saying he had to get in some night flying "for his ticket".

"And where are you going to do that?" I asked.

"In the traffic pattern at Heathrow," he said, and off he went.

Another man more interested in the people than the cars was Peter Ustinov. It must have been early in 1958 when I was introduced to him at the Steering Wheel Club in Mayfair by Peter Scott Russell. Stirling was there and we chatted about people and cars. Some months later, when he returned from a business trip to the US, the celebrated Allard driver, Goff Imhoff, gave me a 33⅓rpm long play disc which was then only available in America. It was *The Grand Prix du Roc*, a brilliantly funny satire based on the motor racing scene as viewed by Ustinov and in which he played all the characters and did all the sound effects. As its title implies, the setting was the Rock of Gibraltar, where the Duke of Edinburgh drives the opening lap of honour, including the watersplash, in his "detuned Morris Minor". Characters included Girling Foss, a gravel-voiced José Giulio Fandango, Count Wolfram von Grips, Commendatore Fanfani, Monsieur Origini, the unmistakable "Schnorschedes" team manager, Herr Altbauer – and a commentator called Roland Thaxter – "Mind my tea – it's right on the edge of the table." I understand that *The Grand Prix du Roc* has been released again recently, on tape and CD: it's a must for anyone with any knowledge of the period – or even without.

Two major personalities not parodied in that masterpiece were Graham Hill and Jim Clark, simply because the recording was before their time. And what a time that was. Their rivalry on the circuits could not have been more close, nor more fiercely contested. Both were extremely popular and likeable personalities – Jimmy, the son and heir of a successful farmer; and Graham, who signed on at the Labour Exchange as an unemployed racing driver before he had even had his first works drive. Jimmy, a quiet but by no means dour Scot; Graham, the total extrovert and member of the London Rowing Club, whose colours he wore on his helmet, as did his son, Damon. Father and son were both Formula 1 World Champions. Jimmy never had time to get married. He drove

164

Real fame at last – every boy's hero!

exclusively for Colin Chapman and was killed by a technical failure in his Lotus Formula 2 car at Hockenheim on 7th April, 1968. Despite their intense rivalry, Jimmy and Graham remained friends, and I never heard one speak ill of the other. In fact when, in an interview, I asked Graham the time-honoured question, "What would you like to see done to improve Formula 1," Graham replied, "Make Jimmy have to do half a lap more than the rest of us."

Both won the Indianapolis 500, considered the birthright of American drivers and big American Offenhauser Specials. It had, by far, the richest prize-money in racing. I suspect, although he never told me, that Jimmy invested the money in the farm. Graham bought a twin-engine aeroplane. He became a proficient pilot as I learned when I flew beside him on more than one cross-Channel trip, and that made his death the more tragic. On 29th November 1975, he was flying back from testing on the Paul Ricard Circuit when he hit a tree at dusk on his final approach to Elstree. With him were five leading members of his Embassy-Hill F1 team – Andy Smallman, Ray Brimble, Terry Richards and Tony Allcock, as well as his immensely talented young driver, Tony Brise. Graham himself had retired from driving a couple of years before to concentrate on running the team.

The investigation suggested an incorrect altimeter setting. Had any other experienced pilot been with him, it is most likely that the accident would not have happened. It is a fundamental of cockpit drill that pilot and co-pilot each set their altimeters to the barometric pressure instructed by Flying Control at their intended arrival point. They then glance at each other's instruments and if there is a discrepancy there is a re-check. Also, had I been with him, I would have strongly urged him to divert to Denham, where there was no mist. We lived within a mile and a half of the airfield. Sylvia could have picked us up and Graham could have joined Bette in time for the reception in London which he was determined to attend. St Albans Abbey was packed for his funeral on 5th December. Morecambe and Wise were amongst the ushers, and of all the friends in motor racing that I lost none grieved me more.

An invasion of talent and determination from Australia and New Zealand introduced Bruce McLaren, Jack Brabham, Denny Hulme and others to British racing. Bruce was not only a top-flight driver, but also a brilliant engineer, and it is fitting that one of Britain's major Formula 1 teams bears his name to this day. He was killed testing at Goodwood, where his monument now stands close to that of Douglas Bader.

Denny Hulme, son of a war hero, was a far cry from the popular image of hell-raising antipodeans. He won the F1 World Championship for Brabham in 1967. In the late 1950s, Jack Brabham had brought tough Australian fibre into the team of his friend, John Cooper. He arrived onto the British circuits straight from dirt-track racing, and his early style, with the tail hanging well out, delighted the crowds. He too proved his engineering ability by building his own succession of Brabhams and was knighted in Australia, following his third World Championship in 1966. He remains the only F1 World Champion to have won the title in a car of his own make. There was no nonsense about Jack, and I liked and admired him very much.

Looking back over the years, names tend to stand out in my memory in pairs: Lofty England of Jaguar and John Wyer of Aston Martin, for example. Both were amongst the most distinguished competition managers of their time – calmly efficient, tactically shrewd, strong on leadership and both perfect gentlemen.

In the early 1950s I persuaded BBC Television that there was a place in its schedules for a series of 30-minute programmes dedicated entirely to motoring. I called it *Driving Club* and it was the first of its kind in Britain, if not the world. Like *Eye On Research*, and for the same reason, it had to come under the wing of the Outside Broadcast Department. Territorial Army drill halls provided ideal accommodation, not least because of their size. It occurred to me that a close-up view of a typical Le Mans-style pit stop, which few viewers would ever have seen, would be interesting particularly if it was a competition. I phoned Lofty and John, who after consulting their bosses, Sir William Lyons and David Brown, agreed.

167

The venue was in West London. A mock up of two adjacent pits was built, two team cars and their complete pit crews were the competitors and their requirement was to change two wheels, check the oil, tip in a churn of fuel, get a driver into the car and start the engine, but not, repeat, not to drive off. The Jaguar team won by four seconds, but that was co-incidental. Health and Safety regulations today would make a repeat performance unthinkable, to say nothing of the cost. Such was the spirit of motor racing in those days, and the still untarnished allure of television, that neither John Wyer nor Lofty England ever mentioned the question of money. My admiration for the two men was unequalled anywhere in the pit lane.

Thinking of Lofty, I remember being given a drive in the prototype E-type Jaguar. Returned to the factory, Bob Berry of Jaguar and I were met by Lofty who asked me what I thought of the car.

"A winner," I said, "but I can't get my feet comfortable." Looking down at me from his height of six foot six, Lofty said, "Don't know what you're talking about," turned on his heels and walked away. That troubled me and I told my rally-driving chum, Jackie Reece about it.

"Perhaps," said Jackie, "if you're as tall as Lofty it mmm...may nn...not have occurred tt...to you that it is pp...possible to be comfortable in a cc...car." Later on, the production E-type had a shallow well below the pedals to accommodate the heels of long-legged drivers.

If ever a pair of motor racing names became inseparable, it would be Mike Hawthorn and Peter Collins, each to the other "Mon ami mate". They might have been called the heavenly twins, but they were far too naughty. Despite their skill, determination and sheer raw courage, they were both over-grown schoolboys at heart, playing with extremely dangerous toys. When they were leading the 1957 German Grand Prix for Ferrari at the Nürburgring, their successful pursuit by Fangio who, recovering from a pit-stop, took the lead with two laps to go and won by 3.6 seconds, is the subject of a masterpiece of motor racing art by Michael Turner.

It was at the Nürburgring a year later, on 3rd August 1958,

that Peter crashed and died in the ensuing fire. Not long after that, on 22nd January 1959 and during his World Championship year, Mike Hawthorn's life ended in a bizarre road accident on the Guildford bypass. Mike had been involved in the major motor racing disaster of my time – Le Mans 1955. I was about to do a live update for BBC Radio when I watched Pierre Levegh's Mercedes hit the roadside bank halfway up the pit straight, fly into the air, land and burst into flames in the middle of the packed spectator enclosure. With little idea of the enormity of the disaster, I was able to assure listeners that no British driver, nor personnel, on the pit side were involved. But my next broadcast the following morning told a sombre tale:

"This is RB calling from Le Mans, where a grey and drizzling dawn has broken over the circuit – weather which I am afraid is fitting to the mood of the event – as news of the casualties in last evening's accident in which Pierre Levegh's Mercedes tore into the crowd – as those ghastly figures mount. The casualty list now shows 72 dead and 100 injured, in the worst accident in the history of motoring.

"At two o'clock this morning, after consultation with the Stuttgart factory, the two remaining Mercedes – driven by Fangio and Moss, in first place with two laps in hand over the pursuing Jaguars – and Kling and Simon, lying fourth – were withdrawn.

"Since then, as the long hours of darkness have dragged on, the number of red crosses on the indicator board, marking the cars which have retired, has steadily increased as the tremendous pace of the race has taken its toll of machinery. Now 28 still run, 32 are out – amongst them all the Ferraris, the Beauman/Dewis Jaguar and all but one Maserati.

"But nonetheless – in the lead – having

completed 195 laps – is the D-type Jag of Hawthorn and Bueb; second – six laps behind – the three-litre Maser of Musso and Valenzano; and third, closing fast, the Aston Martin of Paul Frère and Peter Collins.

"The Kiefts, however, were in big trouble and the Baxter/Deeley 1500 retired at 90 minutes – while the 1100 appeared to be overheating.

"The three-litre Maseratis, which initially joined in the dice at the front, also found the pace too hot – and faded – Mières having two or three pit stops.

"In the two-litre class the Gordini and the two-litre Maser are a lap ahead of the British cars – headed by Peter Wilson and Jim Mayers' Bristol. Both Bristols, Triumphs and Nashes seem happy and are going well, however.

"In the one-and-a-half-litre class the Porsches have galloped away and Polensky is amongst the two-litres. McAlpine's Connaught is one lap down on them.

"Colin Chapman's Lotus was leading the 1100s but had to pit-stop. There is now nothing in it between him – and the Cooper – and Duntov's Porsche.

"Mike Sparken's three-litre Ferrari retired at six o'clock – and the remarkable twin-boom 750 Nardi also went out.

"Les Brooke, almost a lap ahead of the other works TR2s, is grinning happily."

Despite that appalling tragedy and although it was always extremely hard work, our annual outing to Le Mans was enjoyable in a masochistic kind of way, thanks to the excellent company of my colleagues.

Antony Hopkins, the musicologist, conductor and composer wrote to me out of the blue, volunteering to do anything to help during the 24 hours. He proved an excellent and tireless watchkeeper. One year during our drive to the circuit, that inveterate tease Robin Richards said, "I know you write music, Hoppers, but could you perhaps whistle a bit of one of your tunes to give us an idea?" At that moment a factory hooter sounded nearby:

"As a matter of fact, Robin, that is one of my earlier works," said Anthony, "before I got the knack of changing the notes, you know."

A major element of fun was brought to Silverstone when the BRDC/*Daily Express* programme introduced short-distance saloon car races, of about 15-20 laps. From the fall of the flag, keen rivalry broke out between privately entered Mark 2 Jaguars. Amongst the principal players – and it was a game, albeit an extremely expensive one – there was Tommy Sopwith, the son of the legendary Sir T O M Sopwith – pioneer aviator, aircraft manufacturer and America's Cup yachtsman. Tommy, who had himself shown promise as a driver, and who won the Cowes International Power Boat Race, named his Jaguar team Equipe Endeavour after his father's yachts. His principal driver was the well-named 'Gentleman Jack' Sears, Norfolk farmer and landowner, who later became President of the BRDC.

John Coombs had a successful motor business in Guildford and he too had raced. His principal driver was Roy Salvadori, taking time out from his works drives for Aston Martin and others. Ecurie Ecosse, as the name implies, raced Jaguars in the blue and white colours of the saltire at Le Mans and elsewhere. Drivers included Ron Flockhart, who went missing in an attempt to fly a North American P51 Mustang to Australia (this was the aircraft I had ferried from Cairo to India – and I had warned him that single-engined flight over long sea distances was risky, to say the least), Ivor Bueb – a Welshman – Jimmy Stewart and his younger brother, Jackie. Another character from those days was leading journalist and former Brooklands driver, Tom Wisdom, who gave Stirling Moss several victorious drives, notably the RAC Tourist Trophy on the demanding road circuit at Dundrod in Northern Ireland.

Were all the rest not sufficient entertainment, on came the 1275cc Mini-Cooper S. The saloon car races were scratch – no handicaps – with places on the grid allotted by practice times, regardless of class. The result was some monumental dices, not only between the Minis and the Jags but all through the field. John Fitzpatrick and John Rhodes were the principal giant killers, but I remember Peter Harper's works Rapier wheel-to-wheel with Bill Blydenstein's amazing Vauxhall and, later, Peter Procter's Ford Anglia. This got shunted off the road at Goodwood's Easter meeting in 1966, overturned and caught fire. Only Peter's determination got him out of the car, but he was severely burned and became a member of pioneer surgeon Sir Archie McIndoe's Guinea Pig Club at East Grinstead Hospital. Thanks to that, and the never-failing support of his indomitable and loving wife, Shirley, 'Proc' recently took up racing again in Historic events, fearlessly driving a Sunbeam Tiger at the Goodwood Revival and elsewhere.

The advent of colour TV revolutionised our capability on *Tomorrow's World* and added hugely to the spectacle of motor racing. Ironically, for a short while, to me it was a pain. My first experience of a nightmare came at Zandvoort and the Dutch Grand Prix. While viewers at home could enjoy full colour on their screens of whatever size, the monitor in the commentary box had a tiny screen showing only black and white images. That was bad enough anywhere but the 14 miles per lap of the Nürburgring made it all far worse. Although I had, as usual, memorised the numbers of the cars and their drivers, I had only a brief view of the race with the naked eye. When the camera showed a long shot, all I could see was a black dot without even knowing its true colour. I felt like a blind man in a paper chase and I know that my commentary was very below standard. But the advance of technology produced a decent-sized image, in colour, for commentators in all sports – and the nightmare passed.

Some of the personalities I remember from these times include Tony Brooks who was a young dental student when I first met him. A quiet personality, he had a smooth but aggressive style of his own. Tony Vandervell was a self-made millionaire thanks to the Thinwall bearings he produced for the motor industry at his Maidenhead factory. An engineer and a tough businessman of the old school, Vandervell was fiercely patriotic and determined to restore the reputation of British racing following the pathetic failure of the V16 1.5 litre BRM. In character, he could not have been further from Raymond Mays and Peter Berthon of the original BRM story.

Tony began in top class motor racing by producing, and entering in Formula 1, the Thinwall Special. It was a modified Ferrari which paved the way to the Vanwall, a much more original design though still Ferrari influenced. Stirling drove for him and scored a few victories but his most consistent driver was Tony Brooks, so much so that he was snapped up by Enzo Ferrari, along with Mike Parkes, son of the managing director, and later chairman, of Alvis. Tragically, Mike was killed in a road accident in Italy in 1977. By then he was working for Lancia, aged 45 and about to marry for the first time, but back in the '60s Tony married the Italian girl he met at Modena and, as the saying goes, lived happily ever after.

Another of the British drivers hired to ride the 'Prancing Horse' achieved the double World Championship on two and four wheels. John Surtees was by no means born with a silver spoon in his mouth, rather almost with motorcycle chains in a tray of paraffin in his hands. As a boy he accompanied his father, a biker of some repute, around the circuits. Here was an engineer at the wheel.

Thanks to John Surtees, I claim to have been the first commentator to state accurately the gears and speeds around the racetracks, information I had often sought from Graham Hill. Graham was never too preoccupied during practice to answer my questions but he did so vaguely, finger on the circuit diagram in the programme.

Thus, "I change down here direct from fifth to second, so I'm doing a bit under 50 into the hairpin, then I accelerate straight through third and fourth to about 115 here." That was Graham Hill, helpful as ever. At Monaco, in the cool of the pit garage, I put the same questions to John Surtees. "Wait a minute, Raymond," he said. "We've changed the back axle ratio, so I must get my slide rule." He gave me the speeds correct to two decimal points.

John was the driver chosen by the secretive Japanese to introduce Honda to Formula 1 and later he built and entered his own cars. Throughout his epic career, he remained the quiet friend who had invited Sylvia and me to his wedding in Salisbury.

In complete contrast to John Surtees was Innes Ireland, an unquenchable and near untameable wild man of a Scot. Innes was the greatest company, and unfailingly gave his all to whatever he was driving. Tim Parnell, son of former BRM driver Reg, tried his hand behind the wheel but settled for the role of owner and entrant, employing Innes who had already had successful drives at Le Mans and elsewhere, including North America where he had won the US GP for Team Lotus.

But Innes had an awful lot of bad luck. I remember a race at Silverstone when he was lying third and came into the pits. I quickly cued to John Bolster, who was trailing his microphone lead and hurrying breathlessly along the front of the pits. Reaching the stricken car, John said, "Innes Ireland seems to be in some kind of trouble. Nothing serious I hope, Innes?" He thrust the microphone forward. "Depends what you mean by serious, John," said Innes, "That effing wheel is coming off."

Dear John Bolster: like Innes, he was slightly larger than life. With him, as with Jack Reece, I had as much fun as with anyone I ever met. At Le Mans one year, on the morning after the race and the usual celebrations, John and I were having a quiet breakfast together when a crop-headed American enthusiast clapped him on the back and said, rather cheerfully:

"Good morning, Mr Bolster, sir, and how are you today?"

"I'm not at all myself," said John, in his measured, ultra-British and rather nasal intonation, "In fact I'm some other poor bastard... and I don't know who he is... but I think he's going to die."

After Hawthorn had beaten Fangio so narrowly in that enthralling French Grand Prix at Rheims back in 1953, Robin Richards, John Bolster and I celebrated generously with the local vintages that night. A one-way traffic system had been introduced round the city centre which, coupled with the after-effects of the night before, proved confusing. I was driving, Robin allegedly navigating and John was recovering in the back. When we passed the cathedral for the third time John said, "I say, Waymond, if we pass that place again, would you be kind enough to dwaw up, I wish to go in and have myself cwossed off."

To my regret I never achieved with Ken Tyrrell and Jackie Stewart the same warm relationship which I enjoyed with so many others. Strange, because Jimmy Stewart – Jackie's older brother – and I were good friends until Jackie eclipsed him and we lost touch. But personalities aside, there can be no denying that the Tyrrell/Stewart partnership had a huge impact on the motor racing scene. It was not only their victories in the Formula 1 World Championships of 1969, 1971 and 1973, nor was it Tyrrell's readiness to embrace unorthodox design, for his six-wheeler which came after Stewart had retired. It was the influence and consequent power they exercised. It is undeniable that Jackie's refusal to accept the tragic string of fatal accidents in motor racing improved circuit safety out of all recognition and, without question, saved many lives. He even condemned the historic Nürburgring on which he had won the German Grand Prix three times. Many years later, Ken Tyrrell assumed the presidency of the BRDC at a difficult time and was of enormous service to the club. And, at the time of writing, Sir Jackie is facing, as president, a similar BRDC crisis.

Ken Tyrrell's memorial service in Guildford Cathedral was true to the man. The huge building was packed; Dame Kiri Te Kanawa sang and, at the end of the service, the Chris Barber Band led the congregation out, playing *When the Saints....*

And outside, on the lawn beyond the Great West Door, stood the Central Band of the Royal Air Force, playing popular music as the guests exchanged happy memories of the man they had come to honour.

The name of Stirling Moss occupies a unique place in the history of British motor racing. But not just in racing: he first came to notice as an 18-year-old by breaking the 500cc record at the Prescott hillclimb. Backed to the hilt by his parents, he had forsaken a promising start in show-jumping, which he left to his sister, Pat. She in turn took to rallying and, partnered by Ann Wisdom, daughter of Brooklands driver and journalist, Tom, she would have won the ladies championship had there been one. In any case, she repeatedly humbled the male opposition in all the classic international events.

Stirling, too, became a star rally driver. He was second, driving a Sunbeam-Talbot 90 for Norman Garrad's Rootes Group team in the 1952 Monte Carlo Rally and then won the highly prized Coupe des Alpes for a penalty-free completion of the classic of classics, the Alpine Rally. I recorded the commentary to a film of that event. When he got out of the car at the finish he was so exhausted that his knees buckled and he had to hang onto the car door for support. He won everywhere, and lost everywhere, in Formulas 1, 2 and 3 and in sports cars. Free of mechanical failure he was invincible but he was repeatedly dogged by cruel misfortune.

His all-conquering run with Fangio for Mercedes-Benz had its highlight in the British Grand Prix at Aintree in 1955. The two were separated at the chequered flag by less than two seconds; and Stirling never knew whether Fangio had lifted in the last bend to give his young friend victory on his home ground.

I remember his victory at Monaco in 1961 when, through the closing laps, he held off the three pursuing works Ferraris to snatch victory for Rob Walker's privately entered Lotus. It was at Monaco that he refused to protest against Mike Hawthorn for allegedly reversing on the circuit after taking an escape road. It gave Mike the World Championship, which Stirling never won. His record for Jaguar at Le Mans was legendary but perhaps his greatest drive was his famous victory, with Denis Jenkinson as navigator and pace-note signaller, in the Mille Miglia of 1955.

Stirling was, and still is, a good friend of mine. Although I was at Goodwood on the day in 1962, I was not on the air when he inexplicably charged off the circuit, sustaining desperate brain damage. When 'Pa' Moss said it would be okay for me to visit him in the famous Atkinson-Morley Neurological Hospital, he could scarcely complete a sentence.

I secretly wept for the loss of one of the most articulate of men. Three years later, nobody noticed that anything had happened. He had willed his mind to re-orientate its function, to by-pass its damage. He was and still is the epitome of courage, skill and determination as well as being an extremely nice man. Sir Stirling Moss is truly a legend in his own lifetime.

The television coverage of Formula 1 in 2005 is on a different planet from that of my time. The technological advances are breathtaking... multi-camera coverage, instant edited replay, on-board cameras and now eavesdropping on pit-to-driver radio, as well as up-to-the-minute race positions on screen – instead of having to read our pencil-and-paper lap charts.

The current commentary by James Allen, Martin Brundle, Mark Blundell and the rest of the ITV team is also in my view excellent. A principal factor in the quantum leap of audience numbers has been the allocation of time. I had to argue bitterly with the BBC to be allowed five minutes on the air before the start, on both radio and television. I did my best to gabble through the grid – drivers, cars and times – but sometimes failed to include the backmarkers before the starting flag fell. Therefore there was huge pressure to present a proper picture as the tension rose while the seconds ticked by.

More than 30 years ago, I received an extremely civil letter from the mother of James Hunt – later to be World Champion – when he first appeared in Formula 1, driving for Lord Hesketh. "Why," she asked, "did you not mention my son once in your broadcasts?" I could only write an apology. He was then a tail-ender, squeezed out of comment by the necessity to concentrate on the leaders in the time available, and also as dictated by the camera coverage.

Today, the tension before the start of a Grand Prix is brilliantly captured on television. But that tension is not peculiar to Formula 1. I experienced it myself, in what little racing I did, and on rallies and hillclimbs. I once asked Graham Hill about it:

"Sometimes, like at Monaco," he said, "I feel my clutch foot start to tremble."

Chapter 13

Televised Science

In the early 1970s, when we bumped into each other at a television party, Ronnie Barker, one of my favourite comic actors said, "I think the way that you put across all this science and technology stuff is brilliant!"

"Oh, rubbish," I muttered modestly.

"I know it is," he said, "but you do it terribly well."

About the same time I got a letter asking for a couple of signed photographs: nothing unusual about that, but the text of the letter was: "My wife and I greatly enjoy your science programmes and we think your impersonation of Barbara Streisand is out of this world."

I was flattered to be identified, albeit mistakenly, with my namesake, Stanley, whose impersonation of Ms Streisand was indeed remarkable. What really makes my day is when I meet, or get a letter from someone with a lot of letters after his or her name – and quite often wearing a white coat – who says, "You're the guy who got me interested in science, watching *Tomorrow's World* when I was a kid." I suppose that may be true of my son who got a PhD in oceanology, although he hasn't mentioned it to date.

The fact is, in its heyday *Tomorrow's World* attracted a major audience to BBC Television – around 11 million and peaking at 13. Yet, the programme could be fairly described as 'son of *Eye On Research*'.

When Aubrey Singer, an ambitious and self-confident young programme assistant, returned from the BBC's New York office, his reputation preceded him. At the New York Motor Show, microphone in hand, he had asked Sir William Rootes (as he then was), why he was not selling more British cars in the United States – a Jeremy Paxman-type question, forty years ahead of its time.

Aubrey returned to London without loss to his disregard for convention and he had an ambition. It was to bring science to the television screen, but the resources at his disposal were limited, as a producer in the Outside Broadcast Department, whose *modus operandi* was principally to cover sport and other major occasions.

The BBC schedules had recently been increased to include a scientific series called *Horizon*, which was based on film. It is still running to this day. Aubrey's idea was to take the outside broadcast cameras live to the centres of excellence and hence, the title, *Eye On Research*. Its opening title on the screen was the wave-form of four musical notes on an oscilloscope – in those days in itself an unfamiliar sight.

I had done a few broadcasts in the field of science on radio – my first was a visit to the BBC's research centre at Abbey Road, next door to the historic EMI recording studios. After a couple of trial runs, Aubrey invited me to present *Eye On Research* and the series continued intermittently between 1959 and 1962. The script, which ran to a sizeable 'wodge' of A4, was put together in interview form by a remarkable freelance writer named Gordon Rattray Taylor. Arrived on site, my first task was to condense that into a few lines of notes, which I scribbled on the back of the script. Tele-prompt and its successor, autocue, had yet to be invented.

Thus equipped, and with cameras and crews more familiar with horse racing and football, we blithely went where no television man had been before. One of our first visits was to

Dec 4, 1953

Science International

A world-wide report on Scientific Research

2: THE LAST SCOURGE

A report on research into Cancer

Professor Michael Swann and Raymond Baxter
introduce contributions from

EUROPE

Professor Alexander Haddow, F.R.S.,   **E. J. Ambrose**
Professor E. Boyland
of the Chester Beatty Research Institute, London

Dr. R. J. C. Harris,   **Dr. J. Craigie,**   **Dr. P. J. Simons**
Dr. P. Williams
of the Imperial Cancer Research Fund Unit, Mill Hill, London

Dr. J. F. Loutit,   **Dr. C. E. Ford**
of the Radiobiological Research Unit, Medical Research Council, Harwell

Michael Abercrombie, F.R.S.   **Dr. Latarjet**
University College, London   L'Institut du Radium, Paris

Professor M. Stoker   **Dr. J. H. Sang**
University of Glasgow   Agricultural Research Council, Edinburgh

UNITED STATES OF AMERICA

Dr. L. Berwick   **Dr. W. R. Earle**
University of Pennsylvania   National Cancer Institute

Dr. C. Grobstein   **Dr. A. A. Moscona**
Stanford University, California   University of Chicago

Dr. Van R. Potter
University of Wisconsin
American film sequences directed by Derek Burrell-Davis
and made in co-operation with the United States Information Services

★

Design by Stephen Taylor
Production team: Derek Burrell-Davis, Michael Latham, and Mary Popper

Script and research by Gordon Rattray Taylor
PRODUCTION BY
Humphrey Fisher and Aubrey E. Singer

═══AT 9.0═══

A proud moment for the author as he shares the platform with an eminent and world-famous scientist.

Sheffield University where Professor George Porter was doing research in flash photolysis. Years later, as Lord Porter OM, president of the Royal Society and a popular television lecturer, he was kind enough to remind me of his baptism to the camera, as he put it, in my tender care. Another distinguished scientist whom I introduced to the camera was Michael Swann, later to become Lord Swann, chairman of the BBC.

One of the most challenging of these programmes was called 'The First Breath of Life'. Its subject was the birth of a human baby and, as the programme was to be transmitted live, a caesarean delivery was the only way in which it could be guaranteed on time. Whether a British hospital would have co-operated at that time, I doubt. But the leading centre of research on the subject was the then famous Karolinska Institute in Stockholm.

It was the first time anything approaching such real life drama had been shown on British television, but this was far from being a publicity stunt. The tragedies of cot death had yet to make the headlines, but precisely why a baby starts to breathe interested paediatricians because it could well have been relevant to why a baby should inexplicably stop breathing. Anyway, we showed a beautiful and healthy baby safely brought into the world and for me that was satisfaction enough.

In *Eye On Research*, we introduced the viewers to radio astronomy, a somewhat obscure subject still in its infancy. Our task was the more challenging because the leader in the field, Professor Martin Ryle, was well known in scientific circles for his reticence. "You'll never get him to talk," we were told. But we did. He was later knighted as the Astronomer Royal, but I am by no means suggesting that *Eye On Research* played any significant part in that.

'In Pursuit of Absolute Zero', which is a natural impossibility, was an insight into cryogenics – the study of extremely low temperatures and their effect on physical properties. Holding it by the stalk, I dipped a daffodil into a flask of liquid nitrogen and then smashed it into tiny particles with a hammer. More seriously, we reported the development of super conductors and liquid hydrogen as potential everyday fuel.

Konrad Lorenz made a huge impression on me. We visited his research establishment in Bavaria, where his study was the difference between acquired and innate behaviour. Using chicks from the moment they hatched, he could imprint into their minds the first object which they saw and thereby led them into the belief that a shoebox on wheels, making a clucking sound, was their mother hen.

Similarly, he could imprint himself on the chicks of wild geese and, as I saw for myself, could thereafter call them to him from the sky. He discovered that young birds in a wire-mesh pen, who had never known their natural parents, would run for shelter if they saw above them what they considered to be a bird of prey. In fact it was a black paper shape, not necessarily bird like, 'flown' above them on a wire at a critical scale height and speed. His experiments, all relying purely on the observation of birds and animals, brought him into disfavour in certain circles when he applied his conclusions to human behaviour.

One of my first scientific programmes was a visit for radio to the Common Cold Research Unit at Salisbury. Volunteers of all ages were isolated from the outside world and subjected to all the circumstances generally believed to start a cold – sleeping in damp beds, sitting in draughts, wearing wet clothes, etc. None proved to be the culprit. The only certain fact to emerge was that the common cold is highly infectious. But why? It was not until the invention of the electron microscope, which enabled scientists to discover and study viruses by actually seeing them, that the cause of the common cold was identified.

The microscope itself and the never-before-seen images which it produced were demanding subjects for *Eye On Research*. We called one of the programmes 'Smaller than Life' but the astounding capability of the electron microscope provided graphic illustration to several other aspects of research which we explored.

The magnetic linear accelerator was the reason for our visit to the University of Manchester, to meet one of the most remarkable inventors of my time – Professor (later Sir) Eric Laithwaite. The original purpose of his study was technical advance in the textile industry, specifically how better to throw a shuttle in a loom. To demonstrate the principle of his invention, he placed a metal strip about two foot six long by three inches wide by three eighths of an inch thick between two parallel arrays of small electromagnets, and turned on the variable current. The rod shot the full length of his laboratory, about 30 feet, narrowly missing our camera, and imbedded itself in the wall. "Oops, sorry," he said, "a bit too much power that time."

To demonstrate its capability, he ran a small model railway propelled by a linear accelerator. Two or three years later, he persuaded a reluctant government to build a full-scale length of track and travelling vehicle. But instead of running on rails, the vehicle was supported by magnetic hover – the opposite of magnetic attraction. The British government withdrew its support while the project was still in its early stages. It was seized upon and developed commercially in Japan.

But next time you walk through a sliding door or push the button for a lift anywhere in the world, you will almost certainly be employing the all-British invention of a truly remarkable man – Eric Laithwaite's magnetic linear accelerator.

In the *Eye On Research* programmes, I was privileged to meet and work with some of the greatest living scientists – none more so than Francis Crick and James Watson, the discoverers of DNA. I shall never forget my first glimpse of the staggering complexity of their helix model of the molecule, which is the key to the individuality of every human being and all other living things on planet Earth.

On both radio and television I presented a number of science and technology programmes other than *Eye On Research*. The Queen's opening of Calder Hall, later to be renamed Sellafield, the world's first nuclear power station, was an historic royal occasion. So was her opening of the Forties Field, marking the beginning of Britain's offshore oil industry. Other notable events included the live outside broadcast from Goonhilly Down in Cornwall, in which we showed the first transatlantic television pictures via Telstar, the world's first telecommunications satellite. There were also the first Eurovision link-up, the first live television exchange with Australia and the first pictures from the surface of the moon.

But it was the success of *Eye On Research* which persuaded me that a slightly more popular level of a broad range of subjects in a magazine format could win a major audience. I wrote a proposal for an occasional bi-weekly series. Although I did not know it, Glyn Jones, a new recruit to the BBC from the *Daily Mirror*, had presented a far more detailed proposal for a series of live, regular, weekly studio programmes entitled *Tomorrow's World*.

The original brief, written by Jones, and my reply are reproduced below. He invited me to present the programmes

From: Glyn Jones

Subject: "MODERN AGE"

To: Raymond Baxter   17th May, 1965.

Dear Ray,

    Most of this document is for the new members of the staff in order to give them some idea of the mania in which they are about to be involved! However, I thought you might like to have a copy as well, even though much of it will be, to you, like sucking eggs.

                Regards,

                Glyn

FROM: Glyn Jones. Room 4076. K.H.   PABX 6196/7

SUBJECT: "MODERN AGE" - PROGRAMME BRIEF.

TO: Peter Bruce, Michael Barnes, Peter Ryan, <u>Raymond Baxter</u>.
          c.c. H.O.B.F.S. C.A.O.B.F.S.

                           17th May, 1965.

    We have argued for ages the need for a regular magazine devoted to science, technology and their impact on the industrial and social scene. "Modern Age" gives us the chance to prove our point.

    These disciplines are changing the face of the world faster than any others, and will continue to do so. Our brief is to show new developments, to relate them to current affairs and to explain them to the people. This is a plain man's magazine. Subjects, however difficult, must be crisply and simply explained. At least as important for success is to relate them to the viewer's experience. There will be <u>no</u> catering for specialised interests – unless some specialist activity has relevance and news value for the majority of ordinary people.

    Relevance is essential. We know viewers can be excited by spectacular developments in science and engineering. We want to capitalise not only on excitement but on the relevance our subjects

have to the way politicians act and to the way men and women live -
and earn their livings. We are concerned with the source material
for nearly all political, social and industrial decisions. Our
material does not exist in a vacuum.

The programmes are bound to be forward looking. But they
should not be glib. If we have to look, for example, at an aspect
of automation people will just not believe that it will necessarily
be good for them. They know better. While we want to be exciting -
in contrast to so much television output to-day - we do not want
to be easily optimistic in certain areas.

There will be plenty of room to emphasize the spirit and
nature of change. And let's have lots of medicine - since it is
one of the surest ways of interesting people as well as one of the
areas of enormous progress and achievement.

While we shall have to face some issues with a suitable
gravity I would like our general style to be vigorously optimistic
and thrustful. We must constantly hammer away, implicitly, at the
need for adaptation and wholesale change.

"Modern Age" is neither satirical nor burdened with a social
conscience. These ingredients can only enter items if they are
implicit in the scientific, technological or social development we
are showing. If a development in our field cries for this kind of
treatment it can have it. But the prime mover must be the
development itself. I shall need a lot of convincing before
accepting any proposal based on any other premise. There is too
much for us to do in our own way to waste time imitating others.
In any case, imitations always fail because they lack the creative
drive of the originals.

<u>We shall succeed in our own way on our own ground.</u>

- 1 -

- 2 -

More about style: Modern Age is a workshop not a laboratory.
We have no time to experiment. We have to be right from the
minute we take the air.

We have the experience of "Challenge" yearly, and this will
be helpful. Anyone who has not seen these programmes <u>MUST</u> look
at the last two editions this week. Don't waste time analyzing
what was wrong with them. They averaged 7 million viewers and
an R.I. of 80. So concentrate on understanding what was right
about them. Lucidity, editorial compression, pace and pictorial
excitement have a lot to do with it. One important point: I
naturally envisage Modern Age as being more diverse and more
conscious of relevance than "Challenge", which highlights "pure"
research.

Required reading for this series are two new Pelicans
"The World in 1984" - Volumes 1 and 2. They describe the way
scientists and engineers feel we are going. It is our route, too.
Please read them.

I am not, at this time, going to be rigid about the
structure of each programme. But in each I want one strong
medical item (ideally a new surgical technique) and one main
item of 10, 15 or even 20 minutes in length. I also want a
number of 1 or 2 minute "lollipops" of exciting or amusing film.

Let's have plenty of discussion about items - but plenty of

185

action, too. Everybody shall have as much latitude to do good work as possible. But nobody is going to produce a world masterpiece - if you had the talent it would take too long anyway. We want Pulitzer Prize-winning journalism - not film-festival genius. If you hear people say that these programmes are brash, vulgar, lowbrow, Daily Mirror-ish - you have been paid a compliment. If only more of our output were like that ....

I have heard all the complaints about shortage of time. Now we're going to go ahead and do it. Let's by all means be forward-looking, swinging, switched-on - whatever you like. That is the mood we want in this series. The sins are dullness, pomposity and the snide remark. Inaccuracy will be treated as a capital offence - so will overshooting. A time-limit will be set for all filming and it has to be observed.

A full list of possible subjects will follow. After that paperwork will be minimal. Say it, don't write it. And always tell my secretaries your next telephone number.

Three final vital points :-

1. We want to use ALL the resources of T.V. including Early Bird.

2. We MUST be news conscious as well as feature conscious.

3. Always be prepared to throw away a good idea if a better one turns up.

- 3 -

We have a good chance of doing programmes which will make a dent both on television and the national unconsciousness.

(Glyn Jones)

ext. 4284

19th May 1965

03/OB/RB

Dear Glyn,

Thank you for your kindly note about the V.E. + 20 epic. I was very happy to be in on it - and would like to congratulate you again, despite the critics (see Radio Times June 5th - bit by Baxter).

Thanks also for the "Modern Age" brief. But very exciting!

Does the fact that Bruce Maclaren is going quicker than anyone ever has round most circuits with automatic transmission qualify as a "bitser"?

Next step four wheel drive - without question.

Sincerely,

(Raymond Baxter)

SHOT	CAM.	VISION	SOUND

RUN TK-35
& MOVING BP

F/Up TK-35

Music: Job (Vaughan Williams)
Fanfare Scene 7
(Decca LXT 2973, Side 2)

1. FILM 1: 16 mm. sepmag
Opening film

MUSIC S.O.F.

Duration: 0'20"

All B.P.'s on abstracts

2. 1

BAXTER: When Edward White floated
in space outside the Gemini space
craft on its 62 orbit flight round
the world, he achieved something which
seemed impossible as short a time as
five years ago.   Yet within those
five years the beginnings of man's
space flight has developed into a
race to be first on the moon. Great
steps forward have been made in
exploring and exploiting the ocean -
including experiments in living on
the sea bed.   And we have seen
glimpses of a biological revolution
which is likely to change the lives
of our children.   Transplanted
organs, artificial hearts, the
ability to determine the sex of your
child, all these have been achieved
recently, or are just about to be.
These programmes are about the
sweeping changes which are being
made in the world around us by
scientists, engineers and industrialists

(2 next)

- 1 -

and Paul Fox, then controller of BBC1, gave us a trial run of six weeks. The title page of the very first *Tomorrow's World* script is reproduced above. That was in 1965 and the programme ran until 2003.

Originally I was the sole presenter, but during my 14 years

with the programme I was joined by a remarkable team of colleagues. Glyn Jones, who was more a newspaper journalist than a television man, went on to other things after the first six programmes. He was succeeded by two outstanding editors who, consecutively, built the importance and scope of the programme. Each served for three years: they were Max Morgan-Witts and Michael Latham, both close friends of mine from that time on.

Max, a Canadian, had a disarmingly laid-back approach and was determined that everyone should enjoy every programme as much as he did. From *TW* number one our studio floor manager was Joan Marsden. She had been a wartime WAAF ops-room plotter and was later commissioned. We got on extremely well, authoritarian though she may have been. In a totally different sphere, she was a great success with major politicians on the floor and was justly rewarded with an MBE when she retired.

In one programme, I was to demonstrate the application of a material developed by NASA to protect early space rockets from thermal shock when they splashed down into the ocean. I was to heat up a dry frying pan to almost red-hot, then pour cold water onto it. We did not rehearse the item and Joan warned me against slipping on a wet studio floor. I duly poured a kettle full into the hot frying pan and water shot all over the place. But far from slipping, one of my shoes stuck firmly to the floor. Knowing that my feet would not be in shot I stepped out of my shoe and moved onto the next item. After the show, when told of the incident, Max said, "God damn it! If I'd known that I'd have zoomed in on the empty shoe."

Of the many formative contributions made to *Tomorrow's World* by Max Morgan-Witts, for me the most significant was his recruitment of James Burke. Max sent one of the producers in the team to Italy to film an item. Not speaking Italian, as instructed he went to Rome University in search of an interpreter. James was working there as an Oxford postgraduate, and Max was so impressed by his personality and evident capability that he offered him a contract.

I have never more enjoyed working with a colleague and

42   RADIO TIMES *September 14, 1967*

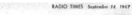

Tomorrow's World

Introduced by
Raymond Baxter
BBC-1 at 7.5

WITHIN the space of ten minutes, the telephone brought in calls from a rocket site at Cape Kennedy, a laboratory in Naples, a lady inventor in Yorkshire, and an enquiry in France about blueprints for a death ray.

Tomorrow's World was back in production preparing for the new series which starts tonight.

Since the first edition a year and a half ago *Tomorrow's World* has filmed hundreds of reports on the most exciting advances and trends in medicine, science, and technology. For the current series, production teams are once again travelling the rarefied world of international research and development, reporting back on anything from plastic igloos for Eskimos to a new way of air-conditioning your home in suburbia.

People often tell us about things that may be included in the programme and we like to hear from them, for it is pleasant to discover that developments going on quietly in British laboratories are often the equal of anything the rest of the world has to offer.

Every Wednesday evening, *Tomorrow's World* will come live from London. Raymond Baxter, as usual, will be there to introduce it and we invite you to join him.   MICHAEL LATHAM

CONFERENCE TALK

Stanley Hyland distils some of the atmosphere of the party conferences—which begin with the Liberals at Blackpool

THE political commentators seem wetter than usual when you read their columns sitting in your bath. You take an early walk on the sea-front (it's the only time you really notice how fresh the seaside air can get) and, as you walk, you think politics.

You return for breakfast and find your table full of people talking politics. You get into the Conference Hall, hear, breathe, cheer (or groan) politics. For lunch it's meat, two veg, fruit pie, custard—and politics.

More Conference with a break for a tea-cup of urn tea sweetened with politics. Then politics over dinner, or at one of those special political rallies where the ginger comes from; politics all evening until your throat is sore and your head is thick.

And then, in bed, too late and too tired, you probably dream—guess what?

That's what thousands of politically committed men and women will be doing off and on in the next five weeks. They love it—otherwise why go to these ritualistic blood transfusion (or blood letting) gatherings called Party Assemblies or Conferences. Many of them give up their annual holidays to be there.

We shall be there too. BBC-2 to let you see the Conference proceedings 'live' from morning to early evening (except for the morning break for *Play School*); BBC News, with its special reporters, will cover them on BBC-1 and BBC-2, and in the Home Service.

When the issues are big and look like getting bigger, *24 Hours* will go down to the seaside; and, late every evening, in *Assembly Talk* Kenneth Harris and Ian Trethowan will assess the day's debates and the political arguments that have buzzed all day around the lobbies of the political hotels. They will talk over the issues of the day with the men and the women who make politics because they cannot help it. They are politics. *Assembly Talk* begins this week among the Liberals in Blackpool, where the new Leader, Jeremy Thorpe, and the Young Liberals will make sure (in their different ways) that the Party Conference season starts off with a change or two.

BBC-1

SEPTEMBER 20

7.30 p.m.
THE VITAL SPARK
starring
RODDY McMILLAN
as Para Handy
JOHN GRIEVE
as Dan Macphail
WALTER CARR
as Dougie
and
ALEX McAVOY
as Sunny Jim
in
Say it with Flour
Written by BILL CRAIG
Based on the Para Handy characters created by NEIL MUNRO
with
Mrs. McKinnon ...... MARJORIE THOMSON
Bunty McKinnon ...... JUNE ANDREWS
Music by IAN GOURLAY
Designer: Guthrie Hutton
Producer: PHARIC MACLAREN
† From Scotland

8.0
THE WORLD FLYWEIGHT BOXING CHAMPIONSHIP
See panel and page 37

8.50
THE NEWS
including a report from the
LIBERAL PARTY ASSEMBLY
at Blackpool
followed by
THE WEATHER

9.5
THE BOSS CLASS
Part 1
BETTER THAN ANY SPORT
We sell goods at £8/11 rather than 10/- because we believe there's something psychological in women that makes it a more attractive price
The Hon. Marcus Sieff
Vice-Chairman, Marks and Spencer
I never work less than eighty hours a week. My wife encourages me. We both act a bit out of it ... to be involved in something that might not happen again.
Jim Houston
Productivity Services Director, Fairfields Shipyard
The first year we lost £5,000. This has been transformed in the second year to a profit of about £1,000. I could run a company fifty or a hundred times longer with not so much energy.
Alan Fletcher
Rico Machine and Tool Co., after three years in business
People don't want to be run by a cipher in London. They want to see somebody, however able ...
Sir Donald Stokes
Chairman, Leyland Group
These insights into the boss, his life, and tough times, all come from men in tonight's programme; the second part, in which workers have their say, is shown tomorrow night.
Produced and directed by
GUYS JONES
See page 39

THE WORLD FLYWEIGHT BOXING CHAMPIONSHIP

Chartchai Chionoi (Thailand)
Champion of the World
v.
Walter McGowan (Great Britain)
The Challenger
Former Champion of the World
from the Empire Pool and Sports Arena Wembley
BBC outside broadcast cameras bring an exclusive recording of the battle the world crown—the fight that top the bill on last night's *Jack Solomons promotion*

Commentator, Harry Carpenter
Television presentation by A. F. WILKINS
AT 8.0 TONIGHT

9.55
TWENTY-FOUR HOURS
Round the clock and round the world with up-to-the-minute coverage of what matters today
Introduced by Cliff Michelmore with Kenneth Allsop
Editor, ANTHONY WHITBY

10.25
ASSOCIATION FOOTBALL
Recorded highlights of one of tonight's top matches
Commentator,
Kenneth Wolstenholme
Television presentation by
Bill Malcolm

11.0
ASSEMBLY TALK
from the
LIBERAL PARTY ASSEMBLY
in Blackpool
Kenneth Harris and **Ian Trethowan** discuss the political ideas of the day with some of the people involved
Directed by RAY COLLEY
Produced by STANLEY HYLAND

11.15
MASTERWORKS
BRAHMS
Trio in C major, Op. 87
played by
Yehudi Menuhin (violin)
Hephzibah Menuhin (piano)
Jacqueline du Pré (cello)
† Producer, PATRICIA FOY

11.45
THE WEATHER MAN

11.47
POSTSCRIPT
by The Rev. David Martin
Close Down

there is evidence enough to suggest we were a creative combination. Indeed, after Mike Latham replaced Max as editor and a *Tomorrow's World* book was proposed, the three of us formed a commercial partnership. Two editions, published by the BBC in 1970 and 1971, went into paperback. As editor, Mike Latham was formidable as well as being a friend. His news sense was as keen as his perception. If we were beaten to a story, Mike would drop it but we scored one major world scoop. A leading producer in our team, and one of the originals, was Peter Bruce. He had an interest in surgery, learned of the work of Christian Barnard in South Africa and won his confidence.

In December 1967, as we approached the end of our programme, Mike Latham left the control gallery and joined me on the floor of the studio.

"In about two minutes time," he said, "that telephone will ring. On the other end will be Christian Barnard. He's done it! Pick up the phone and interview him." This was during our live transmission, remember. And so, within an hour of the completion of the operation and before any release to the news agencies, we announced the first transplant of a human heart.

When Christian Barnard came to Britain some months later, Mike Latham staged a *TW* Special called 'Barnard faces his critics'. In front of a studio audience a panel of medical experts and others, led by Malcolm Muggeridge, questioned the validity of the operation on scientific, moral, ethical, emotional, hereditary and even religious grounds. Other experts we had invited supported it. As chairman I did my best to preserve an appearance of neutrality, but I was sorely taxed!

James and I were joined as presenters by Michael Rodd, John Parry and – later – Judith Hann, who exceeded my 14 years with the programme.

To name all our successes or attempt anything approaching a comprehensive list of our revelations and predictions, let alone the comparatively few times we got it wrong – would require a book of lists, but I remember holding between my fingers a plastic card and saying: "This is the international currency of the future."

I was the first hovercraft passenger to cross the Channel and James, wearing a bowler hat and pinstripes, walked across the Thames to the City in a plastic bubble. Using a Magnum 45 revolver, we shot at point blank range a guy wearing the body armour which he had invented and which is now in general use. We traced the ever increasing power and diminishing size of computers, the growth of transplant and spare parts surgery, the struggle for alternative sources of energy, the introduction of the home video recorder, barcode commerce, hole-in-the-wall banking and robots of all shapes and sizes. We were wrong, however, in predicting throw-away paper clothes and that the standard house-brick was obsolete.

Mike Latham was succeeded by Lawrence Wade, and young producers who started their careers in the *Tomorrow's World* team went on to greater things. James Burke left to launch his *Burke Specials* and to cover the lunar landings with Patrick Moore. He followed that with a series which he wrote, called *Connections*. That met with moderate success here but was a big hit in the States. The BBC dropped him, but public service broadcasting and lecturing provided him with a brilliant career in America.

Lawrence Wade was succeeded as editor by Michael Blakstad and, although it started promisingly enough, our relationship turned sour. For reasons best known to himself, he began deliberately to reduce my part and status in the programme. Matters came to a head when he devoted a whole edition to an attack on Concorde at an important time in the aircraft's future. He was fully aware that I had been an active supporter of the project since its inception and that he was putting me into an untenable position. My contract came up for renewal, senior management declined to support me on principle and I had no alternative but to resign.

It made a few headlines. Blakstad publicly described me as "the last of the dinosaurs". A couple of days later Sylvia and I flew to Washington DC, by prior arrangement, in Concorde. The date was June 1977.

Chapter 14

On and Off the Road

Amongst my modest collection of motor sport trophies, two are rare. A pair of silver-plated tankards, one is inscribed 'BACH, June 1949, Rally Class E, R F Baxter' and the other, after a similar heading, reads, 'Team Award'.

BACH was the British Automobile Club Hamburg. Its members were service or civilian motor sport enthusiasts stationed in or near Hamburg and brought together by Colonel Graham Oates. He was the head of the Road and Road Transport Section of the CCG (Control Commission for Germany) who pre-war had established several motorcycle records, including a ride across northern Canada. I had persuaded him to record his reminiscences, which we broadcast from BFN (British Forces Network). Also working in the CCG was Tom Walkerley, a pre-war motoring journalist with *The Light Car* and brother of Rodney who, under the pen name of 'Grande Vitesse', was sports editor of *The Motor*. Tom kept a lap chart for me when we broadcast commentary on army motorcycle races and he and I were two founder members of the club committee. My team, which won the award, included Captain The Honourable Gerald Lascelles, later the long-serving president of the BRDC.

Sylvia took on the role of my co-driver/navigator and became very good indeed, as she demonstrated when we returned to England. Years later we won our class in the London Motor Club's Dieppe Rally with my 1275 Mini-Cooper S and were all set to do it again the following year. Unfortunately, the wife of a fellow competitor forgot which side of the road to drive on in France and hit us head on, writing off my car, but much more seriously, cutting Sylvia's face and breaking her big toe.

Having left Hamburg in the summer of 1949 and got myself a job in the BBC's Outside Broadcast Department, I lost no time in promoting my enthusiasm for motoring. Attached to Bristol, to gain regional experience, I was able to compile a programme, recorded on discs, called 'The Birth of the Five Hundreds'. The West Country was home to early 500cc racing and introduced me to John Cooper, Colin Chapman and Ken Wharton, amongst many other leading competitors. I also broadcast a report on the Gloucester Trial, introducing listeners to that little-publicised sport, its leading trials drivers and their specials. Wharton was amongst them and also his great rival, 'Goff' Imhof.

It was at Goff's invitation that I drove with him in my first international event, the Lisbon Rally of 1950. Thundering through the night across Europe had a touch of the Bulldog Drummond about it, which excited my romantic imagination. But our car was not a Vintage Bentley, it was an overpowered Allard – and Goff was far from the accepted paperback hero. For a start, he had one blue eye and one brown. When everything was going pear-shaped, the favourite oath which sprang explosively from his lips was, "F*** everybody, including the Archbishop of Canterbury!"

I knew that I was said to be somewhat highly strung. Goff, however, was fundamentally super-tuned, and one of the most remarkable of my friends. His exotic ancestry – he was actually of Swiss extraction, but married to a Russian – was reflected in his mercurial temperament, he was an extremely shrewd and successful businessman and a ruthlessly competitive driver. He had driven fire engines in the London Blitz, had boundless energy and enthusiasm, and a sardonic wit.

We did several continental events together, including the fantastic Dutch Tulip Rallies as well as the Monte Carlo. In those days, at every frontier crossing, one had to fill in an identity form. In the space marked 'sex', Goff would scribble, 'yes please' and against colour of eyes he wrote, 'mixed'. We were off before any question could be raised, not least because there was no time allowance in the rally schedules for frontier formalities.

For him there were two categories of vehicle, 'racers' and 'cooking cars'. I had total confidence in Goff's driving even when, as he put it, we were "ear-'oling" near the ragged edge, ie flat out in the mountains – and he very nearly killed me. It was in the mountains on the third night of the 1953 Monte Carlo. Goff was driving, fresh because Ian McKenzie, our third man in the works Humber, and I had as planned done most of the driving thus far. Climbing away from a village, I noticed a small crowd on the outside of what looked like a long right-hander. It was covered with a sheet of black ice and that was why the spectators were there. Goff lost it in a very big way and we hit an alp extremely hard. Although I was wearing full harness, it was secured to the seat rather than the floor. The seat broke away and threw me against the windscreen, which was laminated, not toughened glass and consequently did not shatter. Crash hats were not yet worn on the Monte and although I was not knocked out, my face and forehead were a mess. I thought I'd lost my left eye, but Norman Garrad, the Rootes Group competitions manager, driving with Leslie Johnson (of pre-war ERA fame) stopped and, after a close look, reassured me. Goff had bent the steering wheel and bruised his ribs but Ian, snuggled in a blanket, just rolled off the back seat and woke up wondering what had happened.

Bob Berry, the Jaguar press officer, drove me to the local doctor. Aroused from bed, and still wearing his pyjamas, after stitching my forehead he began picking glass from my face. As the white-tiled floor below my chair became spotted with blood, I wanted to tell him that if he kept doing that I would faint. But the French word escaped me and I said:

"Monsieur, si vous continuez comme ca, je vais dormir" – I shall go to sleep.

"Ah! Les Anglais", he cried. "Quelle courage, quelle sangfroid!" Bob Berry then drove me on down to Monte Carlo and I did my scheduled live broadcast from the studio that evening. I thought I was talking normally, but later when I heard a recording of that broadcast, I was shocked to hear how shaky my voice was.

Goff told me I should sue him, but I was appalled at the very idea. We did the following year's Monte together in a works Sunbeam-Talbot 90 and finished clean, but not in the money.

KINGSWAY LUNCHEON CLUB

A Luncheon at Shell-Mex House
Monday 24th May 1954

Guest of honour   Raymond Baxter Esq.

Guests	Luncheon
H. E. BRODRICK	*Tomato Juice*
H. J. CLAPP	*Pate de Foie Gras Strasbourg*
H. C. DEAKIN	*Smoked Salmon & Potted Shrimps*
A. S. FOSH	*Cream of Chicken*
A. W. FOX	*Scotch Salmon Mousse Aurore*
J. R. HINE	
G. LAMB	*Tournedo of Beef a la Kingsway*
J. B. OSLER	*Saute Potatoes & Peas*
C. D. POPLE	*Asparagus Hollandaise*
F. G. SMITH	*Strawberry Charlotte Russe*
R. S. SMITH	*Petits Fours*
J. WALTON	*Cheese & Biscuits*
A. V. WYKES	*Coffee*

Guests to the luncheon illustrated overleaf, who no doubt enjoyed this classic 1950s meal.

Goff Imhof introduced me to international rallying, but R W 'Reg' Phillips gave me the unique thrill of driving single-seaters in competition. He introduced himself to me at Silverstone in the late 1950s, when he was racing 500s and running Fairley Steels, a small company making highly specialised steel alloys in Sheffield, which he had inherited from his father. He had served his apprenticeship at 'The Austin', as Longbridge was known before the war. He was commissioned into REME and was in the Dunkirk evacuation. A total motoring enthusiast, Reg was one of the most generous men I ever met, so much so that he invited me to compete against him in speed hillclimbs in cars which he had himself designed and built. Although I got within a second of his times, I never beat him – and that was not for want of trying.

The 'Fairley Special' was a conventional lightweight/big engined, V8 Mercury-powered sprint car, but there was nothing conventional about the 'Fairley Spoke' which he built in 1966. This was based on a BMC Moke, considerably modified and powered by a 1275 Cooper S engine, bored out to 1,340cc and supercharged, and it sure was quick. When 'Phippers', the name given him by Brian Johnston in Monte Carlo, bought himself a pukka Cooper 1100 racing car, he almost literally gave me the Spoke, which I duly shared with my son.

We got second and third in class at Prescott several times,

and once first and second. Then as he started his Finals year at Oxford, Graham said, "Sorry Father, but I think I'd better give up the motoring and do some work, otherwise all the money you've spent on my education will be wasted." I muttered my appreciation and regrets, but heaved a secret sigh of relief. We were not really competing against anyone other than ourselves and were so close that it was becoming dangerous.

Phippers was a trials driver of championship class, and he invited me to drive his home-built trials special in the celebrated Sheffield and Hallamshire Motor Club Kitchen Trophy Trial. I got us both covered in mud and managed to snitch an award thanks to his running-commentary instruction.

I did a couple of Montes with Phippers as my co-driver and Ian McKenzie, a brilliant navigator. One year we had a Ford Zephyr and the next an Austin Westminster. The BBC was not happy if I became closely associated with any one manufacturer. We finished respectably in both, but not well enough for a result. In the Austin we ran into thick fog in daylight in the mountains and even with Ian calling the corners off the Michelin map I simply could not drive fast enough and we dropped a minute on the road. It was following my international rallying debut with Goff Imhof on the Lisbon in 1950 that I got my first works drive in the Monte Carlo Rally.

While I was with BFN, I reported the 1949 event as it passed through the Hamburg control. Now in London with the BBC, I drew up a detailed proposal to cover the 1950 Monte in a nightly series of reports.

"Good idea," said my boss, Charles Max-Muller. "You organise it and we'll get Richard Dimbleby to do the reporting." Swallowing my disappointment, I got on with it. The organisation was quite complicated. I planned an itinerary, short-cutting the rally route, and arranged through the BBC's European Liaison Office a number of locations where French radio would link up with telephone lines to London. I also persuaded Sydney Allard to provide Richard with a car. It was a very hard year, weather-wise, and Richard Dimbleby got stuck at Digne in the Massif Central, but the broadcasts were successful and gave me a start in pursuit of my ambition to compete in the rally and report it from the competitors' point of view.

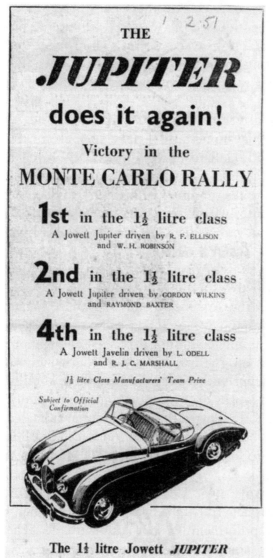

After the war, the historic but minor manufacturer Jowett hired Professor Robert Eberan-Eberhorst, a brilliant German engineer of pre-war reputation with Auto Union. He designed the unconventional Jowett Javelin four-seater and later the two-seat sports version soft-top, the Jupiter. Jowett invited me to Brands Hatch to have a go in the Jupiter with Gordon Wilkins. As a result, we were offered a works drive in the Jupiter in the 1951 Monte Carlo, with me as co-driver.

We finished eleventh, second in class and the three Jupiters won the manufacturers' team prize. I met all my broadcasting commitments, which built up an audience, and I reckoned we were in business.

Sadly for me, the Monte went pear-shaped next year. Gordon and I had a works Jaguar Mark 7. His wife turned up at midnight, at the control at Saint-Claude in the Massif Central, on the last night. It was a snow-bound year and critical that we should make time immediately after that control on some fairly fast roads before the mountains. We left two minutes late! I was furious and Gordon stuffed us into a snow-filled ditch.

At the start of my first Monte in 1951, outside the Royal Scottish Automobile Club in Blythswood Square, Glasgow, I took my live microphone for a walk down the line of competitors and that was how I met Jackie Reece. He and his cousin, Peter, had already won a reputation with their bog standard Ford Anglia. As I approached, Jackie was tinkering at the carburettor with a broken nail file.

"Final adjustments, Mr Reece?" I said.

"I am j..just c..coaxing the last ounce of p..power from the m..mighty m ..motor." I did not know until then that Jackie had a pronounced stammer, but it would clearly have been rude to break off our conversation.

"As your car is standard, you have no rev counter. Won't that be a problem in the mountains?" I asked.

"Not at all," said Jackie. "When the knob on the end of the g..g..gear lever glows cherry red, I change up."

Jackie Reece became one of my dearest friends. When his uncle died he inherited Blakes of Liverpool – "We sell Fords for a living and Aston Martins for fun," he would say, and partly because of that we shared an Aston Martin DB3 on the Monte Carlo in 1958. It was a very hard year indeed and as dusk fell on the third night, we were dropping down out of the Massif towards Castellane, where most of the routes converged. Jackie was driving.

"How are we doing?" he asked.

"Fine," I said, "I can see the lights of Castellane below us; we have three kilometres to run in nine minutes. Do you want anything?"

"Yes," he said, "but we didn't bring it with us."

"Apart from that," I said.

"I'd like an orange juice," said Jackie. I undid my harness and turned, kneeling on my seat, to scrabble about in the back of the car, and felt a tap on my ankle.

"T..t..turn around and f..face the front," said Jackie. I did so and there, 100 yards in front of us, was the biggest *camion* in France, towing an equally huge trailer. It was coming up around the next hairpin, slowly sliding into the middle of the road. Snow-bank on one side, low wall and sheer drop on the other – and the road surface was solid, rutted ice. We were doing possibly around 55mph, steeply downhill.

"I j..j..just wanted you to have a g..g..good view of this accident," said Jackie. Somehow it didn't happen but in the small hours, when I was driving, Jackie missed a critical turn near the village of Chartreuse, of coloured drink fame. We had decided he would navigate that section. It was a crucial mistake. We swapped seats but lost a lot of time, groping round the outskirts of Grenoble. Then our lights started to fade. We made the next control and should have realised that our problem could have been a slipping drive-belt, which it was. When the Lucas service team fixed it in about three minutes, I was ashamed.

We got to Monte Carlo all right and I was quick in the driving test 'wiggle-woggle', but I wrote a profuse apology to John Wyer, the celebrated competitions manager of Aston Martin. For the sake of our friendship, I had to invite Jackie to partner me the next year, when Donald Healey offered me the brand new 'bug-eyed' Sprite, as we called it then though it came to be known as the 'Frog-eyed' Sprite.

Again, we were doing fine until the middle of the last night. The long straight after Saint-Claude was as important as it had been in 1952, when Gordon Wilkins blew it for us. This year the road was being resurfaced the French way, one half at a time. I was dozing and Jackie was driving flat out when we were confronted head on by a big *camion*, lights blazing and horn blaring. Jackie pulled right. We hit a bank of loose stones, delineating the edge of the resurfacing, and took off. I saw a stationary road-roller flash past close as we spun at least three times on landing and our uncontrollable career seemed to go on forever.

Finally stopped, we agreed neither was hurt, the car seemed okay so we pressed on. What we failed to appreciate was that, what was left of the exhaust system was feeding carbon monoxide straight into our hard top and progressively poisoning us. We were reported "continuing slowly after a crash" and we did not qualify as finishers although we got there. Next day, I noticed that Les Leston had drawn a little keyhole on the Sprite with an arrow and the words, 'wind here'. Jackie was far from well and I insisted that he flew home, where concussion was diagnosed. He said on the 'phone:

"The man blew into one ear and a l...l...lot of d...d...dust came out of the other... and I'm fine."

Norman Garrad, the outstanding competition manager of his time, gave me a couple of drives with Sunbeam Rapiers on the ultimate classic rally, the Alpine. The event had one night's stop, crossed and re-crossed the Alps and the Jura, with a speed trial and a race on the Italian Grand Prix circuit at Monza thrown in. My first attempt ended when a big end bearing went on the 9,042ft high Stelvio, Europe's second highest mountain road pass, infuriating because we were amongst few competitors still clean – ie clear of penalty points on the road – and we were on the home stretch.

The following year, the night's stop was in Zagreb. We arrived at our hotel, by coincidence with the Ford team, at about 5pm, covered from head to foot in a thick layer of dust after driving non-stop for 29 hours.

"Welcome gentlemen," said the proprietor. "You come good time. Girls arrive 9 o'clock, dancing until four." We could scarcely stand.

As before, the Stelvio was my nemesis. It was a special section and we knew that the time was extremely tight for the Rapier. At the summit my navigator, Leonard Miller, clutching his stopwatch, yelled, "Sorry, we either made it or missed it by 30 seconds."

It did not matter because on the descent I was taken by

surprise by a wet patch in the last tunnel. We emerged backwards and very bent, and that was that.

Rallying was and, I've no doubt, still is a hard game.

My worst drives were with a Reliant Scimitar – fast and powerful, but not easy. On the Liège-Sofia I went over the edge, but not very far, concluding a nightmare drive in Yugoslavia. On the RAC, later that year, the left front tyre blew out on a special stage at night, landing Ernest McMillen and me deep in the woods, with no teddy bears to play with.

I had three successive very good years as Peter Harper's co-driver in the Rootes Group team for the Monte, one year three up with Peter Procter. We got a result every time – team prizes, class wins or places, best British, best from Starting Point, etc.

The best of those years for us was 1960; with snow and ice all the way, the three Rapiers scored game, set and match – Paddy Hopkirk, Peter Procter and ours. We were highest British – first in class and third overall in the rally, beaten only by two of the three works Mercedes which were heavily favoured by the handicap. We won the Challenge Charles Faroux for a nominated team of three cars of the same make, for the third successive year. So Norman Garrad claimed it for keeps but 'the shruggers', as we had come to call the Monegasque organisers, wouldn't let go.

In a bit of a ceremony at the Piccadilly showroom I was given a silver salver, inscribed 'Presented to Raymond Baxter by the Rootes Group in recognition of an outstanding performance driving a Sunbeam Rapier in the 1960 Monte Carlo Rally. Highest Placed British Car. 1st 1300-2000cc Series Production Touring Car Class.' Peter Harper received one too, of course.

By this time our BBC coverage, which had started with only Brian Johnston and me, had developed. Brian was replaced by Robin Richards as anchor man, with Eric Tobitt as roving reporter and commentator, and Arthur Phillips as producer, doing all the organising. We worked hard and very happily together and I make no apology in claiming that we were a good team in our own right.

My personal best was, without doubt, the RAC Rally of

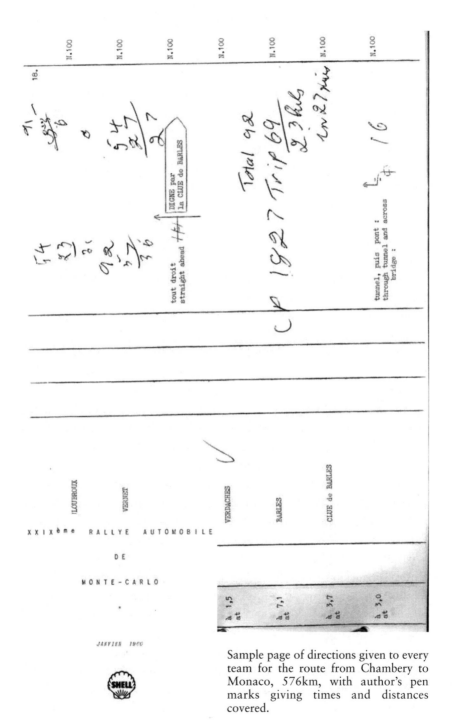

Sample page of directions given to every team for the route from Chambery to Monaco, 576km, with author's pen marks giving times and distances covered.

1961, with Leonard Miller as my navigator in a works Humber Super Snipe. The event had been entirely revamped by Jack Kemsley and his team, transforming it from a gentleman's jolly around the countryside into what Erik Carlsson, who won it with his works Saab, described as "the toughest in Europe."

The BBC Light Programme gave us a nightly spot, my reports coupled with Robin Richards' updating from strategic points. The 2,000-mile circuit started from Blackpool and our first special stage came in the small hours of the morning – 20.7 miles of forest tracks: time allowance 31 minutes. Norman Garrad had assured me that the East African Safari had proved that the Humber's suspension was unbreakable.

"But, Raymond," he said, "look after that engine. It's a gold brick!" Indeed it was. Despite its size, the car designed for luxury motoring fairly flew through the forest, leaping and sliding at 80mph on surfaces which would have reduced its conventional owners to first-gear caution, were they even to attempt them.

Today's television coverage of the Rally of Great Britain, as the RAC came to be called, has familiarised the public with forestry motoring, but this was its introduction. Frankly, to my surprise I began overtaking the opposition and when I saw the times for the first couple of stages I suddenly realised that a class win was on the cards. Five days later that judgement was proved right. Unlike today's RAC event, the road sections between the special stages were also extremely tight, particularly in Wales and the Lake District, allowing no margin for navigational error. I was familiar with the fabulous hillclimb, the Rest and Be Thankful in the Highlands, and also with Prescott Hill, and that helped. I was also quick on the long, loose-surfaced climb up the Eppynt Artillery Ranges in Wales. On one forestry stage I slid wide on a ninety right and the left corner of the rear bumper just clipped a neat pile of logs, scattering the whole lot across the track. Pat Moss, Stirling's sister, who was behind us complained to me at the next control: "Some bastard had spread logs across the road."

We won the class with our lone Humber, beating the Ford and Jaguar works teams, and Peter Harper, Paddy Hopkirk and

Peter Procter won the team prize with the Rapiers. A headline in the motoring press: 'TRIUMPH FOR ROOTES, BAXTER TOP OF THE CLASS' really pleased me.

I first met Ernest McMillen in Monte Carlo after the finish, when the parties started. His magnetic personality radiated fun and friendship, and he had a very good competition reputation. Our first drive together, at my invitation, was the competition baptism of the MG1100 on the Monte Carlo. An Issigonis variant, it had a lateral-mounted engine and front-wheel drive. The heater and wipers failed when we were hit by freezing rain in the final stages and we became totally iced up. Ernest paid the supreme sacrifice by sprinkling the contents of his emergency brandy flask across the windscreen via his side window. It helped but only temporarily. We finished, but way out of the money.

I rounded off my rallying with three consecutive years, starting in 1964, on the Monte with the magnificent BMC team of Mini Coopers. The principal drivers were the Finns, Timo Makinen and Rauno Aaltonen, and Paddy Hopkirk. Stuart Turner, the brilliant competitions manager – my friend ever since he navigated Erik Carlsson's Saab to victory in the RAC – offered me a Cooper in the modified category – the leading three works Minis were standard. I was flattered and delighted, although I realised that I was a 'stop-gap' in case of unforeseen difficulty and also that my broadcasting had publicity value.

My second and third drives were with Jack Scott, a quiet Irishman in contrast to my first partner, Ernest McMillen, also Irish and bubbling with enthusiasm and *craic*. Both were excellent as co-drivers, but my performance was patchy. With Ernest, in 1964, we planned a critical fuel-stop on the final round. When we got there the filling station was shut. Friends came to our aid, but we lost invaluable minutes: we finished 2nd in class but 43rd overall.

The scene for the following year changes to Minsk, then in the Soviet Union. On *This is Your Life*, Ernest McMillen told of our purchase of caviar, in the hope of selling it for profit in Monte Carlo. That did not work, nor did my venture beyond the Iron Curtain in 1965, this time with Jack Scott.

Driving in convoy with our team from Gdansk in Poland to the start, our engine inexplicably put a rod through the side. Despite every pressure, including that of the British Consulate, the Russians flatly refused permission for a replacement engine to be flown in.

Next year, on the road I was within a minute of Paddy on a critical snow-bound section on the last night. But, for some inexplicable reason, I was unable to get the Mini flying on the drier roads of the final circuit. On the Monaco Grand Prix circuit, I surprised Stu with my first-lap time but frightened myself. I eased off slightly, for Sylvia's sake, on the second lap and then missed a gear in the tunnel on the third. Nevertheless, I was second in class in that test to a Pole whom I should have beaten. But then the leading British teams from BMC and Ford were infamously disqualified on an alleged and trivial (lighting) technicality.

Thus, on my last international rally I was not classified. But I had enjoyed my champagne moments as well as my days of despair. Many were unforgettable, especially what I see as the four consecutive Mini Cooper wins of Paddy Hopkirk (1964), Timo Makinen (1965 and 1966) and Rauno Aaltonen (1967) even though the record books show that Timo was disqualified in 1966.

Happier memories, no less unforgettable, include the breathtaking beauty of sunrise in the Alps and the even more longed-for murky first light in November on the RAC; the unequalled exhilaration of getting a car 'flying' on the ice and snow, or the loose surfaces of mountain roads; the sheer luxury of a hot bath, having defied fatigue and distance thanks to determination and a little medical advice; the sense of comradeship, even between rivals; the gut-wrenching disappointment of failure after days and nights of toil; and the pure joy and triumph of winning – sometimes!

No protests

The winter of 1963 was so severe that, from mid-January, all sport in Britain was frozen out. Bryan 'Ginger' Cowgill, the legendary head of BBC Television Sport, in desperation 'phoned me at my office in Broadcasting House to ask if I could lay on "one of your motoring specials".

The Monte Carlo Rally was still fresh in the public mind, so I devised an event, to involve the leading drivers, which I christened the Mini Monte. The first requirement was a course to include snowbound and dry roads. John Webb, MD of Brands Hatch, obliged. My rules required drivers, starting in pairs, to complete one lap over two separate, different but comparable courses. All the major works teams agreed to participate. I have been told since that this was the origin of rallycross.

Böhringer, a jovial hotelier who had won the real Monte Carlo Rally for Mercedes-Benz, was eliminated in the first round, as was Peter Harper's Rapier which had been third, with me as co-driver. I can't remember who won but the event had given the viewers something pretty spectacular to watch when nothing else was available.

Thanks to Erik Carlsson, the next year Saab invited us to a repeat performance at their winter headquarters in Sweden. Snow and ice were guaranteed. The stars included Pat Moss and Rosemary Smith, and thanks to unstinting Swedish hospitality everyone agreed it was a fabulous event, but unfortunately impossible to repeat.

Back in 1952 the first of the motor sport events which Goff Imhoff and I had devised specifically for TV was the Television Trophy Trial. The idea was to tailor the long-established format of trials driving, which is to see who can complete a series of off-road sections, to the requirements of TV broadcasting. We decided to have a series of hillclimbs, each divided by five- and ten-point markers, roughly halfway up and at the top. We drove for miles, seeking a site, because none of the conventional ones was suitable for live camera coverage. In the Chiltern Hills we found a perfect arena adjoining the RAF Apprentices' College, Halton. The CO approved our proposal, thereby providing additional hands to assist the marshals of the London Motor Club. Three teams of four cars, representing the

North, Midlands and South were invited and because of its simplicity viewers were able to follow the progress of what proved to be close and exciting contests.

The gradients went up to one in three and a half and, with some crafty doglegs included, it was a challenge to championship drivers as well as providing pictures of cars at improbable angles.

Because, like all motor sport, the sanction of the RAC Competitions Department had to be gained, the normal trials regulations had to be re-written. In the paragraph headed 'Protests', Goff wrote simply, "There will be no protests."

The event ran annually for several years until the BBC producer, John Vernon, was replaced by a motorcycle enthusiast, anxious to televise scrambles. I do not know what happened to the trophy, which was the original model camera now famous through the BBC Sports Personality of the Year awards.

Another contest we devised was staged by the BBC Midland Region and I called it 'The Ken Wharton Memorial Trophy'. This was a series of timed driving tests, now called autotests, involving high-speed forward and reverse parking, 'wiggle-woggles', stopping on a line and so on. Each team had to include a production saloon, a sports car and a trials special. We had teams from England, Wales and Northern Ireland and that was how I first met Paddy Hopkirk, already a leading competitor in the field.

We were staging the event at Chateau Impney in Warwickshire when the world was shocked by news of the murder of President Kennedy. In search of instant local reaction, BBC News came to us, knowing that we had a live camera set-up. I tried to say something appropriate, as did Paddy and one or two others, but it was a bizarre clash of content and environment.

Perhaps the most outlandish, even outrageous of our off-road adventures was an attempt to match London Motor Club drivers against those of the British army, each driving an assortment of vehicles. On a sandy section of heathland near Aldershot we marked a number of points which had to be reached by any route chosen by the driver. The start and finish were via an extremely steep gradient, vehicles running in pairs. We called it 'autopoint' but it was not so much the competition as the vehicles which made it extraordinary. The army discovered the prototype of a small cross-country vehicle called 'The Bug' – I believe it was the world's first quad-bike. Alec Issigonis had produced an experimental twin-engined Moke. I secured that for the LMC. The largest vehicle was the army's amphibious transport – the Stalwart, I think – and the smallest a club trials car. In between were a standard army three-tonner, the new one-ton Land Rover and the new Austrian Haflinger, both generously provided by the manufacturers. Army co-operation was ensured and organised by Col (later Brigadier) 'Bing' Crosby, another remarkable man who became a personal friend.

Even more strange to relate, we invited Formula 1 world champions to compete – and Graham Hill and John Surtees risked life and limb on the Twinnie Mini.

16mm films

During the late 1950s and through the 1960s I wrote and recorded the commentary to quite a few 16mm films on major motor sport events. Many, but not all, were shot and assembled to order by Stanley Schofield. Principal patrons, or clients, included The Rootes Group, Standard Triumph and Castrol. Shell had their own film unit, for which I also worked.

Stanley Schofield set up his own company, in offices with a small viewing/recording studio and cutting rooms, above a well-known night-club at the bottom end of Bond Street. He was tireless, and skilful with his hand-held clockwork Bolex camera, but the pictures were assembled largely on their image qualities, leaving me to tell the story and make the words fit the pictures. I did have a certain amount of influence on the final assembly, the soundtrack and the music and although hard work it was a useful little earner to add to my meagre salary as a member of staff at the BBC.

I know that some of these films have been shown on TV abroad and I'm told copies are keenly sought by collectors.

Several have been re-released in VHS form in recent years, selling quite well I believe, but sadly I have none myself – nor do I retain any royalties. That's life.

Perhaps the full-blooded warm relationships which enriched the world of motor sport during my time throughout the 1960s were encapsulated in a single event – The Cliff Davis Cars Staff Supper & Smoking Concert. Cliff was a motor trader of the old school. A Territorial soldier, he had spent four years in prison camps after Dunkirk – but his spirit was unquenchable.

He told me that in the heat of summer in Poland the guards would patrol stripped to the waist. He discovered that the prison hut roofs were lined with insulating glass wool. Yes, as early as that! By penetrating the loft space and extending an arm below the eaves it was possible to sprinkle glass wool particles, crushed between finger and thumb, onto the sweaty, naked back and shoulders of a passing sentry. "You could see the hives coming up on 'em!" Cliff said gleefully.

He survived the awful Long March of prisoners to the West, ahead of the advancing Russians and I wonder if his horrific wartime experiences inured him to the risks of motor racing. Certainly he was a fearless driver. Everyone who was anyone on the circuits and in the trade came to his stag nights, which were by invitation only – the proceeds donated to charity. Graham Hill once injured his knee on a glass when dancing on the table, and the comedians were on the cobalt side of blue. During one of those evenings I asked Cliff if he was at all bothered by the law.

"Raymond," he said, "have you met my good friend here, Chief Superintendent ---- ----?" My time in motor sport was good.

Chapter 15

Industrial Interlude

While I was the first (and only) BBC motoring correspondent, I came into contact with many leading figures in the motor industry. My rallying for the Rootes Group introduced me to Sir William, later Lord, Rootes and his younger brother, Sir Reginald.

Another famous individual was Sir Alec Issigonis, creator of the celebrated Morris Minor 1000, the later Mini and subsequent derivatives of the transverse-engined, front-wheel drive theme. He was very generous to me from our first meeting and, similarly, I was able to make my number with other major figures at press conferences, new model launches, motor shows and, by no means least, the BBC's first TV coverage of the London Motor Show in, as I recall, 1953.

Instead of what would have been – at that time – technically limited coverage within Earl's Court, manufacturers with new models were invited under the auspices of the SMM&T to the RAC Country Club at Woodcote Park. Each had an allotted time – about four minutes – to display their wares, introduced by me. There were no showgirls posing for pictures but leading lady competition drivers, Sheila van Damm and Nancy

Mitchell, elegantly dressed, drove their cars into the 'show ring'; and one manufacturer contrived to have his car noticed by having no visible driver at all.

The show was a live outside broadcast, of course, after a morning's rehearsal. What we would have done had it rained I have no idea but, not surprisingly, it over-ran its Sunday afternoon slot by at least 25 minutes and although that was acceptable in those days, the BBC only took the risk for a couple of consecutive years.

I reported on radio from the Geneva Motor Show – which I loved, from the Paris Salon and from the then Independent Scottish Motor Show in Glasgow. Just before the London Show in 1966 I was invited to a meeting by Donald Healey to discuss a project with Sir George Harriman, chairman of BMC, and Lester Suffield, director of sales and later managing director. To my astonishment, they offered me the job of improving the image of the company. I asked for time to consider.

Sylvia had misgivings about me leaving the staff of the BBC but I knew that my next step up that ladder would have been an administrative one. I was reluctant to leave the microphone and the television camera but attracted by such a career move at the ripe age of 44. In detailed discussion Lester Suffield, who was to be my boss, eased my dilemma by telling me that I could continue to present *Tomorrow's World* and any other events the BBC might offer. This was acceptable to the Corporation and, on 1st January 1967, I became BMC's director of motoring publicity. My office was to be at 41, Piccadilly, above BMC's principal London showrooms.

I invited Margaret Cormack, the BBC secretary I shared with Brian Johnston, to accompany me. Next time I saw him, BJ said:

"Pinched any good secretaries lately, Backers?" During the next two years, I never worked so hard in my life. Our office was above the BMC showroom in Piccadilly but I had to drive to head office in Longbridge quite frequently. I grew to like and admire Lester Suffield very much although I know he was not everybody's cup of tea – but it soon became apparent why the company's image was such a problem.

'In-house', there remained a lingering rancour between Longbridge and Cowley following the merger of Austin and Morris, with MG as piggy in the middle. Labour relations and standards of workmanship were poor, particularly at Longbridge. Customer complaints were rife and, recklessly, I took on personal responsibility to tackle that problem, causing some resentment amongst the dealerships.

Soon after I arrived at Piccadilly I got a letter out of the blue from Australia. A young graduate called Des Power wrote to say that he had heard of my appointment – and could I give him a job? It transpired that he was already on his way with his newly married wife, by sea in those days of course. It was the start of a friendship which became a family affair.

From the outset we worked extremely well together and he toiled every bit as hard as Margaret and me. At the same time, his Australian attitude was impervious to pressure and his good humour and sense of fun were invaluable. We normally worked late in my office, not infrequently until 7pm, long after the rest of the staff attached to sales and the showrooms had gone home. And then I would open my liquor locker for a sherry before driving Des and sometimes Margaret to their respective flats.

Home was The Old Rectory at Denham, a lovely Victorian house dated 1858. Its generous space included two self-contained flats on the third floor, under its broad red roofs. I invited Des to come and live in one. Anne, his wife, and Sylvia developed what was akin to a mother and daughter relationship.

He stayed on at BL for a short time after I was sacked. But after returning home, and joining ABC (the Australian Broadcasting Commission) he came back as their London correspondent. He went on to a brilliant media career back in Australia.

Although Sylvia and I were never able to visit Des and Anne and their family in Australia, my grand-daughter as well as my son and daughter-in-law stayed with them on the Queensland Gold Coast. During a working visit to Britain, while this book was being written, Des declared his intention to attend its launch.

Such relationships, born of pure chance and rare as they may be, are of the spice of life.

But, to return to my job at BMC, I was never given a budget. I had a guaranteed account with a splendid little restaurant near the office, for entertaining the press, monitored by Lester.

The historic MG Car Club required roping in and an unknown young man called Maurice Burton had started the Mini-Seven Club. This was my opportunity to launch the first of the Mini Festivals at Brands Hatch: my target, although I never expressed it as such, was 'Fun for the Young'. We invited student participation in 'Stuff a Mini', to discover how many people could be contained inside, doors shut. But the Pop Art Contest was slightly more serious. The students of leading art schools, equipped with aerosols, were invited to decorate a Mini *à la mode*. One entrant was 'The Hairy Mini', its roof covered by a longhaired hearthrug. Alec Issigonis, who was the judge, gave it a special prize.

In addition there was formula racing arranged by the British Racing and Sports Car Club. I explained to Lester and Sir George, both of whom were present, that I could not guarantee that Minis would win every race, and they didn't.

The day ended with dancing on the pit straight, to Chris Barber's band. We did it during the two consecutive years of my job and I know that both were a major success on Sunday 28th May 1967 and Sunday 2nd June 1968. Management could not have been too displeased with me because they appointed Alan Zafer, to increase my personal staff to three – although his official title was PR assistant to the competitions department. Only this year I learnt that Alan remembers his first meeting with me, in my office in Piccadilly, very well because, he claims, I had my feet on my desk and all he could take in was the elegantly cut legend, 'hand made' in the soles of my shoes.

I toured the United States with Lester to introduce the 1100 series – a coast-to-coaster, mainly of one-night stops over ten days. Who'd be an American politician?

It was not my idea, although I welcomed it, to take a party of leading British motoring journalists to the United States and Canada, to see for themselves the very impressive BMC operations there. While we were away the company announced its first financial loss in the annual statement of accounts, and the figures were frightening. It was suggested that the transatlantic trip was cynically timed. The writing was on the wall.

I had long realised that the real purpose of my job was to fend off a takeover by Donald Stokes and his Leyland Triumph Group. It came, he won, and within days I was the first man in British Leyland to be sacked personally by Lord Stokes.

Lester Suffield became head of Defence Procurement, and was knighted. I was offered my company car, an 1800, but dug in my heels for breach of contract. It was a sad and worrying end to a huge personal effort. To my eternal gratitude Sir Paul Fox, then the head of BBC Television, rang to offer me a contract.

Margaret Cormack remained with British Leyland until she could escape to rejoin the staff of the BBC. We have worked together ever since and, at the time of writing she is the honorary secretary of the Association of Dunkirk Little Ships.

As I had briefed the press, Harold Wilson backed the Stokes merger as a convenient prelude to nationalisation. It was the beginning of the end of the once great British motor industry.

Chapter 16

The Little Ships

Despite all the pleasures and little adventures the Otter brought into our lives, in the winter of 1963/4 I decided that I wanted a different boat, a real boat, but, of course, my financial resources were limited. I subsequently realised that what I was looking for was a gentleman's miniature motor yacht of the immediate pre-war period. So I commenced my research: I visited countless boatyards on the Thames and the east coast – and saw more rubbish than you could ever believe.

I was very tempted by the Bates company's Starcraft which was a luxurious small motor yacht, but that wasn't quite right. Then, right out of the blue, I discovered at Tom Jones' yard at Windsor a boat called *Nomad* and the moment I saw her I knew she was what I was looking for. I had her surveyed and unfortunately the report made quite clear that she was beyond my financial capability, let alone skill, to restore. I told Sylvia that, sadly, that boat was not for us.

But, within weeks, returning from an outside broadcast engagement, I was driving along Packhorse Road in Staines. This was my customary route from the south coast back to our home at Horton and in those days there was a gap in the buildings on the left hand side just before the railway bridge. I would always look through that gap towards the river because it was such an interesting view: immediately opposite was the famous Tims' boatyard.

I had already met Stanley Tims, the inheritor of the family business. On that bright, shining afternoon, as I glanced through that gap there on the Tims mooring across the river, I saw 'my boat'. There it was, I thought, *Nomad* – pristine, shining, her brass ablaze in the setting sun.

I had one of the biggest double takes in my life. I realised that, in such a short time, no-one could have restored to such a condition that boat with which I had fallen in love at Tom Jones' boatyard. I crossed Staines Bridge and went over to Stanley Tims' 'yard.

There he was, smoking his pipe in contemplative mood as I shall always remember him. I said, "Stanley, I'm going mad; I have seen a boat called *Nomad* at Windsor which is beyond my reclamation... and there she is!"

"Oh," he said, "you mean *L'Orage*. Yes, she is pretty, isn't she? She's a Dunkirk veteran, you know." Of course, I didn't know and nor had the thought of buying one of the Little Ships of Dunkirk ever crossed my mind. But I said: "Can we have a look at her?"

"Yes, of course," said Stanley, "I'm sure her owner wouldn't mind."

So I went aboard *L'Orage* and, as her outward appearance suggested, she was truly a little classic – the boat for which I had been searching. She offered two single berths in her saloon, with a table between, and two smaller berths in her fo'c'stle, which would have been ideal for the children. So my mind went scampering off in all sorts of exciting directions but all I could do was to say to Stanley: "Thank you very much; should she ever come onto the market, let me know."

"Yes," he said, "of course. She belongs to a bank manager who lives in Strawberry Hill and obviously he is extremely fond of her." So I went home and told Sylvia about this in, I guess, a somewhat despondent frame of mind. But, believe it or not, within a month I had a letter from Stanley Tims, saying:

217

"*L'Orage* is on the market. Are you interested?"

I think I had her surveyed – I am not sure of that – but, in any case, within six to seven weeks of my first sight of *L'Orage* I had bought her for £1,100, including her clinker-built dinghy. She wore what was to become the celebrated brass plate reading, 'Dunkirk 1940', behind the main seating in the cockpit. She was in the 1939 edition of *Lloyds Yachts* and all her parentage and antecedents appeared to be impeccable. She was built by a firm called Cars & Boats, at Kingston-upon-Thames in 1938. That firm was set up with money lent by Sir 'Tom' Sopwith, the proprietor of the Sopwith Aeroplane Company at Kingston. His company was wound up in 1918 at the conclusion of the First World War and he was obliged, reluctantly, to dismiss his entire skilled and devoted workforce. So he lent a small amount of money to three or four of his craftsmen – woodworkers – and they set up Cars & Boats because they also built wooden bodies for Aston Martins and Lagondas, then two separate local companies, and ash frames for Fraser Nash cars in nearby Isleworth.

They had acquired designs by the distinguished naval architect, G H Wainman, MINA, and embarked on a programme of building 30-footers and 45-footers. To my knowledge they only built 11 30-footers, all of which were slightly different according to the purchasers' requirements. I think they had built no more than three to six 45-footers when the war overtook them. It transpired that the original boat with which I had fallen in love, *Nomad*, was a sister ship of *L'Orage*. The former was restored to very good condition but sadly sank on her moorings on the Medway in the early 1970s.

That was how I came to purchase my Dunkirk Little Ship, with no possible comprehension of all that it would lead to. I already knew the epic story of the little ships, of course, and had told it to Graham. In the spring of 1940 the Germans had swept through Holland, Belgium and into northern France. The defending British and French forces were encircled and trapped, with their backs to the sea, within an ever-shrinking perimeter around Dunkirk and the beaches towards La Panne.

Under the command of Admiral Bertram Ramsay, Operation

Dynamo was launched – so-called because his headquarters were in a disused dynamo room within the tunnels long before dug into the White Cliffs, in defence of Dover.

Contrary to the Mrs Miniver legend, the story was not that a handful of gallant yachtsmen leapt into their boats and rescued an army. Operation Dynamo was conceived and executed by the Royal Navy. Little ships were commandeered and almost all were manned by naval personnel, although a few owners did go. Fishing boats, barges, pleasure steamers and other commercial craft were manned by their own crews. It was no place for amateurs. Destroyers played a key role, and suffered severely.

Between 28th May and 4th June, over 338,000 troops were brought back to Britain, including 100,000 French, hundreds of Belgians, Dutch and others. The job of the little ships was to exploit their shallow draught and ferry troops off the beaches to the bigger vessels lying offshore. It has been recorded that approximately one third of the total were rescued in this way.

Over the years I have learnt more and more about Operation Dynamo and, in particular, what happened to *L'Orage*. She was called *Surrey* in 1940 and our short boathook still bears that name. Her owner was a Mr Tudor-Thomas who lived at Kingston-upon-Thames. He took her to Sheerness, as ordered, where she was taken over by the Royal Navy. Crewed by a senior rate and three reservists, she set off for Dunkirk. Precisely what happened thereafter is not known. It was said that she embarked up to 34 soldiers at a time, and Graham and I have worked out how this could have been done.

When she was returned to her owner, a French rifle was discovered in one of her lockers. She was then bought, in 1949, by a Mr Leslie Croucher of Sanderstead, Surrey. I had assumed that she was renamed *L'Orage*, post-war, in honour of a French destroyer which had been sunk. But, in 1998, a letter from Australia told me that the writer had recognised a picture of my boat and that his father had owned her in 1949. Apparently, Mr Croucher had been extremely fond of a little *art nouveau* female figure, whose scanty robe was blown in the wind. It was titled *L'Orage* – 'The Storm' – and because this man regarded it as his other love he gave the name to the boat.

One sunny summer day in August 1964, my family and I were flying over the port and city of Dunkirk at about 3,000ft. Our transport was a trans-Channel car freighter which operated a regular service in those years. We were bound from Southend to Ostend. Flying over the beaches, and looking down, I said to my then 14-year-old son who was sitting beside me: "There, Graham, you see the scene of the epic rescue of Dunkirk." And after a moment he said:

"Do you realise, father, it will be 25 years next year since *L'Orage* was doing her stuff down there? Let's take her back." I confess I was a little shaken because, although I had contemplated taking my boat down the Thames to the estuary and up the Medway and so on, I hadn't seriously thought of taking her across the Channel, let alone across the North Sea and that very tricky approach to Dunkirk.

"Ah," I said, "I guess I'd better have a bit of a think about that, old man." And on we went on our holiday, as we did on so many happy, consecutive summers. But the thought lingered in the back of my mind as we drove on south, to the mountains and the beautiful scenery which I had come to love from boyhood and for which my affection had been stimulated by driving across the Alps and the Jura at maximum speed on various international rallies.

Nevertheless, when we got home I did give this impromptu idea serious consideration. I approached through my good friend, Albert Asher, the special projects manager of the *Daily Express*, and was promised an interview with Max Aitken, wartime flying ace, son of Lord Beaverbrook and then proprietor and managing editor of the *Express*. He was very much into boating and patriotic gestures, but to my disappointment and indeed annoyance he declined any serious interest in my ambitions. I was so cross and disappointed, I didn't even stay for the second gin.

Leaving the *Express* building and turning right to walk up Fleet Street, still in a pretty black mood, I literally bumped into another old friend in the newspaper business, Frank Coven, who was the opposite number to Albert Asher, working for the *Daily Mail*.

"Gracious," he said, "you look as if you're in a pretty foul mood. Let's go and have a glass of champagne together." In those days it was not all that unusual to drop into one of the famous Fleet Street pubs for a glass of bubbly. So I explained to Frank that it was my idea, following my son's suggestion, to get as many as possible of the original Little Ships of Dunkirk together and take them back.

"Ah, Raymond," he said, "I don't work for the *Mail* any more. Since I last saw you, I have started working for Lord Thompson of Fleet, of *The Sunday Times*. May I put this idea to him?"

"Not half," I said.

Somewhat to my surprise, and greatly to my delight, within ten days I was invited to a meeting at the offices of *The Sunday Times*. There I met the now famous editor, Harold Evans, and one of his executives, Jim Lee. It was agreed I should publish a letter, and if *The Sunday Times* received 12 responses, the newspaper would do its best to assist the project with publicity and overall organisation. The date proposed was to be the closest weekend to the actual 25th anniversary of Operation Dynamo, and 43 owners of what they believed to be genuine Dunkirk Little Ships declared their intention of joining the fleet.

We had very much enjoyed our first season with *L'Orage* in the summer of '64, learning how to manage her and make the most of our new pride and joy. We had reached the head of navigation on the Thames at Lechlade and sampled the tidal waters below Teddington Lock. In fact I didn't take her to Bates of Chertsey for her winter lay-up until December. On the advice of Michael Bates, the original American Gray Marine engine was replaced by a similar but new BMC/Newage Navigator. The Gray was clearly past its best work and small marine diesels were noisy and smelly in those days. It was not until mid-April 1965 that we got *L'Orage* back.

I realised that to take my boat and family safely down the Thames, let alone out to sea, I required expert help and advice.

Nothing daunted, I contacted the PLA (Port of London Authority). The Pool of London and the Docks were still busy with commercial traffic, even in 1965. The response I received from the PLA could not have been more generous. The Deputy Harbour Master, Commander Paul Satow, not only gave me advice but he offered to come with us. I also invited my friend Peter Garnier, sports editor of *The Autocar*, who had served in the RNVR aboard MTBs (motor torpedo boats) during the war and at one time had been quartered ashore in the Royal Temple Yacht Club in Ramsgate.

With Sylvia, Graham and Jenny aboard we were a bit pushed for space at our overnight mooring at Kew, in readiness for a 0400 start next morning, 2nd June. There had been a rather sketchy briefing at *The Sunday Times*, where an equally sketchy sailing order was issued. This called for a rendezvous in the sheltered approach to the King George V Dock and there we met our first fellow little ships, including *Gentle Ladye*, one of the best maintained and keenest of our association members to this day.

It was very exciting to see for the first time from my own boat the famous landmarks which I had known from boyhood – the Woolwich Ferry, Greenwich and the Ford factory at Dagenham. Paul Satow was a mine of information. He pointed out the immaculate LCC (London County Council) sludge-boats which dumped sewage into the sea, and the cable-laying ships which, long before satellite and fibre-optic transmission, linked the world by submarine telephone cables. In Tilbury Reach we were joined by the Thames barge, *Cambria*, in full sail, and later, *Braymar*, whose skipper Harry Moss was later to become Commodore of the association. We had a very fair passage and my logbook of the time records, "1100, *L'Orage* dipping prettily, off Southend Pier." Then the tide turned and with it, as so often happens, the sea state. Soon we were rolling heavily, under a grey sky in an unfriendly beam sea, long out of sight of land, in the Prince's Channel. I let Paul Satow and Peter Garnier get on with it while I did my best to keep up the family's spirits.

Not that this was in any way a crisis. Eventually, as we

cleared the North Foreland on a long following swell, Graham was on the helm – and I had learnt a lot. At 1830 we moored to the eastern wall in Ramsgate harbour and it was all hands ashore. Very tired, we made our way to the comfort of the Royal Temple Yacht Club.

However, by the time Sylvia and I had put our feet up for a couple of minutes and made ourselves sufficiently respectable to go downstairs for the evening, we found Jenny, aged eight, already ensconced at the bar, Coca-Cola in hand, recounting her recent adventures to the local stalwarts of the club.

Paul Satow left, to return to his PLA duties, and Peter Garnier for a quick check-up at his office. But my schoolfriend, Bobby Farran, ex-RN Minesweepers in the North Sea, joined us. At 0613 on Friday 4th June, we cleared Ramsgate harbour. Peter Garnier had rejoined us and, encouraged by Sylvia, I had invited our friend and family GP, Dr Derek Roper, to accompany us. So we were seven aboard.

Two starting rendezvous points had been arranged, Ramsgate and Dover, the two fleets to meet off the South Goodwin Light. As far as we were concerned with the Ramsgate flotilla, everything went not only according to plan but also in an extremely satisfactory and enjoyable way. The weather was kind but unfortunately the Dover contingent missed the rendezvous. One of those who missed it was John Knight – not the best start to what was to become a close partnership.

Meantime I had approached the BBC and quite elaborate outside broadcasts had been organised. I had a radio transmitter installed in my boat – it was long before the R/T which of course is now not only common practice but compulsory in sea-going yachts – so this was a BBC transmitter and I was scheduled to make a contribution from mid-Channel. In the event the communication was not established and that was the only bit that didn't work; but Richard Dimbleby was duly installed with outside broadcast cameras to cover the historic arrival of the fleet, between the 'moles' and into the harbour at Dunkirk. Later Richard expressed his annoyance to me, though I think slightly tongue in cheek, that we had not

223

arrived in the order which I had predicted – this, I might say, after an eight and a half hour crossing by a flotilla of total strangers.

For the crossing we enjoyed the protection and guidance of three high-speed patrol boats supplied by the Royal Navy and, for identification purposes, we had all been provided with, and instructed to fly at the masthead, the undefaced Cross of St George. As I subsequently realised, this was a piece of gross impertinence on our part but it led to an interesting sequence of events before many months had passed.

We moored in the Bassin du Commerce, right in the centre of the town and virtually under the shadow of the tower of the Hotel de Ville where we were given an official reception by the mayor. Each owner received a handsome brass plaque, commemorating their vessels' participation in the 25th anniversary of Operation Dynamo, with the appropriate date. This was quite a brave gesture by the mayor, Claude Prouvoyeur, who became a very good friend of ours. In fact in those days there was a strong feeling in France, and in Dunkirk in particular, that the evacuation of 1940 had been a betrayal rather than a major success in turning what would have been, literally, a total disaster into the possibility of living to fight again. I am very happy to record that over the years that attitude diminished steadily and now no longer exists. In fact, quite the contrary. The historically correct version of the evacuation of Dunkirk is now taught to French schoolchildren, the history of the Second World War in France having been considerably distorted immediately after the war and in successive years. There was also a buffet supper and the net result was that this group of owners of a varied assortment of ships already 25 years out of date – this group of very disparate individuals – got to know each other and it was tentatively suggested that this should not be the end of the matter.

We returned in company, as we had crossed out, in a long line-ahead formation – very different from the tactics and practice which we subsequently developed. But the net result was that I had met a man called John Knight and his family. He was a farmer and businessman and I also renewed the

Top left: Honour and glory. Made Freeman of the City of London, 23 November 1976, with the City Remembrancer.

Top right: Order of the British Empire awarded to Raymond Baxter, co-founder and Honorary Admiral, Association of Dunkirk Little Ships. 'For services to Heritage', presented 13th February 2003.

Bottom: Liveryman, Guild of Air Pilots and Air Navigators, clothed by Grand Master, HRH Duke of Edinburgh.

Top left: Left to right: Ted Harvey, Sylvia, George Osborne at the Laying-up Supper, Painted Hall, Greenwich 1990.

Top right: L'Orage braves the waves.

Middle left: Dunkirk Return 2005. Crossing the sea lanes with grandson Tom.

Middle right: 2005 fleet assembled in Dunkirk.

Bottom: Patrick Prince, ex-RAF, back to camera, and Dennis Cox, ex-RN, who crewed *L'Orage* with son Graham and grandson Tom.

The dramatic painting by Michael Turner of the audacious raid on the Shell-Mex building by 602 Squadron on 18th March 1945. Author in the middle Spitfire. *(Courtesy the artist)*

Middle: Battle of Britain Air Display RAF Finningley, with Nick Grace in front of his newly restored Spitfire two-seater, September 1985.

Right: With Air Commodore Simon Bostock, Commandant of the Central Flying School, after a Hawk flight at RAF Cranwell, 1993.

This is Your Life

Top left: The hit. The author is surprised by Stirling Moss and Michael Aspel while working in a Soho recording booth.

Top right: The family arrive. From left to right: daughter Jennifer Douglas, son-in-law Paul Douglas, daughter-in-law Bridget Baxter and son Graham.

Middle left: Closely followed by the grandchildren. Left to right: Anna, Tom with Saskia, Holly and (centre) Rebecca.

Middle right: Close friend and colleague James Burke.

Bottom left: A message from New York courtesy of Carl Andre, the sculptor and author's nephew.

Bottom right: Without whom... Bob Swanson, the author's American flying instructor.

acquaintance of a distinguished naval flyer of the Second World War, Commander Charles Lamb who had written a brilliant book called *War in a Stringbag*. I had met him in aviation circles; I had never met John Knight before, and I became on friendly terms with several other people whom we encountered for the first time on our arrival in Dunkirk. But, subsequently persuaded by John Knight and Charles Lamb – and I confess I was somewhat reluctant because my ambition had only been to get the ships together and get them to Dunkirk – I agreed that the ships and people should not be allowed to simply disperse and the advantage offered should not be just let go to waste.

And so a meeting was called in London of a handful of people who had participated in this great adventure and it was decided that an association should be formed. Other people whom we had met for the first time and whose addresses were available through *The Sunday Times* were contacted and a further meeting was summoned and on 28th November 1966, the Association of Dunkirk Little Ships was formed. As I soon found myself explaining, the association is the most exclusive yacht club in the world which anyone can join provided they own a vessel which is proven to have participated in Operation Dynamo, the miraculous evacuation of Allied Forces from Dunkirk in 1940.

Thanks to the determination and enthusiasm of John Knight and the considerable presence and authority of Charles Lamb, we were able to progress our mutual ambitions in very short order. A formative meeting was called, Charles Lamb was elected Commodore, I was elected Vice Commodore, John Knight was elected secretary and a handful of others formed the committee. It occurred to John, Charles and me that if we were to be a yacht club, it was essential that we should consider the requirement and etiquette of appropriate flags. As I have mentioned, on the original crossing we wore the undefaced Cross of St George, without any authority, and we realised that was actually quite illegal under International Flag Law at Sea.

Nevertheless, it had become very much a symbol in the minds of everyone concerned and so a design was drawn up, largely by John, which consisted of the Cross of St George defaced by the arms of Dunkirk. In order to wear this there were strict formalities which had to be observed. Firstly I acquired from the mayor and council of Dunkirk the right to wear their arms; secondly we applied to the Admiralty for their approval and also I had to take a detail of the design to the Royal College of Heralds for their approval. The net result was that our association house flag duly became the Cross of St George defaced by the arms of Dunkirk and when in company we are authorised to wear the undefaced Cross of St George at the jackstaff in the bow. This entitlement is authorised by warrant of the Admiralty and every member of the association is given that authority by virtue of his membership card.

I then approached the Royal College of Needlework with the request that they might consider making us, as it were, a ceremonial flag; and this they were happy to do but stipulated that I would have to pay for the gold thread involved. I think the total amount of money was some £34, an unbelievable gesture of generosity on their part which of course is in marked contrast to anything which could be achieved today. A small group of us returned to Dunkirk in 1967, unofficially and with no naval escort and I delivered the flag to the mayor of Dunkirk. Very sad to say, I have never seen it since although I believe and fervently hope that it is safely locked away somewhere in the archives of the Hotel de Ville, or maybe the Dunkirk museum.

Meanwhile, our committee, under the chairmanship of the Commodore, Charles Lamb, looked to the future and decided that we would return in strength, and officially, again in 1970. Again we approached *The Sunday Times* but this time sponsorship was declined and so, after some very serious deliberations, we decided that we would go ahead and organise the event ourselves, seeking the support of the Royal Navy and deliberately making a point of denying any opportunity of commercial sponsorship with all the advertising attributes which are inevitably contained in such an arrangement. A policy which remains true to this day.

Again the date selected was the last weekend of May/first in

June. Our members were circulated, all the arrangements were made with the mayor and harbour authorities in Dunkirk and we were all set for the exciting achievement of a return trip. Unfortunately, unlike the weather experienced during the actual evacuation, the skies turned ugly. Indeed, I only got as far as Queenborough on the Medway. Some people got to Dover but, came the morning, and with a howling gale and heavy seas outside Dover harbour we decided reluctantly that the event had to be cancelled. We were determined however that this major setback should not spell the end of the association and so we busied ourselves contriving events to hold it together and thus were born our three official annual functions ashore. We have a formal Fitting-out Supper and a formal Laying-up Supper and of course we have an AGM. But, in addition, we resolved to meet formally afloat every year, not necessarily returning to Dunkirk but executing what we came to call the Annual Commemorative Cruise, intended to visit different ports. Over the years, as a consequence we have visited West Mersea, Ipswich, Dover, Ramsgate, Maidstone, Rochester and Chatham and had three assemblies up the River Thames in London.

But our major goal and ambition was decided. This was that we would return in full glory to Dunkirk every fifth year and in that ambitious plan we have been conspicuously successful even despite the cruel hand of the weather from time to time. Our association with the Royal Navy has been maintained and of that we are extremely proud.

1990 was a very particular year for the Association of Dunkirk Little Ships. David Rolt was Commodore, and his constant reminders of our approaching return to Dunkirk succeeded in assembling our biggest fleet to date. Seventy-five of the little ships returned to the scene of their epic.

After consulting his secretary, I had written to the Duke of Edinburgh outlining our plans and inviting him to pay us a visit. It did not take long to receive a reply. His Royal Highness would come to Dover to see us off. I had immediately to point out that as our time of departure was scheduled for 0700 this might scarcely be convenient. His response was immediate. He visited us mid-morning of the previous day, toured the fleet at our moorings and spoke to virtually all involved, boarding many vessels.

We were obliged to delay our departure by one day because of the weather. Even so, it was very rough outside Dover harbour. The skipper/owner of *Papillon* was quite severely disabled. His helmsman's seat broke and his forward hatch was letting in water. The Dover lifeboat was in attendance and went immediately to assist. I heard the calm voice of our good friend, the Coxswain Tony Hawkins, on the radio: "*Papillon. Papillon.* You have a visitor coming aboard, sir." The crew had launched their Y-boat (dinghy) to take control of the casualty. Shortly after that, Richard Huggett was winched into the ASR (air-sea rescue) helicopter, *Papillon* was safely returned to Dover and the lifeboat continued with us all the way to Dunkirk but then had to return immediately, to be 'on station'.

Ten years later, in 2000, the Duke of Edinburgh came to see us off again. The Dunkirk Veterans Association had announced its intention to disband. The Prince of Wales took the salute at their march past in Dunkirk, and subsequently visited our fleet a second time.

Chapter 17

Bread and Circuses

Actors and actresses profess a fear of becoming typecast, although quite a few have done very well from being just that in successful 'soaps'. I too have had a lot of fun, but not very much money, from being typecast as myself on film, television and radio. Motor racing and the Monte Carlo Rally, aviation and perhaps, rather curiously, science and technology have been the subjects of cameo parts enabling me to indulge my juvenile love of acting – and work with some of the really great performers of my time.

For example, I enjoyed hugely my time spent with James Robertson-Justice at Pinewood Studios. There was an actor whose highly successful career consisted almost exclusively of being himself. But as a slightly larger than life character anyway, with a lot of charm and delightful sense of humour, it is not surprising that he won the affection of his audiences as well as his fellow actors. The 1962 film was called *The Fast Lady*. It was about a classic Bentley and had a remarkable cast including Stanley Baxter, Leslie Phillips, Dick Emery and Julie Christie. I was in another feature film, at about that time, called *The Green Helmet*. It had a motor racing story line and was made by MGM, but was it at Pinewood, Elstree or Shepperton?

No matter: if you've seen the inside of one film studio, you've seen them all and, one way and another, I've worked in most of them in Britain, including Bray – the home of the classic British horror movies. It is said to be haunted, but I never saw a ghost myself. In all my cameo appearances, I always asked the producer/director to allow me to put the proposed lines into my own words, as far as possible, and this all worked extremely well until I met John Frankenheimer. He was an American film-maker with one respectable title to his credit – *The Manchurian Candidate*.

That secured him a blockbuster budget for his feature film, *Grand Prix*, and in 1966 Frankenheimer burst onto the European motor racing scene like a bull into a china shop. He had the temerity, and the money, to hire the Monaco Grand Prix circuit, no less, for two and a half days, cleverly slotting the time into the schedule of the race itself. Graham Hill had a small speaking part and played it beautifully, tongue in cheek. Jack Brabham, John Surtees and many other motor racing people appeared on screen, a form of flattery calculated to win Frankenheimer their support.

There was only one drawback, in my opinion: the plot and the script were rubbish. Again in my opinion Frankenheimer's *Grand Prix* did nothing for the good of the sport, and in those days it was still a sport – just. He squandered an amazing opportunity to make the definitive motor racing film. That was bad enough but what really shook me was the staggering arrogance of the man. I did some filming at Brands Hatch and Monte Carlo as a commentator. Some of this was shot 'in sync' with the action, which was quite tricky. The camera and sound crews were very complimentary – and that pleased me because this was a bunch of hard-bitten Hollywood professionals. I had got my money in cash – Frankenheimer paid everyone in cash – and was feeling, frankly, rather pleased with myself. But a couple of weeks later Frankenheimer 'phoned me from America. He told me I was needed for some further filming and to "get onto a plane and get out here to Los Angeles within 48 hours – all expenses paid." I reminded him that in our first discussions I had told him I was contracted to present a weekly television programme live for the BBC, and that his request at such short notice was therefore impossible.

He became extremely angry and offered me twice the money which the BBC would have paid me, which wasn't very much anyway. But he simply refused to accept that I was not prepared to betray my obligation to the *Tomorrow's World* team and the BBC. His attitude embittered me, and he had to get Anthony Marsh – a colleague who did most of the top PA motor racing commentary at that time, to provide a substitute English accent. It was Frankenheimer's arrogance that offended me as much as his waste of the opportunity to make an important film. Since then, I have always reacted strongly against anyone who seems to me to be trying to take me for granted.

A national hero whom I got to know quite well – and admired enormously – was the British and world champion boxer, Freddy Mills. In conversation I mentioned that I was concerned to ensure that my son had the necessary aggression to stand up to the rough and tumble of adult life. Almost by return, so to speak, he sent me two pairs of practice gloves, duly signed "with best wishes". My son has made a successful career in the oil industry – not the most gentle of environments.

Freddy was found shot outside a West End nightclub. The verdict was suicide. I found that impossible to accept and remain convinced that he was the victim of a gangland murder.

I presented the gloves, as a trophy, to the National Association of Boys' Clubs, with which I was closely associated during the 1950s and 1960s.

Brian Johnston, that icon of the world of cricket, and I shared an office in the OB department of BBC Radio for 14 years. We worked well together, on both radio and television, and became friends. There was even a time when we considered leaving the staff of the BBC to work in England in the summer and Australia in the winter, he doing the cricket and me the motor racing. It was a pretty wild idea, which we abandoned, not least because although Sylvia and I had at that time only one child; Pauline and BJ, as he was then known, already had four. Pauline used to say that Brian had but to look at her and she was pregnant!

It was impossible not to have fun in his company, and we had a lot in a wide variety of contexts. In our office there was a large green, baize-covered notice board. We used to send rude picture postcards to each other from wherever we happened to be – the usual gaudy 'fat lady at the seaside' type which were popular at that time. By the time our ways parted, when I left the BBC, the board was almost completely covered. It must have been a remarkable collection and both my son and daughter remember it from their childhood visits to Daddy's office.

When an edition of *Hancock's Half Hour* was devoted to the Monte Carlo Rally, Brian and I recorded some appropriate 'cod' commentary. I met the Great Man only briefly, but Sid James and I became quite good friends and Sylvia and I were invited, on more than one occasion, to remarkable parties at his luxuriously furnished house when we lived at Denham and he at nearby Iver. His performance in *Carry On up the Khyber* still makes me laugh, only thinking about it, but he was always brilliant while remaining totally unassuming and roguishly delightful company – another example of stunningly successful permanent typecasting.

In the 1950s and 1960s, the circus was a very popular entertainment. I loved it, and Brian and I worked together quite often in that wonderful world of glamour, humour, skill, courage, family traditions and just plain hard work. There were three big travelling circuses at that time, all playing under canvas in the traditional big top, and touring the length and breadth of the country, complete with lions and tigers, elephants, sea lions, performing dogs, chimpanzees, high wire and trapeze acts – and almost cavalry regiments of beautifully turned out and superbly ridden horses.

I never considered it cruel and never saw anything seriously to question that judgement. It brought high-class entertainment, at affordable prices, close to people's homes and boundless delight to millions of children, including mine, before the deluge of contemporary television swamped live entertainment.

The three major circuses performing very soon after the war were Bertram Mills, Billy Smart's and The Chipperfields. The founder of the former had been sufficiently successful in the 1920s to send his two sons to Harrow. When I first met them in the mid-1950s, they were running the circus. Cyril was responsible for the business and the constant search for new acts, and Bernard was in charge of the animals, particularly the horses. As well as being skilled entrepreneurs, both were cultured and charming and our professional relationship became a friendship based on mutual confidence and regard. When war broke out in 1939, Cyril's knowledge of Europe, including the languages, clearly qualified him for recruitment into Intelligence. Over a lunch arranged to discuss programme details with my boss, Charles Max-Muller, Cyril told us a strictly off-the-record story.

The scene is a deserted stretch of moorland near the Scottish border, at night. An aircraft is heard passing overhead. There is a soft swishing sound and as the parachutist recovers his balance after touchdown he is confronted by Cyril Mills, revolver in hand. In faultless German, he says,

"Good morning, Herr Oberleutnant. We were expecting you."

On Boxing Day, 1951 Brian Johnston and I were at Bertram Mills Circus at Olympia for what had become a routine traditional live radio broadcast. What happened was far from routine, as reported by *The News Chronicle,* reproduced overleaf.

As the artiste, Arno Wickbold rode, arms extended, round and round in his wall of death, suspended 30 feet above the arena, to my surprise he began peeling off his shirt. I distinctly saw a corner of the crimson silk catch in the back wheel. Realising the inevitability of disaster, I immediately cued "over to Brian Johnston, backstage." I knew that BJ would smoothly pick up the cue even though it was unexpectedly early, and so our listening audience knew nothing of the tragedy which

233

7,000 SEE CIRCUS CYCLIST CRASH
70ft. fall into ring
NEWS CHRONICLE REPORTER

Arno Wickbold motor-cycling round the wall of death, 70ft. above the circus ring. Yester-day, when his engine cut out he fell with his machine through the bottom of the cage

A CIRCUS crowd of 7,000 at Olympia yesterday saw Arno Wickbold, a 34-year-old German trick motor-cyclist, fall with his machine from an aerial "Wall of Death" and crash 70ft. to the ring.

He missed a safety net—to which he had objected—by a foot, and was picked up unconscious with multiple injuries.

Millions of radio listeners heard the motor-cycle's engine splutter as commentator Raymond Baxter told them: "If he loses speed he's going to lose altitude very quickly—and I hate to think what would happen . . ."

Then it did happen. . . . But radio listeners were not told of the crash. Many rang up newspapers to ask if there had been an accident.

First a clown . . .

The matinee was almost over. The programme had been re-arranged for the broadcast, and "Wickbold's Aerial Sensation" was to bring the show to a peak of excitement.

Ten clowns pranced into the ring—Wickbold among them, wearing an extravagant wig, a big nose and moustache, and gay clothes. He went hand-over-hand up the 70ft. rope to the big steel-lattice hoop suspended in the roof.

The hoop then had a floor, also of steel lattice, and Wickbold mounted his cycle and rode around it for a few seconds checking over his machine.

He went higher, until he was spinning round the sides of the hoop. He signalled, and his assistants folded back the floor beneath the hoop.

Caught in wheel

Wickbold shed his clown's make-up and garb to show lilac silk shirt and black riding-breeches beneath. Seven thousand watched him. . . .

Two-thirds of the way through the 4½-minute act clothing was caught in the wheel and Wickbold could not steer. The machine spun out of the hoop and fell. It hit the floor with Wickbold still holding it upright. Ringmaster Frank Foster, jun., and his assistants rushed forward and carried Wickbold away on a stretcher. "His lips were moving, but he could not say anything," said Mr. Foster.

Two doctors came from the audience to tend Wickbold before an ambulance took him

Few realised . . .

There was no announcement in the hall. . . . A party of chimpanzees ambled into the ring, two minutes ahead of their time . . .and the show went on. . . .

One of the audience, Mr. A. D. Lissauer, of Beckenham, Kent, said: "I think most of us thought the fall was part of the act and that he would be caught by the net. My own children—Frank (11) and Annaliss (5)—noticed nothing odd, and before anyone could think about it the man and the machine had been picked up, music started and the next act had begun."

One or two people fainted when they realised it was an accident.

Disliked net

Mr. Cyril Mills, one of the circus principals, said after the show: "I first saw Wickbold doing his act in Hamburg last June and I offered him an engagement at once. He had only just begun to perform the act in public, though he had been a 'Wall of Death' rider for 13 years.

"When he came here I insisted he used a net—he had never used one before. When he fell he missed it, but how I cannot tell."

Wickbold—a German—did not like the net. Last week-end he told a News Chronicle photographer: "Please, please, ask Mr. Mills to take the safety net away. It spoils the act."

The B.B.C. explained last night why Raymond Baxter did not mention the accident. "Our commentators would always avoid anything that might cause distress or unpleasantness."

26
24 12 51

CHRISTMAS is the season when the great circuses come to town and on Boxing Day Brian Johnston and Raymond Baxter will take Home Service listeners to the ringside and behind the scenes at Bertram Mills' Circus. Cyril and Bernard Mills, the two sons of the founder, will be there. Bernard, who buys all the animals for the show, is much in demand as a horse show judge and is now one of the few people in Britain who can drive a four-in-hand coach. Cyril is the talent finder and must have visited more circuses all over the world than anyone else in the business. This year he has found several new acts, among them young Wickbold who rides a 'suspended' Wall of Death high above the ring and the Flying Condoras who perform their somersaults blindfold.

How the *News Chronicle* reported the tragedy (above), and (above right) the *Radio Times* preview of BBC coverage. Taken from the author's scrapbook.

would otherwise have cast a dark shadow into the Christmas enjoyment of a million families.

In later years, when BBC Television visited both Billy Smart's Circus and the Chipperfields, I was the commentator and followed the practice, which BJ and I had established, of seizing any excuse to get in on the action. The 'lunge' is a time-honoured circus device used to protect equestrian artistes from a fall in practice. It consists of a safety harness attached to a light rope, passed through a pulley suspended above the centre of the ring. So, on one end of the rope is the performer and on the other end the trainer or ringmaster.

Wearing the lunge, Brian Johnston and I stood upright on bare-backed horses trotting steadily around the ring. They are called rosin-backs because of their broad, flat backs which provide as good a platform as you can get for the soles of rosined slippers. It was, of course, inevitable that sooner or later Brian and I would fall off to be left dangling in mid-air by the ringmaster, to screams of delight from the children.

The Smarts had a well-loved elephant called Burma, whom

Burma carries RB around the ring.

Burma, the elephant begging, Billy Smart obliging with Derek Burrell Davies, TV producer.

I got to know very well and of whom I became very fond. Amongst other tricks, she carried me round the ring holding my left knee in her mouth while I lay back, arms extended, in the best I could do towards a relaxed and elegant pose.

In cameo roles, I appeared twice on television with Michael Bentine and his Potties, and twice with Spike Milligan in his Q series. Although I hugely enjoyed working with both these comic geniuses, they were the despair of their production staff, and not above abrasive comment to members of the cast during rehearsal. In one episode, Spike created the wonderfully bizarre concept of 'Funeral by Rocket – Bury Your Loved Ones in Space'. The setting he chose was one of the huge Victorian cemeteries in North London.

Having parked my car, I was walking past a chapel in search of the camera and crew amongst the forest of gravestones when I was passed by a Roman Catholic priest.

"Good morning, Father," I said respectfully.

"Oh, 'ello Raymond," he said, "has Spike got you into this one too?" It was Bob Todd, a staunchly supportive regular in Milligan's casts. My role was to report what it would be like to be shot into space in a coffin, and there one stood, vertically, complete with brass handles.

"Speak your lines to camera," said Spike. "Then get into the box, shut the lid and sing."

"Sing what?" I said.

"Oh, I don't care, Raymond. Er, Rule Britannia," said Spike.

So I did just that, until I had to pause and say,

"Sorry Spike. I don't know any more words." Dead silence. Cautiously, I opened the lid and peered out. No one in sight. No camera, nothing, just a deserted cemetery on a grey winter's morning. Then up they popped from behind the gravestones, Spike and the whole crew, roaring with laughter at my apparent bewilderment.

I'm Sorry, I Haven't a Clue was amongst my favourite radio listening from its inception, and my two appearances on the show are amongst my happiest memories. In the first, the idea was a major feature programme based on the game Mornington Crescent, which I was to present. In my mock interview with Humphrey Lyttleton, whom I greatly admire, the question of corruption in the international game was raised. Humph's line was:

"I have heard of large sums of money changing hands. Up to £10,000." My line, as scripted, was, "As **much** as that." Instead I said dismissively, "As **little** as that." And that nearly corpsed Humphrey Lyttleton. (The word in showbiz language, means to make a fellow artiste laugh inadvertently.)

To celebrate its 30th anniversary in April 2002, the show was staged as a special programme in the Playhouse Theatre, where I had first trod the boards when my school friends and I, with our own production, won the Peoples' National Theatre Youth Festival. This time I was to do a running commentary on a critical game of Mornington Crescent in the competition for the Armitage Shanks Bowl. The players were Barry Cryer, Tim Brooke-Taylor, Graeme Garden and Stephen Fry. During my carefully-timed *sotto voce* comments on the play, Barry ad-libbed:

"I'm sure I can hear someone talking." I should have said, "I think I had better close the window of my commentary box." But I didn't think of it until later. Always the way.

I appeared three times in drag on television, a statement which has been known to cause surprise. The first time was with Bruce Forsyth in a Christmas edition of *The Generation Game*. Henry Cooper, Terry Wogan and I were dressed and heavily made up as pantomime dames. The challenge was to identify us. Try hard as we did, Henry and I were soon spotted, but Wogan was not. He was quite annoyed, because it was in the early days of his career and he was disappointed by the lack of recognition.

The first of the other two occasions came when I was invited to do my party piece on *Pebble Mill at One*. I chose Noel Coward's 'I've been to a marvellous party' – a bit of a shock for a lunch-time audience. Laurie Holloway did an ad-lib accompaniment without a score. But when, a few months later, I was asked to do a repeat performance in the *Russell Harty Christmas Show*, I invited my friend, Antony Hopkins, the distinguished musicologist and pianist to accompany me. He had recently been honoured with a CBE, so I addressed him throughout as commander. Tony really entered into the spirit and obtained the original score, which he played with great *bravura*. And, with my outrageous costume and make-up, on which a lot of care and attention had been lavished by those backstage, we got a very good reception from the audience and, indeed, our host.

Like *I'm Sorry, I Haven't a Clue*, I had admired *The Goodies* from its debut. It reminded me of the Establishment Club, of which Sylvia and I were early members when John Cleese and the original 'Monty Pythons' were forging the excellence of British satirical comedy.

Tomorrow's World provided their reason for inviting me to

present a report on the varied, but much overlooked, qualities of string. To add emphasis to the point, I wore string socks, a string singlet and underpants, which got a big laugh for a start. I demonstrated that, as a conductor of electricity, string was extremely economical because (attaching string to light bulb): "It doesn't work." I then visited a hospital ward in which string had been applied in various surgical techniques (Seize patient's leg, protruding from above the bed covers, and wave it wildly round and round in the air). I continued:

"In building and general construction work, string can replace conventional cement and glue, even in furniture making." (Sits on stool which collapses). The platform and the whole set literally fell about my ears. The Goodies – Graeme Garden, Tim Brooke-Taylor and Bill Oddie, the principal writer – have told me subsequently that of their material the string sketch was repeated more often than any other – on Japanese television.

Chapter 18

Postscript

Despite doing my best to avoid them, this book may contain errors. If they are to do with aircraft my attention will be swiftly drawn to them by aviation enthusiasts whom I hope to number among my readers. But as I write this postscript during the second week of June, the Little Ships have just completed their 2005 Return to Dunkirk, escorted by HMS *Severn* and a whisper of happy ghosts whom I heard laughing in the wind. So many friends, so many memories....

For example, no skipper of a small boat could ever have been more fortunate with his crews. Family apart, many memorable moments aboard *L'Orage* were in the company of Ted Harvey and George Osborne – Ted 'n George. Cousins in one of the long established families of cockle fishermen at Leigh-on-Sea, Essex, they were almost soulmates though each had his individual characteristics. Even their nicknames were part of local folklore: Ted was 'Edgey', taken from his father's saying, "Edge 'er up to windward a bit" when they were under sail in the cockleboats. By the same token, his father had been known as 'Nudger'. George's nickname was 'Pie': when he was less than two he fell out of an attic window and rolled down the slope of the roof, just like 'a little pudden'. Miraculously he was caught by his uncle, hence 'Roly-poly, pudden and pie.'

Ted joined the Royal Navy in 1939. He took three vessels to Dunkirk, two of which were sunk off the beaches and their third sunk on her return to Dover harbour. George did not go to Dunkirk because he had been hit on the head by a winch handle and had tonsillitis. The family cockleboat, *Renown*, one of the five which sailed from Leigh, struck a mine on the way home. All aboard were killed instantly, including George's uncle and two cousins. Ted 'n George served throughout the war in small boats. Their yarns, including those of boyhood, were our delight when 'holed up' by the weather, and their seas wisdom was boundless. Both were aboard when *L'Orage* made her longest non-stop voyage at the end of May 1980 – Dunkirk to Teddington in twenty-four hours exactly. Graham (my son) assured me we had just enough petrol; he was anxious to rejoin his wife, Bridget – my grand-daughter, Anna, was born a few weeks later. We cleared Dunkirk at 0630, left the ADLS fleet at Ramsgate, dropped off Ted 'n George at Tilbury and carried on up river through the night, in company with *Janthea* and *Doutelle*, two other Dunkirk Little Ships. The engine stopped as we moored ....

On that trip, Jenny produced the most wonderful Irish stew I've ever tasted. Asked what was in it, she said, "Angostura bitters and George's blood." He had cut his thumb, opening a tin. Ted 'n George were succeeded as my crew by Ron Toby and Patrick Prince. Ron had a stroke at the end of January, from which he is recovering. His place was taken on the 2005 trip by Dennis Cox, ex-National Service Fleet Air Arm, a staunch member of the Association of Little Ships and the Restoration Trust. Patrick, trained as an RAF cook, can produce bacon and egg 'banjos' at first light, with one hand holding the kettle on the hob.

Despite very severe weather, our fleet assembled at Ramsgate from as far apart as Plymouth, the Medway, the Thames and east of Clacton. At 0600 on Thursday 26th May we sailed, led by David Knight, our Commodore and the son of my co-founder of the ADLS. He has restored *Chico*, one of Sir Malcolm Campbell's original Bluebirds. With Dennis and Patrick, I also had aboard my son, Graham, who has never missed a Return since 1965 and my grandson, Tom, who first came with us as a young teenager.

As on previous occasions, we were escorted by the RNLI – the Ramsgate lifeboat was a star attraction on the quay in Dunkirk. The sea showed us every expression of her fickle face, from 45-degree rolls, to visibility of less than a mile to a long, blue following swell as we closed Ramsgate to be greeted by crowds and later a civic reception. Our welcome in Dunkirk could not have been more warm, from the mayor, M Delebarre, to the hundreds of passers-by who stopped to read the individual potted histories, in French, displayed beside each boat, thanks to our archivist, John Tough (yes, same family, Tough's of Teddington). Fifty-six Dunkirk Little Ships now wear the handsome brass plaque presented in the historic Hôtel de Ville. It was my eighth Return and in this *L'Orage* is unique.

I am a believing Christian and I cannot end this book other than with the words, "Thank God. Amen."

Index

The abbreviation RB is used for Raymond Baxter in references in the index such as (RB son).